Mind

Body

Spirit

Mind
Body
Spirit

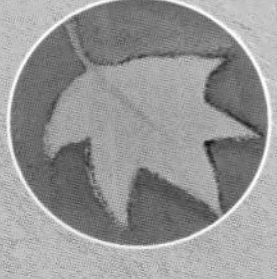

**A practical guide to
natural therapies for
health and well-being**

Contributing Editor: Mark Evans, B Phil. FNIMH

LORENZ BOOKS

Paperback edition published by Lorenz Books
an imprint of
Anness Publishing Limited
Hermes House
88-89 Blackfriars Road
London SE1 8HA

This edition distributed in Canada by
Raincoast Books
8680 Cambie Street
Vancouver
British Columbia V6P 6M9

ISBN 0 7548 0766 5

A CIP catalogue record for this book is available from the British Library

PUBLISHER: Joanna Lorenz
PROJECT EDITOR: Emma Gray
DESIGNER: Jo Hill, Balley Design Associates
PHOTOGRAPHER: Don Last
PRODUCTION CONTROLLER: Wendy Lawson
ILLUSTRATORS: Giovanna Pierce and Anna Koska

Previously published as eleven separate volumes: *Instant Herbalism, Instant Homeopathy,
Ayurveda, Instant Massage, Instant Aromatherapy, Instant Reflexology, Instant Shiatsu, Instant
Stretches, The Alexander Technique* and *Instant Meditation*

Printed and bound in China

© Anness Publishing Limited 2000

contents

preface

Health is, or should be, the most natural state of being. The origins of the word are linked with those of wholeness and healing, and it is that complete sense of harmony, of being in tune physically, mentally and spiritually, that brings true health. This is the ultimate aim of systems of natural healing, those that adopt a holistic view rather than the reductionist perspective that is evident in some conventional modern medical practices.

The holistic approach takes into account the physical, mental, emotional and spiritual well-being of a person when assessing health problems. It recognizes that physical symptoms, such as headaches and insomnia, and emotional ones, such as depression and mental strain, can all weave together to create disease, or rather, dis-ease – a lack of harmony.

Many Eastern cultures, such as those of China and India, have retained a strong tradition of therapies aimed at balancing energy. Much of Eastern ideology is an energetic one, with all parts of the human body interconnected and infused with vital energy, and all life-forms similarly interdependent on an exchange of energies. These concepts have led to the development of systems such as acupuncture in China, shiatsu and acupressure in Japan, and

yoga in India. In recent years in the West there has been increasing interest in these therapies, both in recognition of their intrinsic value and as a move away from the impersonal approach and unwelcome side-effects of allopathic medicine. At the same time, traditional Western forms of treatment, such as herbalism and massage, have undergone a resurgence in popularity, and research projects are now confirming their value. The physical benefits of meditation are also quantifiable. They include relaxation, improvement of sleeping patterns, lower blood pressure, better recovery from fatigue and a general beneficial effect on most stress-related disease.

In a world of ever-advancing technology, people feel the need for a human, individual touch. Touch is an absolutely primal, vital requirement that is sadly neglected in many modern societies. It provides the most immediate way to affect another person, and its therapeutic effects range from the alleviation of physical pain to reduced brain cell deterioration and memory loss with ageing. In the infirm, it often acts as a complement to exercise as it improves circulation and remedial massage and shiatsu can improve mobility to a limited extent.

The holistic approach to health seeks to enhance life rather than dissect illness. Many people think of medicine as a crisis treatment for when they are sick, but one of the strengths of natural therapies is their value in helping to prevent illness. By reducing the impact of worries and stress, natural systems of treatment can work to restore your vital energy and inner harmony, reducing visits to the orthodox doctor or medicine counter.

Life follows a natural rhythm, with periods of activity followed by periods of rest. This is as it should be. Too much stimulation, or an over-reaction to stimulation, leads to a state of stress. Over time, you may reach a state of exhaustion, reducing your ability to react and cope appropriately with new stresses and jeopardizing your general health in many different ways.

Stress is recognized as one of the major factors affecting health in modern society and nearly everyone has felt its grasp at one time or another. Human beings have a wonderful natural system for maintaining balance, and the body is always striving to achieve this state. But its balancing, adaptive energy is tested by stress, and is constantly being challenged. The increasing pace of modern life, the complexity of many professions, juggling the demands of work and family, changes and strains in relationships, all place considerable burdens on natural stress-management systems.

Stress is a normal part of life: in fact, a certain amount will do you no harm and is actually essential to motivation and personal development. But if you are under pressure for a long time, the cumulative impact of events may sometimes mean that, eventually, you cannot go on coping and your body takes the strain.

There are plenty of things that you can do to help yourself cope better when life presents a challenge. The first step to improving the situation is to recognize it, and to accept your own limits. Actively reducing the amount of external stress you are under will help, of course, as

well as looking at ways of easing its effects in the long term. Both diet and exercise are vital elements in maintaining optimal health, but most fundamental of all is to remove the causes.

Natural therapies can be used at home for many common complaints. However, it should not be forgotten that more complex conditions should be treated by professional practitioners of these therapies, and if you are in any doubt about a problem you should always seek qualified advice.

calming

wellbeing

refreshing

harmony

natural healing

One of the key issues today is knowing exactly how to look after yourself, and that does not just mean steering clear of all kinds of excesses that are known to be bad for you, such as coffee, alcohol and stress. It means knowing the many subtle and sophisticated ways in which the body works which are largely ignored by conventional medicine. Knowing, for example, how the deft use of herbalism can quickly help you to revive after a tiring, difficult day, how using homeopathy can bolster your body's well-being, and how the ancient Indian healing technique, Ayurveda, can help you tackle all kinds of illnesses holistically. using colours, gems and crystals.

herbalism

herbalism herbalism

All over the world, people have used plants not only as food but also as medicines. Traditional knowledge of herbal remedies used to be passed from generation to generation, but nowadays this is rare.

Fortunately, the countryside still produces wonderful herbs and many can be grown in the garden. Getting to know the plants growing around you can be a relaxing pleasure in itself. If you learn about their various properties, you can use them to help you feel more healthy and better able to cope with everyday problems. Very simple remedies can easily be made from dried or fresh herbs, and substituting an excellent herb tea for stimulating drinks such as tea, coffee and cola will help you to relax and reduce your tension levels.

Herbs, like people, are complex and variable organic structures. Each plant contains many different constituents which together give a unique taste and range of actions. Particularly active constituents have been isolated and copied by pharmacists to produce medicines such as aspirin. However, using the whole plant has a much more subtle effect, and generates far fewer side effects. Herbalists therefore prefer to use the whole plant to treat the whole person. We are all unique and react to life in different ways; just as we all have special preferences for various foods, each of us responds best to particular herbs.

the nervous system

It is easily overlooked, but the nervous system is like the key component in a highly complex computer. It regulates and fine tunes, analyses information and decides on the best course of action; it is an extremely sophisticated kind of mechanism. That is why looking after the nervous system is one of the most important things you can do. Here are some excellent ways of making sure that you relax and keep feeling well.

The Effects of Stress

The involuntary or autonomic nervous system has two divisions. The sympathetic part prepares you for action and initiates the "fight or flight" response. The parasympathetic system is responsible for the body's "housekeeping", ensuring good digestion, assimilation of nutrients, detoxification and elimination of waste products. The sympathetic system allows you to respond to any stimulation, making the heart and lungs more active when necessary and suppressing natural processes such as digestion.

All life follows a natural rhythm, with periods of activity followed by periods of rest. This is as it should be. Too much stimulation, or an over-reaction to stimulation, leads to stress. If you are subjected to excess stimulation, sympathetic activities become dominant or habitual and may reach a state of exhaustion, reducing your ability to react and cope appropriately with new stresses. This can cause forgetfulness, panic, exhaustion or increased vulnerability to infection. At the same time, reduced parasympathetic activity can cause all sorts of digestive and nutritional debilities as well as poor elimination, which in turn can result in problems with the skin, muscles or joints.

Lavender oil rubbed into the temples will encourage relaxation, and gradually ease a headache.

Helpful Herbs

The nervous system co-ordinates all the highly complex activities that manage to keep us functioning efficiently and well. They help us rapidly, unconsciously adjust to all kinds of constantly changing stimuli. The following pages clearly describe some of the highly valuable, beautiful plants growing right across the world which, among their many properties, help give back-up and support to the nervous system. Herbalists have named these very important plants, the nervines.

Choosing the Right Remedies

Like all herbs, nervines have a wide range of actions. It is important that you choose the one that applies to your own symptoms of stress, and to which you feel naturally drawn. Knowing, growing, harvesting and drying herbs (which is quite easily done) will help you to appreciate them much more. You may well discover that a symptom that is particularly troubling can in fact be treated by several different remedies.

Simply meandering down paths of richly scented lavender can quickly help to raise the spirits.

Nervous Tonics

These plants are used to aid recovery from stress and are particularly useful when we feel in any way debilitated and exhausted after an illness, prolonged pressure or even a trauma. They will improve the health and functioning of nervous tissue by invigorating and restoring it.

Some act as gentle stimulants while others are in fact slightly more sedating. Your choice will depend on whether nervous debility makes you hyperactive (in which case choose relaxing nervines) or restless, depressed and tired (in which case you must choose stimulating nervines).

Stimulating Tonics:

- Mugwort (Artemisia vulgaris)
- Wild Oats (Avena sativa)
- St John's Wort (Hypericum perforatum)
- Sage (Salvia officinalis)
- Damiana (Turnera diffusa)

Relaxing Tonics:

- Wood Betony (Stachys betonica)
- Skullcap (Scutellaria lateriflora)
- Vervain (Verbena officinalis)

Stimulants

Some plants, such as coffee and tea, stimulate our nervous system without nourishing it. Since such over-stimulation is exhausting, additional herbal stimulants are rarely used. But there is a place for gently stimulating nervines. For example, Mugwort is beneficial during convalescence and Rosemary, by helping stimulate blood flow to the head, is used to tackle and reduce tension headaches.

- Rosemary (Rosmarinus officinalis)

Relaxants and Sedatives

You can use relaxing nervines to calm yourself down and prevent over-stimulation. All these valuable herbs will help encourage rest and sleep. In any event some, like the Passion Flower and Lime Blossom, are excellent garden plants and help create a marvellous soothing atmosphere; a garden made for quietly walking round, inhaling the excellent scents, filled with a wide range of colours.

- Lady's Mantle (Alchemilla xanthochlora)
- Pasque Flower (Anemone pulsatilla)
- Chamomile (Chamaemelum nobile and Chamomilla recutita)
- Californian Poppy (Eschscholtzia californica)
- Hops (Humulus lupulus)
- Lavender (Lavandula spp.)
- Motherwort (Leonurus cardiaca)
- Lemon Balm (Melissa officinalis)
- Peppermint (Mentha piperita)
- Marjoram (Origanum vulgare)
- Passion Flower (Passiflora incarnata)
- Lime Blossom (Tilia x europaea)
- Cramp Bark (Viburnum opulus)
- Valerian (Valeriana officinalis)

Adaptogens

- Siberian Ginseng (Eleutheroccocus senticosus)
- Korean Ginseng (Panax spp.)

Other useful Herbs

- Borage (Borage officinalis)
- Licorice (Glycyrrhiza glabra)
- Evening Primrose (Oenothera biennis)
- Chaste Tree (Vitex agnus-castus)

Taking Herbal Preparations

Like other medicines, herbal remedies must be taken at the appropriate time and in a suitable manner tailored to the individual. For example, in cases of pregnancy, no strong herbal teas should be taken during the first trimester, even if they would otherwise relieve stress because the body is in too sensitive a state. Likewise, young children, whose bodies are also very labile, should not take Peppermint or Sage tea, they may suffer an adverse reaction. It is commonsense to avoid ready-made herbal mixes that contain sugar, the sugar will only create an additional burden for the body, reducing its ability to cope. Where it is possible, the cause of the stress should be removed, and everything done to support the person at this time.

Herbal teas are easily made in a wide range of flavours. They are a gentle and simple way to soothe both body and mind.

the herb garden

Herb gardens are easy to make and quickly stocked. Get a catalogue from a specialist seed supplier and you will probably find that they have eight or so different kinds of Basil from Europe and the Far East, with herbs like Coriander and Cumin. Growing them is incredibly easy. In most cases, pick regularly to encourage plenty of fresh, new tasty shoots. You will quickly see the benefits in the kitchen and your health.

PLANTING HERBS

You do not need very much space to grow herbs: a small border, or even a collection of containers, will provide a perfectly good supply. But if you do have the room, a large herb garden offers the chance to try fun designs like a circle of triangular beds pointing in to a focal point such as a small statue or painted urn.

Soil and Site

Most herbs are undemanding and quick to grow. They are essentially wild plants, and do not require rich, highly cultivated soil. Many of the most useful herbs, such as Sage, Thyme, Rosemary and Lavender, are natives of southern Europe and will not survive heavy clay soils or water-logged conditions. Many moisture-loving plants, such as Lemon Balm, Mint and Valerian, will grow happily in a light soil, though not in conditions of total drought. A sunny, sheltered position protected from strong biting winds will suit all the plants, though some, such as the more tender Lemon Verbena and Bay, will need protecting in bad winters.

Design

A formal layout of small beds dissected by paths provides a satisfying framework for the lax, untidy growth of many herbs. It also makes sure that you can easily tend and pick when necessary. A single species to each bed can look highly effective, evoking the magical, atmospheric style of medieval herb gardens. In contrast, an informal cottage garden provides plenty of scope for imaginative, exuberant planting with herbs cleverly mixed in with flowers. Raised beds or a lively collection of attractive containers make easy-to-control, self-contained areas.

A perfect example of a well-tended herb garden, with symmetrical beds and wide paths for easy access. The plants thrive in this warm, sheltered corner of the garden.

EXPERIENCING HERBS

Identifying, growing and harvesting herbs can be a marvellous, healing experience itself. Handling herbs brings you closer to nature and increases your appreciation of the vitality of plants.

Growing

The quickest way to acquire herbs that will help you stay healthy is to grow them yourself. You can easily grow most from seed. This means that you will be sure what they are, and that they will have been grown safely and organically, without the use of any chemical sprays. Most of the herbs used in the remedies on the following pages will grow extremely well in temperate climates. In fact many are often regarded as weeds, and actually thrive on patches of spare ground despite getting no care and attention whatsoever.

Gathering

The aerial parts of herbs (the flowers, stems and leaves) should be gathered for use or for drying when the plants are in bud and totally dry. That means early morning when the sun has dried the dew. Roots should be dug in the autumn, cleaned and roughly chopped into very small pieces.

If you harvest from the wild, make quite sure that you have identified the plant correctly (use a good wild flower book) and that it has not been polluted by fertilizers, pesticides or car fumes. Never pick so much that you reduce next year's growth.

Many of the culinary herbs we use today were distributed throughout Europe by the Roman army.

Drying

Spread out your herbs on a rack to dry naturally in an airy position, out of direct sunlight. Alternatively, tie them in loose bundles and hang them from a beam, or dry them in an oven at a very low heat.

Storing

Always make sure that you store dried herbs in airtight containers, kept well away from the light, and do not forget to label and date them. They will keep for up to six months, but the sooner they are used the better and fresher the flavor. (When they are kept for too long they look dull and taste of sawdust.) If you are in any way worried about over-drying your herbs, try storing them in a freezer instead. This is a particularly good technique for herbs such as Lemon Balm and Parsley, which quickly lose their flavour when they are dried.

Buying

Many shops stock dried herbs. Buy these only if they seem fresh – they should be brightly coloured and strongly aromatic.

Some herbal remedies are now readily available over the counter in the form of capsules, tablets or tinctures. These are usually of good quality. Choose the simpler ones that tell you exactly the type and quantity of herb involved.

Lime Blossom is abundant for easy picking in both the countryside and urban areas during early summer.

herbal preparations
Herbs are multi-talented. They can be used in the kitchen, fresh or dried, and to tackle a wide range of ailments from hyperactivity to insomnia. They even provide a refreshing tonic when you are feeling down-and-out. In fact, you can take herbal remedies internally as teas, decoctions and tinctures, or applied externally as soothing, relaxing oils and conditioners. Best of all, they guarantee gorgeous perfumes.

MAKING TEAS

Herbal teas are also called infusions or tisanes. They are a simple and delicious way of extracting the goodness and flavour from the aerial parts of herbs. You can use either fresh or dried herbs to make such teas; note you need to use twice as much fresh plant material as dried. If you find the taste of some herb teas rather bitter, then try sweetening them with a little honey. Alternatively, try adding extra flavour by stirring the tea with a Licorice stick, or adding ginger.

1 Put your herb(s) into a pot. Standard-strength tea is made with 1 tsp dried or 2 tsp fresh herbs to 1 cup of water.

2 Strain and drink as required. Teas can be drunk cold as well as hot. Cold teas are thoroughly invigorating.

MAKING DECOCTIONS

Infusing in boiling water is not enough to extract the constituents from roots or bark. This much tougher, harder, inflexible plant material needs to be broken up into far smaller pieces by chopping or crushing with a sharp knife.

Next, place every tiny scrap of this rough-cut material into a stainless steel, glass or enamelled pan, but absolutely not aluminium. Fill up with cold water, and gradually bring to the boil. Finally cover and simmer for about 15 minutes. The resulting liquid is what is called a decoction. Strain it and flavour, if necessary, and drink while it is still warm.

Nervine Decoctions

- Cramp Bark
- Licorice
- Valerian

Avoid using Licorice if you suffer from high blood pressure.

1 Harvest root and bark in the colder months. Trim the aerial parts of the plant away from the root.

2 Wash the roots thoroughly in cold water, ensuring they are perfectly clean, then chop into small pieces.

3 Fill a pan with cold water and add 1 tsp of the chopped herb per cup. Boil and simmer for 10–15 minutes.

4 Strain and cool before drinking. Decoctions can be kept for 24 hours in the fridge. Drink reheated or cold.

MAKING TINCTURES

Sometimes it is more convenient to take a spoonful of medicine than make a tea or decoction. Tinctures are made by steeping herbs in a mixture of alcohol and water. The alcohol extracts the medicinal constituents, and it also acts as an excellent preservative.

Herb syrups make good remedies for giving to children. They also improve the taste of herbs that might be bitter, such as Motherwort and Vervain.

1 Place 100 g/3½ oz dried herbs or 300g/11 oz fresh herbs in a jar.

2 Add 250ml/8fl oz/1 cup vodka and 250ml/8fl oz/1 cup water.

Making Syrups

1 Place 500g/1¼lb sugar/honey in a pan; add 1 litre/1¾ pints/4 cups water.
2 Heat gently, stirring to dissolve,
3 Add 150g/5oz plant material and heat gently for 5 minutes.
4 Turn off the heat; steep overnight.
5 Strain and store in an airtight container for future use. Since the sugar acts as a preservative, a herb syrup will keep for 18 months.

3 Leave the herbs to steep in the liquid for a month, preferably on a sunny windowsill. Gently shake the jar daily.

4 Strain and store the tincture in a dark glass bottle where it will keep well for approximately 18 months.

COLD INFUSED OILS

Herbal oils are suitable for external use when having a massage, or as bath oils or hair and skin conditioners. Cold infused oils are quite simple to prepare. Macerate freshly cut herbs in vegetable oil for up to two weeks, but no more. Give the jar a daily shake. Finally drain off the oil, and squeeze the excess liquid out of the herbs. You will find that chamomile invariably gives excellent results.

1 Fill a glass storage jar with the flowers or leaves of your chosen dried herb.

2 Pour in a vegetable oil to cover the herbs; try sunflower or grape seed oil.

Herb Oil Infusions

- Chamomile
- Lavender
- Marjoram
- Rosemary
- St John's Wort

Do not put St John's Wort oil on the skin before going into bright sunshine for fear of an adverse reaction.

3 Stand the jar for two weeks on a windowsill to steep. Shake daily.

4 Strain. For a stronger infusion, renew the herbs in the oil every two weeks.

herbal recipes

herbal recipes

herbal recipes

In today's high-tech, high-speed world it is virtually impossible not to encounter stress, and stress at even alarmingly high levels. It can strike going to work when you get stuck in a gridlock traffic jam, at work with faxes, e-mails and meetings, and when you get back home and suddenly have to cope with meals and children. In fact, many people find that getting quality, quiet time for themselves is becoming increasingly difficult, if not impossible. But while you cannot always avoid stress, there are plenty of things you can do to help yourself cope better when life suddenly presents a barrage of testing, difficult challenges.

A good, healthy diet really does make a significant difference. It is therefore absolutely essential that you eat proper, healthy meals packed with vitamin-rich fruit and vegetables, and totally avoid artificial additives. If you miss these extra flavours, you will find that you get a far greater range using fresh or dried herbs, and of course they offer plenty of extra goodness.

Also, try as hard as you can to reduce your intake of such stimulants as tea, coffee, alcohol and cola. Instead, drink plenty of water and invigorating herbal teas. All kinds of flavours are becoming increasingly available. You simply choose what you like, and that can include Anise, Chamomile, Lemon Verbena, Lime Blossom, Mint, and Sage. They are all incredibly refreshing. Even better, you can grow these herbs in pots or in the garden, where you know they have been organically raised.

Exercise is equally important for all kinds of reasons. It dispels excess adrenaline and improves relaxation and sleep. Swimming prevents your joints from becoming stiff and gives the body a marvellous feeling of freedom. Exercise also tones up your muscles, keeps you in shape, and helps shed excess weight. In short, it keeps you feeling alert, well and able.

One of the biggest problems of stress is that it can all too easily disrupt your appetite and your ability to rest. In turn, such disruption makes you even less able to cope with any setbacks and problems. You get pulled into a depressing, downward spiral. One of the best ways to break out of this pattern is to use herbal remedies to improve your digestion, to help you relax, and to improve your adaptability.

The recipes that follow are designed to help you through difficult times. As long as you do not exceed the doses stated, and are sure that you are using the right plant, it is safe to experiment with these suggestions. But do seek professional help if a problem persists.

key stress symptoms

While some degree of stress is an inevitable part of modern life, there are fortunately several significant ways of tackling it. They should help make sure that your day is not ruined by a tense neck or a nervous stomach. In fact some ways, such as using using excellent massage oils, are so incredibly relaxing, refreshing and enjoyable that they could well become part of your daily routine.

CALMING ANXIETY

Everyone knows exactly what it feels like to be excited, but inappropriate or excessive excitement, often combined with frustration, creates anxiety. In this state, the body produces too much adrenaline. It is primed for "fight or flight" but neither is possible. The heart races, muscles tense and the chest expands. Anxiety can cause many symptoms, including palpitations, sweating, irritability and sleeplessness. In these situations, Rescue Remedy, which is bought ready-made, is useful.

Two drops of Rescue Remedy on the tongue can help prevent a panic attack, and give you ease of mind.

RELAXING TENSE MUSCLES

Muscles can tense as a result of anxiety which often causes slightly raised shoulders or contracted back muscles. The effort of maintaining your muscles in this semi-contracted state is tiring, possibly causing spasms and bad postural habits. The neck stiffens and the back may ache. Tight neck muscles can also hinder blood flowing to the head, creating tension headaches. Moving frequently will release the muscles. Rotate your head or stand and stretch, and take breaks from working or driving. Gently massaging the neck with oil can help.

Tension can build up in the neck and shoulders, causing stiffness.

Cold Infused Oil of Lavender

Fill a glass jar with lavender heads and cover with clear vegetable oil. Allow to steep on a windowsill, shaking the jar every day. Strain and bottle.

The oil can be used for massaging into a stiff neck or back. It can also be added to the bath to keep your skin soft and perfumed, while also encouraging relaxation.

Lavender is an extremely talented herb. It has traditionally been used as a sedative helping combat anxiety and tension. A few drops of infused oil added to your favourite massage oil will also help relax your over-tense muscles. Similar oils can be made from Marjoram (which is anti-spasmodic) and Rosemary.

Herbal Remedies

To help your nervous system readjust and adapt, consider the value of:
- Skullcap
- St John's Wort
- Vervain
- Wild Oats
- Wood Betony

Choose whichever one suits you best and combine it with a specific remedy for the symptom that is causing you most problems.
- To ease palpitations:
  Motherwort or
  Passion Flower.
- To reduce sweating:
  Motherwort or Valerian.
- To help you sleep:
  Passion Flower.

Chamomile tea makes an ideal after-dinner drink.

DIGESTIVES

Many people suffer from digestive upsets when they are stressed. This is because the "fight or flight" activity of the sympathetic nervous system tends to suppress digestive processes. The result may be indigestion, loss of appetite, wind, diarrhoea or even an irritable bowel.

The three recipes below have all been specially designed to help relax the nervous system, encouraging parasympathetic activity and reducing any signs of spasm in the gut.

To Calm Butterflies

Nervous stomachs can be quickly settled by Chamomile, Hops and Lemon Balm combined in a tea, or simply select the best combination for you. Lemon Balm and Chamomile can be taken as frequently as you like.

Put 1 tsp each Lemon Balm, dried Chamomile flowers and Peppermint into a small tea pot or cafetière. Fill with boiling water and allow to steep for at least 10 minutes. Strain and drink at least three times a day or after meals.

Herbal Remedies

- Chamomile
- Cramp Bark
- Cumin
- Fennel, Caraway, Dill
- Hops
- Lemon Balm
- Licorice
- Peppermint

To Relieve Wind and Colic

In a small saucepan, boil 1 tsp each Fennel seeds and Cramp Bark with about 300ml/½ pint/1¼ cups water. Add 1 tsp dried Peppermint. Allow to steep for 10 minutes. Strain and drink.

To Ease Constipation

Make a decoction of Cramp Bark and Fennel as above, but add 1 tsp Licorice root. If the constipation is proving to be an unpleasant, recurrent condition, 1 tsp Linseeds added daily to your breakfast cereal can be very helpful.

The same amount can also be soaked in hot water for about two hours, and drunk before going to bed and again, if necessary, early the next morning when you wake. If the problem is not eased or solved then it is important that you consult your doctor at the first opportunity. Generally, the best way to avoid an attack of constipation is to make sure that you are regularly having a balanced, healthy diet which includes plenty of fresh fruit, vegetables and roughage on a daily basis.

Contraindications

Some herbs should only be used at certain times and not if you are suffering certain other symptoms. For example, since Hops are a sedative, they should only be taken at night, and are not suitable if you are depressed or lacking in sexual energy. Likewise, Licorice should be avoided if you have high blood pressure or oedema. Always consult a medical doctor if in any doubt.

revitalizing recipes

You do not have to be so ill that you are completely confined to bed to take some of the excellent revitalizing herbal remedies now available. Many are purpose designed as a refreshing pick-me-up or tonic to get you through testing emotional and physical times – the bad, dark days – when the mind and body might otherwise become tired and sluggish. Such recipes are nature's way of keeping you healthy.

NERVOUS EXHAUSTION

It is much more likely that you will get ill or depressed after or during a long period of hard work, or from a whole battery of emotional demands. This can easily happen to teachers, for example, at the end of term, or to those who have to care for disabled or sick relations on a long-term basis. You will find that herbal remedies help to give your nervous system plenty of vital support at such testing, difficult times. To make a revitalizing tea, mix equal portions of all the dried herbs listed. Put 3–4 tsp of the mixture into a pot with a lid. Add 600ml/1 pint/2½ cups boiling water. Steep for 10 minutes, strain, and drink 3–4 cups a day.

Herbal Remedies

- Borage
- Licorice
- Skullcap
- St John's Wort
- Wild Oats
- Wood Betony

Make a relaxing herbal tea from a blend of supportive herbs whenever you are feeling exhausted and too tired to cope.

Borage, like Licorice, restores the adrenal glands.

TONICS FOR CONVALESCENCE

Remember that even if your symptoms have gone, your body needs time to recover after an illness. A tonic is extremely useful. Wild Oats and St John's Wort support the nervous system, Vervain promotes relaxation and digestion, and Licorice restores the adrenal glands. Vitamin C supplements should be continued for several weeks after an illness. Alfalfa sprouts are also high in vitamins and minerals. Also note that rest is very important.

Tonic Tea

Put ½ tsp of each of one of the dried herbs listed below into a small pot. Add boiling water. Flavour with Peppermint to taste. (Avoid Licorice if you suffer from high blood pressure or oedema.) Allow to steep for 10 minutes. Strain. Drink three or four cups, warm, each day for at least three weeks.

Herbal Remedies

- Borage
- Licorice
- St John's Wort
- Vervain
- Wild Oats

St John's Wort thrives in a bright, open sunny position.

RELIEVING WINTER BLUES

The old herbalists thought that the appearance of a plant held a clue to its healing action. For instance, Pilewort (Lesser Celandine) has roots that resemble haemorrhoids, and it does indeed make an effective ointment for piles. The flowers of St John's Wort resemble nothing so much as the sun. The plant thrives in sunlight and is known to have anti-depressant effects. There is no better herb than this to take if you are depressed in the winter, when sunlight is in short supply.

Wild Oats also help by strengthening the nervous system and keeping you warm. Rosemary, an evergreen plant, will improve circulation to the head and keep the mind clear. Also, Ginseng capsules can be taken for a month in the early autumn to help you adapt to the difficult transition between seasons.

Winter Brightener

Combine 2 tsp dried St John's Wort with 1 tsp dried Rosemary. Add 250ml/8fl oz/1 cup boiling water. Allow to steep for 10 minutes and then strain. One cup alone is not enough. Drink three times a day throughout the winter.

Herbal Remedies

- Ginseng
- Rosemary
- St John's Wort
- Wild Oats

LIFTING DEPRESSION

Depression is a very good illustration of the close connection that exists between the body and mind: physical and emotional energy are both depleted when you are in a depressed state. Both will benefit from a healthy diet that includes plenty of raw, vital foods, nuts, seeds and B vitamins. A multi-vitamin and mineral supplement is an effective kick-start that will give you an excellent lift. But do not undermine its effect by indulging in stimulants, such as caffeine, because they tend to exhaust both the body and mind.

The refreshing, restorative tea described below is a marvellous, tasty way of restoring the health of your nervous system. It has a slight, barely noticeable, stimulating effect.

Restorative Tea

Mix equal parts of each of the dried herbs listed in the box below. Put 2 tsp of the mixture into a pot. Add 600ml/1 pint/2½ cups boiling water. Allow to steep for 10 minutes and then strain. Drink one cup of this excellent tea three times a day.

Herbal Remedies

- Damiana
- St John's Wort
- Wild Oats

There are many tasty ways of incorporating the goodness of Oats in your diet, including home-made snacks such as biscuits.

headache and night-time remedies

From time to time everyone suffers from headaches and bad sleepless nights. Occasional attacks are just about bearable, but when they become a regular feature and interrupt your life, especially your sex life, it is clearly time to act. All these herbal solutions, ranging from baths and teas to massages, have one aim: to give you back your healthy life as quickly as possible.

RELIEVING TENSION HEADACHES

Headaches are a common symptom of stress. Often they are caused by tension in the neck and upper back muscles. This can prevent adequate blood supply to the head and thus lead to pain. Both massage and exercise can ease this kind of headache.

Scented Baths

Pour a few drops of essential oil or infused oil into a hot bath, lie back and relax. Better, tie a bunch of herbs under the hot tap as you fill the bath. Rub two drops of essential oil of Lavender mixed with 1 tsp water on the head when stressed.

Soothing Tea

Put 1 tsp dried Wood Betony and ½ tsp dried Lavender or Rosemary into a cup. Top up with boiling water and leave for 10 minutes, before straining and drinking. Repeat hourly.

Herbal remedies

- Lavender
- Rosemary

Hang a muslin bag of fresh or dried herbs under the hot tap.

Help yourself beat a hangover by taking a herbal remedy.

HANGOVER REMEDIES

Most people know what a hangover feels like – a combination of headache, nausea, fuzzy head and depression. Most of these symptoms are connected with the liver being overloaded. Bitter herbs stimulate the liver and speed up its ability to detoxify. Vervain is bitter and Lavender aids digestion; both herbs also lift the spirits. If you have a hangover it is also advisable to drink plenty of water and take extra vitamin C.

Morning-After Tea

Put 1 tsp dried Vervain and ½ tsp Lavender flowers into a pot. Add 600ml/1 pint/2½ cups boiling water and cover to keep in the volatile oils. Steep for 10 minutes. Strain and sweeten with a little honey. Sip through the day until you start to feel better.

Herbal Remedies

- Lavender
- Vervain

REVITALIZING THE LIBIDO

Depression or anxiety can all too easily hinder and interrupt your sex life. This may be because your energy is too low, or it may in fact be connected with a hormone imbalance. Damiana stimulates both the nervous and hormonal systems, and it has vital constituents which convert to hormones in the body. Vervain is good at releasing tension and stress, and it was traditionally used as an aphrodisiac. Wild Oats and Ginger root are both considered stimulating too.

Energizing Tea

Put 1 tsp dried Damiana and 1 tsp dried Vervain into a pot. Add 600ml/1 pint/2½ cups of boiling water. Leave to steep for 10 minutes. Strain and flavour with Licorice, Ginger or honey, as you prefer. Drink two cups a day.

Herbal Remedies	
• Damiana	• Vervain
• Ginger	• Wild Oats

Teas or decoctions made with the right herbs can help restore energy of all kinds, including sexual energy.

ENHANCING SLEEP

There are many different types of insomnia, and the causes are varied. If you really cannot sleep then it is best to experiment with the remedies below to find the one herb or combination of herbs that suits you best. If the problem is long term and you have not been sleeping well for a period of time, then take a nervous system tonic to improve your well being.

In the evenings, drink teas that have been made from relaxing herbs. Lavender oil in a hot bath before bed and on the pillow will also help. You could even try using a Hop pillow. Furthermore, it is important to give yourself plenty of time at the end of the day to relax and wind down. Exercise, meditation and yoga are all good at helping you fall asleep.

You can make or buy a herb pillow to encourage sound sleep.

Sleepy Tea

Put 1 tsp each dried Chamomile, Vervain and Lemon Balm into a pot. Add about 600ml/1 pint/2½ cups boiling water. Leave to steep for 10 minutes. Strain and drink one cup after supper. Warm the rest and drink before going to bed.

If you continue to have problems sleeping, add a decoction of 1 tsp Valerian root or ½ tsp dried Hops or Californian Poppy to this blend of herbs.

Chamomile tea is not only beneficial but extremely refreshing.

Herbal Remedies	
• Californian Poppy	• Passion Flower
• Chamomile	• Valerian
• Hops	• Vervain
• Lemon Balm	

guide to herbs and their uses

It has long been known that herbs are an essential part of the kitchen, adding all kinds of flavours, and for helping to relieve and cure a range of problems from migraines to wind (gas). The early physic gardens in monasteries were really basic pharmacies stocking many of these essential plants. Do not try and compete. Just grow those herbs that you know will help you feel much better.

USING HERBS

The herbs described on the following pages are a particularly useful group for helping tackle stress and various other common conditions. Reading the notes and studying the pictures will help you decide which would be most beneficial for you and your garden. After all, they should also help make a special relaxing feature. If planting them in groups, remember to put the tallest in the centre and the smaller ones around.

You may well want to try several as remedies before deciding which you find most helpful. Note that herbs do not usually work instantly, so do not be impatient and give them at least two weeks to take effect. If you do not feel better in three weeks, seek the help of a qualified practitioner. Herbs can also be used in various combinations, and you will find suggestions for putting them together to give additional benefits.

Since most of us would benefit from a nerve tonic during stressful times, choose the herbal remedy best suited to you.

For example, if when stressed you start to feel depressed, then look for a stimulating herbal tonic such as Wild Oats. If, however, stress makes you feel anxious and you start developing symptoms such as palpitations, sweating and sleeplessness, then turn to those herbs that have a relaxing effect.

Rescue Remedy, because it is not strictly herbal, but a Bach Flower remedy is not included in this directory, but it is readily available over the counter.

It is quite clear that some herbs are multi-talented. Borage gives a marvellous show of flowers and adds to the cottage garden, attracting plenty of bees. The leaves add a cucumber flavour to drinks, the flowers can garnish salads, and the oil lowers blood pressure. Lavender is another all-purpose herb, essential for pot-pourris and for a range of soothing treatments. If you find some plants do not succeed in certain parts of the garden, move them around until you find a more suitables place and you may well find that they perk up.

LADY'S MANTLE

Alchemilla xanthochlora syn.
A. vulgaris, Virgin's Cape

The unusual leaves of this plant resemble a cloak, hence its common names. The name Alchemilla derives from the Arabic word for alchemy, signifying its power to help make a change. A larger species, Alchemilla mollis, is grown as a foliage plant. Lady's Mantle is a women's herb and helps balance menstrual cycles. As a douche or wash, an infusion helps sooth any itching or inflammation.

n o t e s • Parts used: Leaves and flowers.
• Dose: 1 tsp dried/2 tsp fresh to a cup of boiling water three times a day.

PASQUE FLOWER

Anemone pulsatilla, Wind Flower

One of the most beautiful medicinal herbs with purple spring flowers. The common name comes from *Pasch* meaning Easter. Pasque Flower is a sedative, bactericidal, anti-spasmodic painkiller used to treat the reproductive organs. It is used against all types of pain affecting male and female genital organs.

n o t e s • Parts used: Dried leaves and flowers.
• Dose: A very low dose is needed – it is advisable to consult a herbalist.
c a u t i o n : Do not use the fresh plant.

MUGWORT

Artemisia vulgaris

The "mother of herbs" grows robustly along roadsides and is said to protect the traveller. It is best described as a tonic with particular application to the digestive and nervous systems; it reduces nervous indigestion, nausea and irritability. As a womb tonic it helps regulate the menstrual cycle, reduces any associated period pain and PMS. It is also used to repel insects, including moths.

n o t e s • Parts used: Flowers and leaves.
• Dose: ¼–½ tsp three times a day.
c a u t i o n : Avoid in pregnancy.

WILD OATS

Avena sativa

Oats are an excellent tonic to the nervous system. They slightly stimulate and are a long-term remedy for nervous exhaustion. They also help cope with shingles and herpes. Oats contain vitamin E, iron, zinc, manganese and protein and help reduce cholesterol.

n o t e s • Parts used: Seeds and stalks.
• Dose: There are many ways to take oats – in gruel, porridge, flapjacks, oatcakes and other dishes, as well as tea.
c a u t i o n : Oats are not suitable for those who are sensitive to gluten.

BORAGE
Borago officinalis

A strapping plant with lovely, luminous blue flowers. They make an attractive garnish to ice cream and cold summer puddings. Borage boosts the production of adrenaline and is useful in times of stress. It is also very nutritious, and helps to treat skin diseases and rheumatism.

n o t e s • Parts used: The leaves, flowers and seeds. The leaves need to be dried quite quickly and are best heated very gently in a cool oven until they are crisp.
• Dose: I tsp dried/2 tsp fresh to one cup of boiling water.

CALIFORNIAN POPPY
Eschscholzia californica

The beautiful, delicate flowers last for one day and are then replaced by long pointed seed pods. The stunning hot orange, yellow and pinkish colours of the blooms might account for its French name, *globe de soleil*. Californian Poppy is a gentle painkiller and sedative which reduces spasms and over-excitability.

n o t e s • Parts used: The whole plant
• Dose: I tsp dried herb to a cup of boiling water.
c a u t i o n: It is important to avoid this herb if you suffer from glaucoma.

CHAMOMILE
Chamomilla recutita or
Chamaemelum nobile

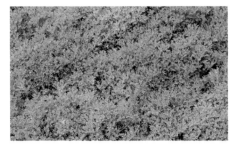

This pretty daisy is one of the better known herbs, possibly because it is so useful. Use the flowerheads alone in a tea or tincture to relax both the digestive function and those gut feelings that may sometimes disturb you. It makes a very suitable tea to drink late in the day because it has quite the opposite effect to that of coffee, which actually exacerbates tension and anxiety.

n o t e s • Parts used: Flower heads.
• Dose: I tsp dried/2 tsp fresh to a cup of boiling water.

LICORICE
Glycyrrhiza glabra

A highly useful herb which has been cultivated since the Middle Ages for its sweet, aromatic roots. It aids digestion and reduces inflammation along the gut, loosening the bowels. Licorice heated in honey makes a soothing syrup, helping to soothe attacks of bronchitis and asthma.

n o t e s • Parts used: The root (Licorice sticks) or solidified juice in the form of black bars.
• Dose: I tsp to a cup of boiling water.
c a u t i o n: Not recommended for those with high blood pressure or oedema.

HOP
Humulus lupulus

The name Hop comes from the Anglo-Saxon *hoppen*, "to climb": the twining fibrous stems may top 4.5m/15ft. Hops are taken as a bitter tonic helping both to improve digestion and to reduce any restlessness. It also has a sedative effect and will provoke deep sleep. The action is partly due to its volatile oils.

n o t e s • Parts used: Dried flowers from the female plant, called "strobiles".
• Dose: Not more than I tsp a day.
c a u t i o n: Avoid the use of Hops during any depressive illness.

ST JOHN'S WORT
Hypericum perforatum

To be sure that you have the right plant, hold a leaf to the sun; the oil glands look like little holes. The plant is now well known for its anti-depressant action. It is a nerve tonic which helps nervous exhaustion and damage to nerves caused by diseases such as shingles.

n o t e s • Parts used: Flowering tops.
• Dose: I tsp dried/2 tsp fresh to a cup of boiling water, three times a day.
c a u t i o n: This remedy is best avoided when you are spending any time out in the garden when there is bright sunlight.

GINSENG

Korean Ginseng, *Panax spp.*

By improving the production of adrenal hormones, Korean Ginseng helps the body to adapt to stress and resist disease. It should only be taken for short periods though. It benefits ME sufferers.

n o t e s • Parts used: Dried root.
• Dose: 1g per day.
c a u t i o n : Avoid the use of Ginseng during pregnancy or when taking other stimulants. Do not take high doses for more than six weeks without seeking expert advice. Stop taking Ginseng if it makes you feel agitated or if you develop a headache.

LAVENDER

Lavandula spp.

Everybody knows this fragrant plant. Herbalists call it a thymoleptic, which means it raises the spirits. This, combined with its anti-infective action and relaxing properties, makes Lavender a powerful remedy. The essential oil is used externally for relaxation and to heal sores and burns. Lavender can also be taken internally in a tea or tincture. It is also an ideal remedy for irritation, indigestion and for the onset of a migraine attack.

n o t e s • Parts used: Dried root.
• Dose: 1g per day.

MOTHERWORT

Leonurus cardiaca

The Latin name refers to the leaves shaped like a lion's tail. It is a great calmer if tension is causing palpitations or sweats. It improves the circulatory system and is also used to relieve any menstrual and menopausal problems. Motherwort can also help to lower blood pressure.

n o t e s • Parts used: Leaves and flowers.
• Dose: 1 tsp dried/2 tsp fresh to a cup of boiling water three times a day, or 2 tsp syrup.
c a u t i o n : It is important that it is avoided in the first trimester of pregnancy.

LEMON BALM

Melissa officinalis, Bee Balm

This plant has so much vitality that it can spread all over the garden. It makes a suitable drink for every day; hot in winter and iced in summer. Lemon Balm aids digestion and relaxation, and sensitive digestive systems. It is much used for irritable bowels, nervous indigestion, anxiety and depression. It makes a good bedtime drink, promoting peaceful sleep and a sense of relaxation.

n o t e s • Parts used: Leaves and flowers.
• Dose: 1 tsp to a cup of boiling water, taken up to three or four times a day.

MINT

Mentha spp.

Peppermint (Mentha piperita) is a hybrid between Spearmint and Watermint. It is antiseptic and anti-parasitic, and will reduce itching. It has a temporary anaesthetic effect on the skin and gives the impression of cooling. It is included in lotions for massaging aching muscles, and makes an effective footbath.

n o t e s • Parts used: Leaves and flowers.
• Dose: 1 tsp dried/2 tsp fresh to a cup of boiling water.
c a u t i o n : It is important that it is avoided in the first trimester of pregnancy.

EVENING PRIMROSE

Oenothera biennis

A beautiful plant, luminous in the twilight, which freely self-seeds in the garden. It is used externally for eczema and other dry skin conditions. Taken internally, Evening Primrose oil reduces cholesterol levels and benefits the circulation. It has a decent success rate on women with PMS, and can help calm hyperactive children. It also helps regenerate livers which have been damaged by alcohol.

n o t e s • Parts used: Oil from seeds.
• Dose: Capsules as directed.
c a u t i o n : Avoid in cases of epilepsy.

MARJORAM
Origanum vulgare

There are many species of Marjoram, and they are used in potpourris and cooking. Medicinally, Marjoram reduces depression and helps tackle nervous headaches. It contains volatile oils which are antispasmodic, making it useful when soothing digestive upsets. The infused oil can be used in the bath to relieve stiffness, or rubbed on to soothe sore and aching joints or muscles.

n o t e s • Parts used: Leaves.
• Dose: I tsp dried/2 tsp fresh to a cup of boiling water, taken twice a day.

PASSION FLOWER
Passiflora incarnata, Maypop

This is a climbing plant which produces spectacular flowers. It is often included in sleeping mixes, and is very helpful when tackling restlessness and insomnia. It counteracts the effects of adrenaline, which may cause anxiety, palpitations or nervous tremors. It is used to ease the pain of neuralgia.

n o t e s • Parts used: Dried leaves and flowers.
• Dose: ¼-½ tsp dried herb twice a day, or I tsp at night, or take an over-the-counter preparation as directed.

ROSEMARY
Rosmarinus officinalis

A familiar plant containing several active, aromatic oils. Like Lavender, it can be used both externally, in the form of an essential or infused oil, and internally as a flavouring, tea or tincture. The actions of Rosemary are centred on the head and womb. It increases the supply of blood to both. In the head it helps tackle cold headaches and in the gut eases spasms due to poor circulation.

n o t e s • Parts used: Leaves and flowers.
• Dose: I tsp to a cup of boiling water taken up to three times a day.

SAGE
Salvia officinalis

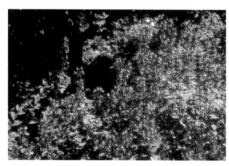

A beautiful, evergreen plant with fine purple flowers in early summer. Like many culinary herbs, it aids digestion. It has antiseptic properties and can be used as a compress on wounds that are slow to heal, or as a gargle or for infections of the mouth or throat. It is also said that it will help reduce night sweats and menopausal hot flushes, and can darken greyish hair.

n o t e s • Parts used: Leaves.
• Dose: I tsp dried per cup of boiling water.
c a u t i o n : Avoid during pregnancy.

SKULLCAP
Scutellaria lateriflora

This herb is another nervous tonic. It was traditionally associated with the head, because it produces skull-like seed pods. It is very calming. Skullcap can help reduce anxiety and restlessness. Its bitter taste encourages the liver to remove toxins from the body, as well as excess hormones which can cause degrees of premenstrual tension.

n o t e s • Parts used: Aerial parts, which are harvested after flowering.
• Dose: I tsp dried/2 tsp fresh to a cup of boiling water.

WOOD BETONY
Stachys betonica syn. S. officinalis, Betonica officinalis, Bishop's Weed

An attractive plant with purple flowers. Wood Betony aids the nervous system, especially if sick headaches and poor memory are a problem. It also encourages blood flow to the head. Always a popular remedy throughout Europe, it is certainly well worth trying if you get headaches or migraines.

n o t e s • Parts used: Aerial parts.
• Dose: I tsp dried/2 tsp fresh herb to a cup of boiling water.
c a u t i o n : It is important that you avoid high doses during pregnancy.

LIME BLOSSOM

Tilia x europaea, Linden Blossom

The tall upstanding Lime tree has honey-scented blossom. Medicinally it is relaxing and cleansing. It makes a helpful tea for fevers and flu, especially if combined with Yarrow and Peppermint. It encourages sweating and aids the body through fevers. It is also used to reduce hardening of the arteries and high blood pressure, and to relieve migraines.

n o t e s • Parts used: Flowers, including the pale yellowish bracts.
• Dose: I tsp dried/2 tsp fresh to a cup of boiling water taken three times a day.

DAMIANA

Turnera diffusa

Damiana grows in South America and the West Indies. It was previously called Turnera aphrodisiaca and is a tonic to the nervous and reproductive systems. It is useful if the sexual function is impaired. It is taken as a remedy by men, but the stimulant and tonic work equally well for women. Damiana is harvested when in flower, and is dried for use as an anti-depressant, and to relieve anxiety.

n o t e s • Parts used: Leaves and stem.
• Dose: 2 tsp to a cup of boiling water, which can be taken twice a day.

VALERIAN

Valeriana officinalis, All Heal

This is a tall herb with whitish-pink flowers which grows in damp places. The root has a powerful sedative effect on the nervous system, and effectively reduces tension. It can be used to reduce period pains, spasms, palpitations, and hyperactivity. It is good if anxiety makes sleep difficult.

n o t e s • Parts used: Dried root.
• Dose: I tsp to a cup of boiling water at bedtime.
c a u t i o n : High doses taken over a long period may cause headaches.

CRAMP BARK

Viburnum opulus, Guelder Rose

A decorative wild bush which produces glorious white and pale pink spring flowers, followed by autumn red berries. Writer Geoffrey Grigson said it had a smell like crisply fried, well-peppered trout. Therapeutically, the use of Cramp Bark is a good illustration of the connection between body and mind. It reduces spasms whatever the cause and helps tackle constipation, period pains, and high blood pressure.

n o t e s • Parts used: Dried bark.
• Dose: I tsp to a cup of boiling water.

CHASTE TREE

Vitex agnus-castus, Monk's Pepper

The common name reflects a slight anti-oestrogen effect which can cool passion: perhaps this property may account for its other common name, Monk's Pepper. Small doses of this herb can re-balance the hormones and reduce some of the symptoms of PMS, menopausal change, infertility, post-natal depression and irregular periods. It also increases milk production after birth.

n o t e s • Parts used: Dried ripe fruits.
• Dose: 10–20 drops of tincture which are taken first thing in the morning.

VERVAIN

Verbena officinalis, Herb of Grace

An unassuming plant with tiny flowers. Vervain is a nervous tonic with a slightly sedative action. It is useful for treating nervous exhaustion and symptoms of tension which include headaches, nausea and migraine. It has a bitter taste and has been used for gall bladder problems. It is quite often recommended for anyone who has depression, and works well with Wild Oats.

n o t e s • Parts used: Leaves and flowers.
• Dose: I tsp dried/2 tsp fresh to a cup of boiling water.

homeopathy

homeopathy
homeopathy thy

The name "homeopathy" was coined by Samuel Hahnemann from two Greek words meaning "similar suffering", or "like cures like". Appalled by the savage medical practices of the day, Hahnemann, a German doctor and chemist, started on a course of study that led to the development of homeopathy. His philosophy of disease and its cure through natural processes has changed very little from that day to this. The traditional approach is today's approach.

The principle of like curing like, or "the law of similars", as it is sometimes called, decrees that if a substance can cause harm to a healthy person in large doses, it also has the potential to cure the same problem in tiny doses by stimulating the body's own natural energy, enabling it to heal itself.

The law is best illustrated by example. In the 19th century it was a custom among German women to take the herb Valerian as a stimulant. The practice was abused and overtaxed the nervous system. Yet, given in minute doses, Valerian relaxes the nervous system, and is one of homeopathy's main remedies for insomnia.

The doses used in homeopathy are so minute that they cannot be acting directly on the physical body. Hahnemann considered that what they did was act dynamically: in other words, the energy of the remedy stimulated the natural healing energy of the body. If it had been in a state of disharmony, then it would be propelled back to its former, healthy state.

homeopathy and health

Homeopathy is not only an energy medicine, it is also holistic. Homeopaths convincingly argue that the body is much more than the sum of its various parts, and that the mind, the emotions and indeed the organs are somehow intricately interconnected. Consequently, the treatments they give are more "rounded" than those found in traditional medicine. They are not just aimed at the symptom, but at the whole person.

ENERGY WITHIN

The mechanics of this interconnection are elaborate and hard to explain, but it is clear that the process really does work. The key point is that underlying the physical and mental systems of the body is a refined system of energy which is self-regulating. It generally works extremely well. You sense it in action when you become ill. We usually get better even without taking a medicine. The body heals itself though it might need support when its own natural energy is low.

Treatment

The healing process is like running a car. Modern cars are so efficient that, provided you maintain them properly, give them the right fuel and drive them sensibly, problems seldom arise. Then one night you forget to turn off the lights and the next morning the battery is flat and your car incapacitated. The only way to get it moving again – the only cure – is to get a transfer of energy, in the form of a jump start from another battery. Homeopathy is in many ways just like getting an energizing jump start.

Homeopathy is becoming increasingly popular because of the serious concerns about drugs-based orthodox medicine. Many drugs are toxic and the side-effects in susceptible people can actually be quite unpleasant. Even if the side-effects are not observable, the long-term consequences from the excessive use of drugs are not always fully appreciated. In fact modern medicine seldom cures, and it does not even pretend to. What it does do is alleviate and palliate the symptoms, and manage the illness, but since it addresses the symptoms and rarely the cause, the results are not entirely satisfactory.

Homeopathy is different because it is safe and it does not treat the removal of symptoms as an end in itself. Symptoms are considered as signs of distress or adjustment. The correct remedy removes the cause of the problem; the symptoms will then fade away. Homeopathy is highly rated because it takes into account the nature of the person. It knows that when two people have been diagnosed as having the same illness, they can actually become ill in quite different ways and will require different remedies to effect a satisfactory cure.

Sometimes our bodies just do not seem to be firing on all cyclinders, and we need a carefully chosen homeopathic boost to revive them.

DEFINING DISEASE

We become ill when our energy is depleted or when we are out of harmony. In fact the word "disease" could be more accurately written "dis-ease", indicating that we are definitely not at ease, and for a disease to be cured it is not necessary to give it a name. To cure homeopathically depends on a sensitive, accurate analysis of the symptoms. There is usually no need for a diagnosis, for it is widely said that there are no diseases, only what might be called people who are "dis-eased".

Symptoms

Except for any life-threatening situations, symptoms are not the primary problem. They reflect a picture which shows how the system is making adjustments to heal itself. For example, both diarrhoea and vomiting are the body's way of ridding itself of unwanted "material", and the intolerable itching of eczema does not specifically mean that you have a skin disease. Rather it means that there is an imbalance in your whole system, and that your body is pushing the problem to the safest possible place, well away from the essential organs. The skin becomes an organ of elimination.

Treating the Whole Person

Some people are very robust and seldom become ill, others are over-sensitive and become run-down and sick after a slight chill or an emotional upset. For some, the chest is the greatest weakness: winter colds quickly turn to bronchitis. With others digestion is the problem: the slightest unusual change to their diet causes an immediate upset. Homeopathy acknowledges these many differences and adjusts all treatments accordingly. The professional homeopath will always prescribe "constitutionally" to try to strengthen the weak areas, as well as the whole system.

Causes of Illness

There are many causes of disease. Some are obvious, such as being run-down and poor nutrition, but illness might have an emotional cause. Stress creates disharmony which manifests itself in physical ailments. Homeopathy takes such factors into account and, if possible, tries to mitigate them and strengthen the sufferer.

Mental and emotional stress, often at work, can surprisingly quickly lead to a range of physical problems.

CHRONIC DISEASES

With so much battering from within and without, it may seem a wonder that we are not all permanently ill. Of course, many people are. Although many of the acute infectious diseases of the past have ceased to be a serious problem, their places have now been taken by today's chronic diseases. Never has there been so much cancer and heart disease, eczema and asthma, or even digestive problems such as irritable bowels. Our immune systems are overstretched in combating these problems.

The Immune System

It is all too easy to ignore the incredible adaptability and intelligence of the immune system, which appears to make heroic efforts to keep us up and running despite considerable adversity. One writer shrewdly called this intelligence the "vital force". He described it as "the spirit-like force which rules in supreme sovereignty". It has also been well described as "the invisible driver", overseeing the checks and balances that are needed to keep us in the best possible health.

The Vital Force at Work

Most of the time we are completely and utterly unaware of this sophisticated balancing process which is entirely automatic and pre-programmed through our genetic make-up. We can certainly observe it in action when we contract an acute illness (i.e. one that arises suddenly) such as a fever or a cough. What we may not always realize is that the fever is really a necessary, natural function and that it actually "burns up" the infection, and that the cough exists to prevent any active accumulation of mucus in the lungs. The body is extremely resourceful. However, chronic diseases (i.e. those that develop slowly, or are of long duration) might well need outside help, and a consultation with an experienced, professional practitioner.

Reading the Symptoms

When trying to cure a disease, the vital force causes the body to produce symptoms. Homeopaths call this "the symptom picture". These symptoms accurately reflect exactly what is happening inside, and they also indicate what outside help or extra energy is therefore now required.

For example, during a flu epidemic two children in the same family become ill. The first child catches the flu very suddenly, overnight, and develops a high fever with a red face and a dry burning heat all over the body. The second child's symptoms might be very different, appearing quite slowly over several days. This child's fever is much lower, but he is shaky and shivery and his muscles ache all over. Both children have the same flu, but the vital force has produced completely different symptoms. Each child therefore needs to be treated in quite a different way. The homeopath will certainly understand this and give the first child the remedy Belladonna, while the second child receives quantities of Gelsemium. Homeopathy is well known for excelling at individualizing such treatments.

While it is quite true to say that in homeopathy we do not treat symptoms but the individual sufferer, we are still extremely interested in the symptoms. For it is through careful observation of the complete symptom picture that we can discover which remedy is required. In acute ailments the vital force will eventually effect a cure, given sufficient time, but by giving a helping hand from an accurate reading of the symptoms, that is by giving the body an "energy fix", the process can in fact be speeded up considerably.

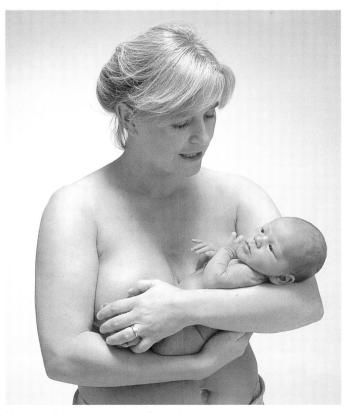

We are all born with a vital force that oversees our health.

using remedies

When first taking a homeopathic remedy, you might well be totally bewildered how anyone could possibly know that a certain recipe of mixed ingredients is the one that is best for you. In fact there is no guesswork. The exact remedies for all kinds of problems have been known and listed for hundreds of years. The technique is precise and proven, and the beauty of it is that remedies can be subtly fine-tuned to suit your particular ailment.

REMEDY SOURCES

The remedies used in homeopathy are derived from many sources. The majority are prepared from plants, but many minerals are also used and a few remedies are even prepared from insect and snake poisons and other toxic substances. Do not be alarmed about the toxins because they have been diluted so that no danger remains. The Law of Similars shows that the most powerful poisons can be turned into equally strong remedies. In fact about 2,000 have now been described and documented, but in practice most professional homeopaths use only a fraction of that surprisingly high number.

In homeopathy every symptom is fully taken into account when trying to apply the right remedy.

The process that turns a substance into a remedy is called "potentization", and consists of two main procedures, dilution and succussion (or vigorous shaking). When you buy a remedy note a number after its name, usually 6, but also other numbers rising in a scale: 30, 200, 1M (1,000). Sometimes a "c", standing for centesimal (one hundredth) appears after the number. It shows how often the remedy has been diluted and succussed.

A remedy is prepared by dissolving a tincture of the original material, usually in alcohol. On the centesimal scale, the 6th potency means that the original substance has been diluted six times, each time using a dilution of one part in a hundred. This results in a remedy that contains only one part in a million million of the source material. Yet the greater the potency (number of dilutions), the greater the remedy's power.

Between each dilution, the remedy is succussed. When the potentization is complete the remedy is preserved in alcohol, and a few drops can be added to a bottle of milk-sugar pills or a cream. The remedy is now ready to use.

Tissue Salts

The 19th-century German doctor Wilhelm Schussler identified 12 vital minerals, or "tissue salts", essential to health. According to his theory, many diseases are associated with a deficiency of one or more of these substances, but they can be cured by taking the tissue salts in minute doses, singly or in all kinds of different combinations.

PROVINGS

Almost all homeopathic remedies have been "proved", or tested, although practitioners gain additional knowledge of them from clinical experience. In a proving, a remedy is tested on a group of healthy people over a period of time, until they develop symptoms. Neither the supervisor nor the group should know what remedy they are proving. This is a double blind test, conducted on sound, regulated principles. The symptoms that the provers develop are accurately collated until a complete symptom picture has been obtained. Consequently, we know exactly what the remedy can cure.

Once proved, remedies can be used for all time. Hundreds of original remedies are still in use today. The remedy pictures are described in great detail in volumes called *Materia Medica*. Because thousands of symptoms for thousands of remedies have been proved over the last 200 years or so, no one homeopath could possibly remember them all. They are therefore listed in another impressively detailed book called *The Homeopathic Repertory*. It is, in effect, an index to the *Materia Medica*. Between them, these two astonishing books cover most symptoms.

In homeopathy, physical examinations are seldom necessary, but bright, sparkling eyes are a sign of good health.

Even members of the same family will have different susceptibilities to illness and react differently.

CHOOSING THE CORRECT REMEDY

With a copy of the *Materia Medica*, the homeopath is now well equipped to match the symptoms with the symptom picture. This is usually known as finding the similimum (or similar).

The Symptom Picture

Finding the correct remedy is like trying to arrange a perfect marriage. If the two partners are compatible, success is almost certain. If the remedy is a good match to the symptoms, the patient is going to feel a good deal better, the natural way. The words "I feel better in myself" are like music to the ears of the prescribing homeopath, because it means that the natural healing processes have been stimulated successfully, even if some of the physical symptoms remain. It should be only a short time before they too disappear.

The prescriber is like a detective looking for clues. Apart from the obvious general symptoms, such as fever, headache or a cough, you should note what are called the "modalities" – that is, what aggravates or alleviates the symptoms, or makes the person feel generally better or worse. They might include the need for warmth, or cool air, sitting up or lying down. Notice whether the person is thirsty or sweaty; whether the tongue is coated, and the state of the breath. What kind of pain is it: throbbing, stitching or sudden stabs of intense agony?

It is also important to note if the symptoms have an obvious cause? Did they arise after an emotional shock, or after catching a chill in a cold wind? Did they arise dramatically and suddenly in the middle of the night, or have they developed in rather a nondescript way over a number of days?

It is also very important to note the person's state of mind. For example, irritable people who just want to be left alone may need quite different remedies from those who want to be comforted and are easily consoled. The homeopath has to be sensitive in all kinds of ways.

HOW TO USE REMEDIES

Many minor and self-limiting acute problems can be treated safely at home with a basic first-aid kit. However, for more serious long-term ailments, or if you feel out of your depth and really worried – especially if young children or old people are ill – seek help from your own homeopath or doctor. Access to professional homeopaths is now much easier, and they can often do wonderful things for persistent and chronic disease. Be assured that qualified practitioners will have completed three or four years' training.

What the given remedy is doing is helping your body to help itself. Sometimes there may not be a great deal you can do – a well-established cold is going to mean several days of suffering whether you intervene or not. In other cases, the sooner you act, the better: for instance, if you take Arnica (either in pill form, or rubbed-in cream if appropriate) immediately after a bad fall for the bruising and shock, the results will be very impressive with the healing time being be much shorter.

You can often limit the duration or intensity of suffering, as in fever, sepsis (pus-forming bacteria), pain, indigestion and many other conditions. Moreover, there will be many satisfying times when the problem is aborted or cured altogether.

Once you are confident of an improvement then the vital force needs no further help, and you can stop taking the remedy. You will do no harm if you do in fact carry on, but there is really no point in trying to aquire far more energy than your mind and body actually require. In homeopathy it is perfectly true to say that less is actually more.

You may feel rather hesitant and uncertain about treating very young children, but it is known that homeopathy usually works extremely well on them, and can be safely used from birth.

remedies for common ailments
remedies for common ailments

remedies for common ailments

Many straightforward problems can be treated at home using homeopathy. For each one, the following pages list a number of remedies that are likely to be the most helpful in the situation. Read the remedy picture carefully and choose the one that best seems to match the symptoms that you have observed. Then, when you have selected your own particular remedy, double-check it very carefully with the more detailed description which you will find listed in the Materia Medica section. Rescue Remedy is often used by homeopaths, though it is not strictly homeopathic, for that reason it has not been included in the Materia Medica.

How to Take the Remedy

Carefully empty one pill into the cap of the bottle. If more than one tumbles into the cap, tip the others back into the bottle without touching them. This is quite important. If you are shaky, use a folded piece of paper to help if necessary.

Next, drop the pill on to a clean tongue – that is, you should take the remedy at least ten minutes before or after eating, drinking or cleaning your teeth. The pill should be sucked for about thirty seconds before being crunched and swallowed. Remedies for babies can be crushed to a powder in an envelope and given on a teaspoon.

Giving the Remedy

The 6th and 30th potencies are most useful for home use. As a rough rule of thumb, use a 6c three or four times a day, or a 30c once or twice daily until symptoms improve. One pill at a time is all that is necessary; there is no need to reduce the dosage for children.

In serious situations such as a high fever or after an accident, you can give a remedy every half-hour if necessary. Since the active content of the remedy is so small, you cannot overdose in acute situations and if you do not get a good reaction within a day or overnight, you may want to consider a second remedy. Never worry about giving the wrong remedy: it will either work or it will not. If it does not work you will have done no harm to the patient.

Sometimes the symptoms may change after giving a remedy, so that a new picture emerges. You then need to find a new remedy to fit the new picture. If the situation improves, or the picture is unclear, watch and wait. Only intervene if you feel you need to.

Until you get used to the method of diagnosis, you may find it helpful to consult a practitioner on the first few occasions, this is also a good idea if symptoms persist. The Homeopath will also be able to give other effective advice.

colds, flu and toothache

Most colds, unless nipped in the bud, take their natural course and they should clear up in about week. Even so, they can make life pretty uncomfortable, as can a throbbing toothache. Flu, however, can be much more debilitating, though a good remedy can often help ameliorate the symptoms, soon reducing the effects of aching bones, weak legs, headaches, high temperatures, shivering and even dizziness.

Colds and Flu

If flu comes on suddenly, often at night and perhaps after catching a chill, with symptoms of high fever and profuse sweating, Aconite is a perfectly good remedy. If the symptoms are similarly sudden and with a high temperature, but accompanied by redness, burning heat and a headache, then the remedy is much more likely to be Belladonna.

For flu that appears more slowly, accompanied by extreme thirst, irritability and the desire to be left alone, Bryonia will be very useful. Probably the most widely used remedy in flu, though, is Gelsemium. The most pronounced symptoms are shivering, aching muscles and general weakness. Where aching bones are prominent, use Eupatorium.

For head colds with sneezing and an acrid nasal discharge, Allium cepa or Arsenicum should be very helpful. If the sinuses are also affected and there is a lot of yellow-green mucus which appears in globules, or if it looks sticky and stringy, then use quantities of Kali bich.

For a general tonic, both during and after the flu, when your symptoms are not very well defined and there is a general feeling of malaise, try using Ferrum phos.

Kali bich can be a good remedy for blocked sinuses where there is pain and a green stringy discharge.

The most useful remedies at the start of a high fever in children are Aconite and Belladonna.

Fevers

Fevers, particularly in children, whose temperatures may be quite high, may seem alarming, but it should be remembered that they are the body's own efficient, natural response to dealing with and burning up infection.

The two main remedies for high fevers that appear suddenly are Aconite and Belladonna. Thirst and sweat characterize the Aconite picture, while Belladonna cases will reveal a dry skin, redness, and a throbbing pain in the affected area. If the fever appears more slowly and the person is irritable, wants to be left alone and is very thirsty for cold water, try Bryonia. For flu-like fevers, with shivering, weakness and aching muscles, use Gelsemium. Ferrum phos can be used in milder fevers, with no particularly distinctive symptoms. Pulsatilla is really useful in children's fevers, where the child soon becomes very emotional, clingy and weepy, and wants to be comforted.

If the period of fever is made more uncomfortable by poor circulation and chilblains, the former can be helped by herbs that stimulate the circulatory system. Angelica and Ginger have a good track record, taken with the likes of Yarrow. The latter is best treated by a tincture of Arnica.

At the first sign of a head cold, try Arsenicum or Allium cepa.

Coughs and Croup

For very harsh, dry, violent coughs, which may appear suddenly and may be worse at night, use Aconite. For a hard, dry painful cough, which seems to be helped by holding the chest very tightly and also by long drinks of cold water, use Bryonia.

For deep-seated, dry, spasmodic coughs that may end in retching or even vomiting, use Drosera. Painful, barking coughs, which produce thick yellow-green mucus, may be helped by Hepar sulph. For coughs that are really quite suffocating, and which sound sharp and rasping, like a saw going through wood, try Spongia. Where there is a lot of mucus seemingly trapped in the chest, try Ant tart.

Croup is a horrible sounding dry cough that affects small children. The main remedies are Aconite, Hepar sulph and Spongia. Try each one of these remedies in turn if it is in any way difficult to differentiate between the symptoms.

Sore Throats

If a sore throat starts suddenly, often during the night, perhaps following a chill and accompanied by a high temperature, try Aconite. If the throat burns and throbs painfully and looks very red, it may be eased by Belladonna.

For a sore throat that looks very swollen and puffy, with a stinging pain, try Apis. Hepar sulph can be used for an extremely painful throat that feels as if there is a fish bone stuck in it, making it very difficult to try and swallow.

If the sore throat feels worse on the left side and swallowing liquids is particularly painful, use Lachesis. Use Lycopodium if the throat is worse on the right side or the pain moves from right to left; warm drinks may be comforting.

For a sore throat which is accompanied by offensive breath and saliva, with a degree of sweatiness and thirst, then you should try Mercurius. For throats that appear dark, raw and red, and feel as if a highly uncomfortable, unpleasant hot lump has got stuck inside, try taking quantities of Phytolacca. That usually proves quite effective.

Relieving Toothache

There is probably no worse agony than the pain of toothache, as the area is so sensitive. In most cases, a visit to the dentist will be essential, but the following remedies may well help you cope with the pain in the meantime.

For sudden and violent pains, perhaps precipitated by a cold, Aconite may be helpful. If the area looks very red and throbs violently, Belladonna should be used. For abscesses, where pus is obviously present and the saliva tastes and smells foul, the best remedy is likely to be Mercurius. If you are prone to abscesses and your teeth are generally not very strong, Silica should be used to strengthen the system.

For pain that lingers after a visit to the dentist, take Arnica or Hypericum. If the pain is in any way accompanied by extreme irritability, Chamomilla should be used.

Hepar sulph is a suitable remedy for extreme septic states (infected areas), where bad temper is a prominent symptom. Another remedy for toothache where there are spasmodic shooting pains is Mag phos.

Though there are several remedies that can help with toothache, you will still need to visit the dentist.

eyes and ears

Any problems with the eyes and ears can be immediately quite distresssing, especially for young children who do not appreciate what is happening. Their world can suddenly be turned upside down. Fortunately, there is a wide range of proven remedies for helping ease such discomfort, for example reducing puffy, swollen eyes, styes, burning sensations, and even the debilitating effects of a sudden, throbbing ear infection.

SOOTHING THE EYES

Overwork, pollutants, viral and bacterial infections can all affect the delicate tissues in and around the eyes. Stress and fatigue tend to aggravate these problems by weakening the immune system's ability to fight off infection.

Aconite helps when the eye feels hot and dry, perhaps after catching a cold. The eye may feel irritated, as if it has got a piece of grit. Apis is a good remedy to use when the eyelids look puffy and swollen; the discomfort can be reduced and relieved by applying a cold compress.

Belladonna is a very good remedy for eyes that look in any way red and bloodshot, and which are over-sensitive to light. Euphrasia is one of the very best remedies for sore and burning eyes, and it can also be used in an eyebath because it can be obtained in a diluted tincture.

One of the best remedies for styes is Pulsatilla, which should be used when the eye has an infection which results in what is best described as a sticky yellow discharge. When treating eye injuries, Symphytum can be used where there has been a blow to the eyeball. For general eye injuries, Arnica will ease the bruising. Ledum helps when the eye is cold and puffy.

Eye irritants cause a lot of discomfort and need tackling quickly.

An effective cure for children's earaches is Verbascum oil.

EAR INFECTIONS

Acute earaches are most common in young children. They need to be treated quickly, as an infection within the middle ear can be both painful and damaging. Speedy home help can be very useful, but you must get professional medical help if the earache worsens or if it in any way persists.

One of the most soothing remedies is Verbascum oil. Pour a few drops into a spoon that has been pleasantly warmed, and drip gently into the child's ear.

For sudden and violent pains, accompanied by fever which usually start at night, use Aconite. Where there is a fever with a sudden and violent appearance, and the ear throbs and looks very red, Belladonna will effect a cure.

For earaches where there is great pain and the child is exceptionally irritable, use Chamomilla. Ferrum phos is required where the pain comes on slowly and there are no other significant distinguishing symptoms. For very painful, sore earaches with some discharge of yellow-green mucus, when the child is also clearly chilly and irritable, use Hepar sulph.

allergies

Over the last 20 or 30 years there has been a highly significant increase in all kinds of allergies, which might be better described as the body's sensitivity to an excess of substances that cannot be easily assimilated. Sadly, many such substances are the product of our time. Hay fever, eczema, asthma, irritable bowel disease and other chronic diseases have now reached almost epidemic proportions. Fortunately, homeopathy can offer you essential help.

HAY FEVER

Hay fever is rather a misnomer, for there are many other substances apart from hay which can trigger the well-known symptoms of watering eyes and runny nose, itchiness and sneezing. The problem may last for a few weeks, a few months or even all year, depending on the cause.

Euphrasia and Allium cepa are two of the most effective acute remedies. If the problem is centred in the eyes, with even the tears burning, Euphrasia is the remedy to use. However, if the nasal symptoms are worse, with constant streaming and an acrid discharge, then try Allium cepa. Another remedy that is sometimes useful when there are constant burning secretions from the mucous membranes is Arsenicum.

To build up your immune system, it is best to act about two to three months before the time when hay fever usually begins. There are plenty of tasty aids. Garlic, in pill form or meals when it can even be eaten whole if roasted in the oven, imparting a new, sweetish flavour, works well. So too do regular applications of honey. Inhaling over a steam bath using lemon balm reduces the chances of an allergic attack.

Red onion, the source of the remedy, Allium cepa.

CHRONIC DISEASES

No one knows precisely what causes these problems. Further research is required. Quite clearly there are many different reasons. Toxicity overload is almost certainly one. The body simply cannot cope with the increasingly large number of chemicals and drugs that it was never designed to absorb. Another likely reason is deficient nutrition. Many of our foods are now so over-processed (apart from being sprayed with all kinds of chemicals) that they do not contain sufficient minerals and vitamins to allow the body to function efficiently.

Homeopathy can often work wonders in correcting the many weaknesses that result from such causes. Obviously, you should also take care to avoid toxic substances wherever possible, and eat a healthy, varied diet. The homeopathy that is needed to cure chronic ailments is complex and beyond the scope of this book; seek advice from a professional homeopath.

Allergies, or over-sensitivity to certain foods, are becoming increasingly common. Research shows that dairy products and wheat-based foods seem to cause the most problems.

acute illnesses and upsets
There is nothing quite as frustratingly disabling as a sudden upset stomach, whether it be diarrhoea, lingering indigestion, niggling cramps or even quite painful bouts of trapped wind. But with the use of homeopathy you do not have to keep on suffering. It actually offers several well-proven ways of helping you tackle such problems, so that you can resume a normal life, quickly getting out and about.

SETTLING GASTRIC UPSETS
The main symptoms of stomach and intestinal infections are pain, wind (gas), nausea, vomiting and diarrhoea. Bear in mind that vomiting and diarrhoea are actually natural processes by which the body rids itself quickly of any unwanted material. Consequently these symptoms need to be treated only if they are persistent. Such problems can arise at any time and may be due to food poisoning or just a sudden reaction to unfamiliar food; this invariably seems to happen on vacation.

Upset Stomach
The great standby remedy is Arsenicum. Other symptoms which may accompany diarrhoea or vomiting are excessive weakness, coldness and restlessness. Mag phos is an excellent remedy for general abdominal cramps which are soothed by doubling up and making sure that you keep warm.

For constant nausea which is unrelieved by vomiting, use Ipecac. Nux vomica is a very good remedy for gastric upsets where nothing really seems to happen. The undigested food lies like a horrible dead weight in the stomach and refuses to move or be expelled, causing plenty of discomfort.

Phosphorus can be a useful remedy for diarrhoea, and it is particularly effective if attacks are accompanied by a sensation of burning in the stomach. While you may crave a cold drink, it is actually vomited as soon as it warms up in the stomach.

A piece of Arsenopyrite used in the remedy Arsenicum.

Indigestion
The symptoms of indigestion are heartburn, wind (gas) and cramping pains. They are usually caused by eating too much or in fact eating too quickly. The symptoms are usually much more marked when you are eating very rich food and drinking large quantities of alcohol. The most useful remedy is Nux vomica. The digestive system seems heavy and sluggish and the feeling is that you would be much better if the undigested food would move. Another good remedy that can help is Lycopodium.

CALMING BOILS AND ABSCESSES
Sometimes, an area of skin becomes inflamed and gathers pus. This usually happens around a hair follicle. The build-up of pus can cause acute pain before it comes to a head as a boil or abscess, or until the pus is absorbed by the body.

In the early stages of a boil or abscess, when it looks red and angry and throbs painfully, Belladonna is often the best remedy. Later when it starts becoming septic (infected) and even more painful as the pus increases, use Hepar sulph. If the boil seems very slow in coming to a head, Silica should be used to speed up the process. This remedy is also helpful as a daily tissue salt for unhealthy skin that keeps producing boils. The nails may also be unhealthy, breaking and peeling too easily.

Belladonna is highly effective against a wide range of complaints.

emotional issues
We underrate at surprisingly great risk the incredible part that our emotions can play in our health. Diseases can easily arise from any disharmony in our lives. This is even more likely if we are repressed, unable to express and articulate our more difficult, upsetting emotions, feelings staying trapped and locked within us. Just as joy can bolster and keep us in good health, a big build-up of grief can result in all kinds of illness.

Emotional Turmoil

It is not unusual for a homeopathic practitioner to hear words like "I've never really got over my father's death," or "I've never properly felt well since my divorce." It is important for good health not to allow such wounds to fester. Homeopathy can often help chronic and acute conditions when needed.

In any emotional situation where you feel that you really cannot cope, the Bach Flower Rescue Remedy is useful. Although it is not strictly homeopathic, it works well with homeopathic remedies, and can be taken as often as you wish.

Grief and Fright

Ignatia is the number-one remedy for acute feelings of sadness and loss. It can calm both the hysterical and over-sensitive and those who tend to keep their grief bottled up. Children and emotionally dependent people can be helped by Pulsatilla. Aconite is considered the major remedy for helping people who need to get over a shock or a terrifying experience.

Anticipation

The worry brought on by a forthcoming event such as an exam, appearing on the stage or meeting someone new can severely affect some people. Fortunately, there are a number of remedies that can help ease any anxiety and panic.

The most useful remedy for dealing with emotional upsets is Pulsatilla, combined with plenty of security and love.

Gelsemium is best used when you start trembling with nerves and literally go weak at the knees. Arg nit is a good all-round anxiety remedy, where there are symptoms of great restlessness. It also has a claustrophobic picture and could help those who suffer from a fear of flying or even travelling on underground trains. The panic often causes diarrhoea, and another anxiety remedy that can help the bowels is called Lycopodium. Strangely, people who need Lycopodium are often found to excel at the ordeals that they have been worrying about, once they have overcome the panic barrier.

Insomnia

There can be many causes of sleeplessness including worry, habit, and bad eating. For the "hamster on the wheel" syndrome, where your mind is rushing around in never-ending circles, Valerian can be a magical aid helping you quickly fall asleep. For those sufferers who constantly wake too early, especially if they are people who live too much on their nerves and eat large quantities of rich food, try Nux vomica.

A Pasque flower, used in Pulsatilla.

women's health

Two of the greatest concerns to most women are their reproductive systems and the effects of their associated hormones, but many find they are treated in quite a heavy-handed way by traditional modern medicine. Fortunately, homeopathy offers another route and a range of different treatments which can include important aspects of your diet. Homeopathic self-help can ease the distress for various non-persistent conditions.

Anaemia

Anaemia is usually caused by an iron deficiency and manifests itself through weakness, pallor and lack of stamina. The most vulnerable times are during pregnancy or after excessive blood loss due to heavy periods. Since iron pills supplied by your doctor can often severely upset the bowels, gentler methods are actually preferable. Eat foods rich in iron and try organic iron preparations which can be obtained from health food shops. Ferrum phos should also be used on a daily basis.

Cystitis

Many women are familiar with the burning agony of urinating when they have a bladder infection. Cranberry juice or sodium bicarbonate can often help. Two of the most useful remedies are Cantharis and Apis. Use Cantharis as a general remedy. Apis can be helpful when the last drops in urination hurt the most.

Mastitis

Mastitis means an inflammation of the breast and it occurs commonly during breast-feeding. It can be painful but is not normally serious. Fortunately, breast-feeding does not have to stop because of it. Homeopathy is usually very successful in curing the inflammation. Phytolacca is the most important remedy aiding breasts that may feel lumpy and swollen.

A good diet is essential for good health. Fresh organic apples and other fruit are especially good for you.

PMT mood swings are not uncommon and should not alarm you. Check your symptoms to find a remedy that might help.

Pre-menstrual Syndrome (PMS)

Most women are familiar with the mood changes that arise just before an oncoming period. For an unfortunate few, more extreme symptoms of depression, anger and weepiness can appear, sometimes as much as a week or more before the flow begins. A visit to a professional homeopath can certainly be of great benefit, but there are several remedies that you might like to try yourself at home in order to alleviate some of these sudden, extreme symptoms.

Pulsatilla is an excellent remedy if weeping and the feeling of neediness is prominent. Sepia should be used where there is anger and exhaustion, and even in cases of indifference towards your family. Lachesis is very helpful in minimizing the more extreme symptoms of violent anger, jealousy and suspicion.

Period Pains

If your period pains are consistently bad, you will need to consult a homeopath. For occasional pains, there are a number of self-help remedies from which you can choose. The three PMS remedies mentioned above, Pulsatilla, Sepia and Lachesis, should be considered when applicable, and if your symptoms seem significant and over-riding. All three might also be of some help during a difficult menopause.

children's health

Children tend to respond very well and quickly to all kinds of homeopathic treatments, and they are a joy to treat. However, while there is actually no substitute for constitutional treatment from a professional homeopath who will try to boost the immune system as much as possible, there is no reason why you should not keep a good stock of remedies at home in case of a sudden, acute situation. You too can do a lot to help.

Children and Homeopathy

The best start you can possibly give a child is plenty of confidence, with love and security, breast milk for as long as is practical, a healthy, varied diet, as few drugs as possible, and homeopathy. Young children invariably have rather dramatic, acute conditions, such as fevers. Usually there is nothing for you to worry about if you are well informed, have professional support and have access to remedies. The dosage is the same as for adults, but remember to crush the pills first for babies.

Teething

The most widely used remedies for teething pains are Chamomilla and Pulsatilla. Chamomilla is an "angry" remedy and suits bad-tempered babies best. These are the ones that drain you of sympathy because you have had so many sleepless nights making you feel irritable and guilty for becoming bad tempered, and helpless. Only constant attention, picking them up and carrying them round, soothes them in any way. Pulsatilla children respond differently – they are softer, weepy and are constantly in need of your sympathy. They feel better and are significantly soothed by being given plenty of cuddles.

For babies, it is essential to crush the tablet first.

Give your child the right start with love and a healthy diet.

Fevers

Many small children get fevers with very high temperatures, as they burn up infection in the most efficient way. Seek help if the fever goes on for more than 24 hours, especially if there are any signs at all of a violent headache or drowsiness. Aconite and Belladonna are the best, general high-fever remedies.

Croup

This harsh, dry cough is very disturbing in small children, but usually sounds far worse than it really is. There are three main remedies for croup. Aconite can be used for particularly violent and sudden coughs, which are often worse at night. For harsh coughs that sound like sawing through wood, Spongia is the remedy. For a rattly chest with thick yellow-green mucus, possibly marked by irritability and chilliness, use Hepar sulph.

Colic

Trapped wind can be very upsetting for a baby. It comes without warning, and for no apparent reason the baby will cry. Sometimes babies try to curl up to ease the pain, and warmth and a gentle massage should help. Mag phos is a useful remedy to try.

first aid

Homeopathic remedies are extremely useful as first-aid treatments in all kinds of situations, but dangerous, serious injuries should always receive immediate, expert medical attention. If you are in any way alarmed or concerned, you must first call for help, at which point it might just be possible to start giving an appropriate remedy. In more minor cases, such as bruising, cuts and sprains, homeopathy can certainly make quite a difference.

Bruises

The very first remedy to think of after any injury or accident is Arnica. For local bruising, where the skin is unbroken, apply Arnica cream, and whether you use the cream or not you can give an Arnica pill as often as you think necessary, until such time as the bruising starts to go down.

Arnica is also wonderful in cases of shock. If the person is dozy or woozy, or in fact unconscious, crush the remedy first and place the powder directly on to the lips.

Where there is serious shock, or in any real emergency, use Rescue Remedy. This can be used either alone or with Arnica in cases of physical trauma. Place a few drops of the Rescue Remedy straight on to the lips or tongue, every few minutes if considered necessary. If the injury results in pains shooting up the arms or legs, try using Hypericum.

This remedy is also very useful where sensitive areas have been injured and hurt, such as the toes, fingers, lips and ears. If the joints or bones have been hurt, Ruta may be more effective than Arnica, which is more of a soft tissue remedy.

Cuts, Sores and Open Wounds

Clean the area thoroughly to remove all dirt. If the wound is deep, it may need stitches and you must seek instant medical help. Once the wound is clean, apply some Calendula cream.

Calendula cream is a widely available, excellent remedy to use if you have got any open cuts and sores.

Puncture Wounds

Such injuries can easily occur in all kinds of ways: from animal or insect bites, pins, needles and nails, and even from standing on a sharp instrument such as a garden fork or rake.

If the wound becomes puffy and purple and feels cold, with the pain being eased by a cold compress, Ledum is the best remedy. If there are shooting pains, which travel up the limbs along the tracks of the nerves, then Hypericum should be used.

Sprains, Strains and Fractures

For general muscle strains, resulting from lifting heavy weights or excessive physical exercise such as aerobics or long hikes over hilly countryside, Arnica will almost always be extremely effective. For deeper injuries where the joints are affected, as a result of a heavy fall or a strong football tackle, use Ruta.

For even more severe sprains, especially to the ankles or wrists, where the pain is agony on first moving the joint but eases with gentle limbering up, Rhus tox should be very helpful. For injuries where the slightest movement is extremely painful and hard pressure eases the pain, Bryonia will provide relief.

Once a broken bone has been set, use Symphytum daily, night and morning, for at least three weeks. This will not only ease the pain but speed up the healing of the bones.

For bites that come up as any kind of bruise, small or dramatic, apply Arnica cream. For many it is very effective.

The herb St John's Wort, used in the remedy Hypericum.

Burns

Severe burns need urgent medical assistance: do not delay, especially in the case of children and babies. For minor burns and scalds, Calendula or Hypercal cream can be very soothing, especially if applied straight away. If the pain remains, or the burn is severe, take one pill of the remedy Cantharis every few hours until the pain eases. In the case of shock or a hysterical child, also use Arnica (in pill form) and/or Rescue Remedy.

Bites and Stings

For minor injuries, you can apply Calendula or Hypercal cream. If the wound looks in any way bruised, use Arnica, either as a cream or in pill form. However, if the wound becomes dramatically swollen and starts looking red and puffy, then use Apis. For any injuries to quite sensitive areas, such as the fingers, especially when shooting pains can be felt, Hypericum is a useful remedy. Ledum is preferable if the wound looks puffy and feels cold to the touch, and is helped by the application of a cold compress.

Travel Sickness

Many people end up getting seasick even when the waves are not too rough, and some, especially children, are also air-sick or car-sick. The symptoms are eased by the remedy Cocculus.

Fear of Flying

Use Aconite and/or Rescue Remedy before you go to the airport and then as often as you need during the flight. If you actually find yourself shaking with anxiety, try Gelsemium. If the problem is more a question of claustrophobia, the fear of being trapped in a narrow space, Arg nit should be very useful.

Visits to the Doctor or Dentist

For any pre-visit nerves, to which we are all prone at some time, take Arg nit. For surgery or dental work where bruising and shock to the system might well have been involved, you cannot go wrong with Arnica. Take one pill before the treatment, and one pill three times a day for as long as you actively need it.

The Homeopathic First-aid Kit

It is a good idea to keep a basic first-aid kit in the house so that you are well prepared for any sudden emergency. Many remedies are now available from health food shops and even some chemists, but for many of us there might not be a nearby source, and it is amazing how many emergencies arise outside shop-opening hours. Stock up and be safe.

Your first-aid kit should include:
Arnica cream – for bruises
Calendula cream – for cuts and sores
Echinacea tincture – for the immune system
Rescue Remedy tincture – for major emergencies

Plus these bottles of pills:
Aconite – for fevers, coughs and colds
Apis – for bites and stings
Arnica – for bruising or shock following accidents
Arsenicum – for digestive upsets and food poisoning
Belladonna – for high fever and headaches
Bryonia – for dry coughs and fevers
Chamomilla – for teething and colic
Ferrum phos – for colds, flu and anaemia
Gelsemium – for flu and anxiety
Hepar sulph – for sore throats and infected wounds
Hypericum – for injuries

Although not strictly a homeopathic treatment, Rescue Remedy is one of Dr Edward Bach's Flower Remedies. These flower essences are a series of gentle plant remedies which are intended to treat various emotional states, regardless of the physical disorder.

Ignatia – for grief and emotional upsets
Ledum – for puncture wounds, bites and stings
Lycopodium – for anxiety and digestive problems
Mercurius – for sepsis
Nux vomica – for hangovers, nausea and indigestion
Phosphorus – for digestive problems and nosebleeds
Pulsatilla – for ear infections, fevers and eye problems
Rhus tox – for sprains, strains and rashes
Ruta – for injuries to tendons and bones

the materia medica

There are something like 2,000 remedies in the homeopathic Materia Medica, though most of them are actually best left to the professional practitioner. However, there are a surprising number of remedies that can safely be used by the lay person in low potencies for acute and first-aid cases. These remedies cover a wide range of not too serious, non-persistent problems. It is well worth seeing just how much you can achieve.

HOMEOPATHIC CURES

Use this section to back up and confirm your choice from the remedies that were recommended for ailments earlier in the chapter on herbs. If your choice still looks good, then you are almost certainly on the right track. However, if it does not, then consider trying one of the other remedies which are described for the ailment. Do note, though, that not every particular symptom of the remedy has to be present. Homeopaths use the expression "a three-legged stool"; if the remedy covers three symptoms of the condition, then it is more than likely to be well indicated.

Note that you must always keep your supply of remedies in a cool, dark place or cupboard. Also do keep them well away from any strong, pervasive smells and young children. Fortunately, homeopathic remedies are known to be extremely safe, so even if a child does actually swallow a number of pills, even as much as a whole bottle, you need not be unduly alarmed or concerned.

ACONITE
Aconitum napellus

Monkshood, a beautiful yet poisonous plant with blue flowers, is native to mountainous areas of Europe and Asia. It is widely cultivated as a garden plant.

n o t e s • Symptoms appear suddenly and violently, often at night. • They may appear after catching a chill or after a fright. • Fear or extreme anxiety may accompany symptoms. • An important remedy for high fevers with extreme thirst and sweat. • Major remedy for violent, dry croupy coughs. • It is most effective when used at the beginning of an illness.

ALLIUM CEPA
Allium cepa

The remedy comes from the onion, whose characteristics are perfectly well known and obvious to anyone who has ever had to peel a strong one: it directly affects the mucous membranes of the nose, the eyes and throat.

n o t e s • Sneezing, often repeatedly, accompanied by a streaming nose. • The nose and eyes begin to burn and become irritated. • Nasal discharge is acrid while the tears are bland. • Major remedy for hay fever (when the nose is affected more than the eyes) and also for colds.

ANT TART
Antimonium tartaricum

Ant tart is prepared from the chemical substance antimony potassium tartrate, and is traditionally referred to as tartar emetic. Ant tart affects the mucous membranes of the lungs.

n o t e s • A wet, rattling cough from deep in the lungs, with shortness of breath and wheezing. • Helps to bring up mucus from the lungs.

APIS
Apis mellifica

The remedy is prepared from the honey bee. The well-known effects of its sting describe the remedy picture very well.

n o t e s • A useful remedy after injuries, especially from bites or stings where there is subsequent swelling, puffiness and redness. • The affected area feels like a water bag. • A fever appears quickly and without any thirst. • The person appears restless and irritable. • The symptoms are often relieved by the application of a cold compress, or exposure to cold air.

ARG NIT
Argentum nitricum

Silver nitrate, from which this remedy is derived, is one of the silver compounds that are used during the photographic process. It is good at helping to soothe an agitated nervous system.

n o t e s • Panic, nervousness and anxiety. • Feeling worried, hurried and without emotional and practical support. • Fears of anticipation which might include stage fright, exams, visiting the dentist, flying, and many others. • The nervousness may cause diarrhoea and wind (gas).

ARNICA
Arnica montana

Arnica is a well-known herb with yellow, daisy-like flowers. Its native habitat is mountainous areas. It has a special affinity with soft tissue and muscles, and is usually the first remedy to consider after any accident. Where there is bruising but the skin is not broken, use Arnica cream. (When the skin is broken, use Calendula or Hypercal cream.)

notes • The most important remedy for bruising. • Shock following an accident. • Muscle strains after strenuous or extreme exertion.

ARSENICUM
Arsenicum album

Arsenic oxide is a well-known poison. However, when used as a homeopathic remedy it is extremely safe and works especially well on the gastro-intestinal and respiratory systems.

notes • Vomiting, diarrhoea, abdominal and stomach cramps. • Often the first remedy in cases of food poisoning. • Asthmatic, wheezy breathing, often worse at night. Head colds with a runny nose. • Chilliness, restlessness, anxiety and weakness. • Warmth gives great relief.

BELLADONNA
Atropa belladonna

The valuable remedy Belladonna must be prepared from deadly nightshade, whose poisonous berries are best avoided. However, they produce a medicine which is one of the most important fever and headache remedies.

notes • Violent and intense symptoms appearing suddenly. • Fever with high temperature, little thirst and burning, dry skin. • The face or the affected part is usually bright red. •Throbbing pains, especially in the head. •The pupils may be sensitive to light.

BRYONIA
Bryonia alba

Bryonia is prepared from the roots of white bryony, a climbing plant which is found in hedgerows right across Europe. The roots are surprisingly large and store a great deal of water. Bryonia patients often seem to lack "lubrication".

notes • The symptoms tend to develop slowly. • Dryness marks all symptoms: in the mouth, membranes and joints. • Extreme thirst. • The condition feels worse with the slightest motion.• Bryonia coughs are dry and very painful. • The person is irritable.

CALENDULA
Calendula officinalis

Calendula has long been known to herbalists as a major first-aid remedy for injuries. It is prepared from the common marigold, and the simplest way to use it is as a cream. When combined with Hypericum it is known as Hypercal.

notes • Use this cream on all cuts, sores and open wounds. (For bruises where the skin is not broken, use Arnica cream.) • Calendula is a natural antiseptic and keeps the injury free of infection, as well as helping to speed up the healing process.

IPECAC
Cephaelis ipecacuanha

Ipecacuanha is a seemingly small, insignificant South American shrub. The remedy works mainly on the digestive and respiratory tracts, and the most important symptom it treats is nausea, no matter what the ailment.

notes • Persistent nausea, not helped by vomiting. • Coughs that are accompanied by feelings of nausea. • Outbreaks of morning sickness during pregnancy. • Asthma or wheeziness accompanied by degrees of nausea. • Development of "sick" headaches.

COCCULUS
Cocculus orbiculatus

The remedy is prepared from the Indian cockle, a plant that grows along the coasts of India. It profoundly affects the nervous system and can strengthen a weakened and exhausted system. Because it can also cure nausea and dizziness, it is considered an important remedy for all kinds of travel sickness, whether on a boat, plane or in a car.

n o t e s • Nausea, vomiting, and dizziness, as in travel sickness.
• Exhaustion and nervous stress, perhaps due to lack of sleep.

DROSERA
Drosera rotundifolia

Drosera is a remedy prepared from an extraordinary insectivorous plant, the round-leaved sundew. The plants are often called "flypapers" because the leaves are tipped with sticky glands. The insect prey gets more embroiled the more it struggles, and is finally dissolved. Drosera affects the respiratory system and is an important cough remedy.

n o t e s • Deep, barking coughs.
• Prolonged and incessant coughs returning in periodic fits or spasms.
• The cough may result in retching.

EUPATORIUM
Eupatorium perfoliatum

Eupatorium is a North American herb found growing in marshy places. It is used as a herb as a flu remedy, to lower fevers and even relieve congestion and constipation, as well as boosting the immune system. Its common name, boneset, gives a clue to its homeopathic use. Whatever the other symptoms, the bones usually do ache.

n o t e s • Flu-like symptoms, with aching all over, but pains that seem to have lodged deep in the bones.
• There may be a painful cough.

EUPHRASIA
Euphrasia officinalis

Also known as eyebright, Euphrasia has long been known as a remedy with a specific application to the eyes. It is a very pretty little meadow plant, much used in wild flower plantings, with colourful flowers that open wide only when there is direct sunshine.

n o t e s • Eyes that are sore, red and inflamed. • The eyes water with burning tears. • In cases of hay fever, the symptoms are sneezing, itching and a runny nose, but for most the eyes are most usually affected.

FERRUM PHOS
Ferrum phosphoricum

Iron phosphate, from which Ferrum phos is prepared, is a highly valued mineral that manages to balance the iron and oxygen in the blood. It is also a tissue salt and can be used actively as a tonic for anaemic patients who are beginning to feel rather weak and feeble.

n o t e s • Flu and cold symptoms that are not well defined.
• Weakness and tiredness. • General anaemia: the remedy can be very useful for women with heavy periods or during pregnancy.

GELSEMIUM
Gelsemium sempervirens

The remedy is prepared from a North American plant known as yellow jasmine. It acts specifically on the muscles, the motor nerves and the nervous system. It is also quite probably the most important acute remedy for helping to treat an attack of flu.

n o t e s • Aching, heavy muscles which will not obey the will.
• Tiredness, weakness, shivering and trembling. • Fever with sweating but little thirst. • Headaches concentrated at the back of the head.

HEPAR SULPH
Hepar sulphuris calcareum

The remedy was developed by Samuel Hahnemann, the first homeopath, from calcium sulphide, which is made by heating flowers of sulphur and the lime of oyster shells together. It strongly affects the nervous system and is good in acute septic states (infected areas) and in respiratory system problems.

n o t e s • Extreme irritability and over-sensitivity. • Coldness, especially around the head. • Hoarse, dry coughs with yellow mucus, croup. • Evidence of unusually heavy sweating.

HYPERICUM
Hypericum perforatum

Prepared from the herb St John's Wort, Hypericum is primarily an injury remedy. It is particularly effective on any areas that have an abundant supply of sensitive nerves. They include the fingers, toes, lips, ears, eyes, and the coccyx at the base of the spine. Apply Hypericum instead of Arnica for bruising in such sensitive areas, although Arnica may work perfectly well if Hypericum is not available.

n o t e s • Pains are often felt suddenly shooting up the limbs, travelling along the tracks of the nerves.

IGNATIA
Ignatia amara

Ignatia is prepared from the seeds of a tree, the St Ignatius bean, which grows in South-east Asia. It is well known as a major "grief" remedy, and it can strongly affect the emotions.

n o t e s • Sadness and grief following emotional loss. • Sudden changeable moods: tears following laughter, or hysteria. • Suppressed emotions, when the tears will not flow. • Pronounced bouts of sighing following a period of emotional unhappiness, particularly anxiety, fear or grief.

KALI BICH
Kali bichromicum

The source of Kali bichromicum, potassium dichromate, is a chemical compound involved in many industrial processes which include dyeing, printing and photography. It especially affects the mucous membranes of the air passages, and is an important sinusitis remedy.

n o t e s • Highly unpleasant thick, strong, lumpy green discharges from the nasal passages or mouth. • Headaches in small spots as a result of catarrh. • Dry cough accompanied by sticky, yellow-green mucus.

LACHESIS
Lachesis muta

Lachesis is prepared from the venom of the bushmaster snake which is native to South America. It is a chronic remedy best left to expert, professional homeopaths, but it does have an acute use when treating sore throats and also various menstrual problems.

n o t e s • Sore throats, much worse on the left side. • Painful throats where liquids are more difficult to swallow than solids. • Menstrual pains and tension improve when the flow starts. • Hot flushes around the menopause.

LEDUM
Ledum palustre

The small shrub known as marsh tea, from which Ledum is derived, grows in boggy places across the cold wastes of the Northern Hemisphere. It is primarily a first-aid injury remedy when cold rather than warmth soon brings welcome, soothing relief.

n o t e s • Puncture wounds from nails or splinters, bites and stings, when pain is eased by cold compresses. • Wounds that look puffy and feel cold. • Injuries to the eye which looks cold, puffy and bloodshot.

LYCOPODIUM
Lycopodium clavatum

This remedy is prepared from the spores of club moss, a strange prostrate plant which likes to grow on heaths. It is generally prescribed constitutionally for aiding chronic conditions but it can also be very helpful for digestive problems and sometimes even acute sore throats.

n o t e s • Conditions which are worse on the right side, or move from the right to the left side of the body.
• Flatulence and pain in the abdomen or stomach. • Problem is aggravated by gassy foods such as beans.

CANTHARIS
Lytta vesicatoria

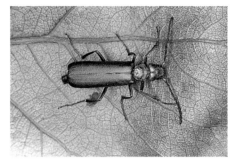

Cantharis is one of a few homeopathic remedies prepared from insects. It is derived from an iridescent green beetle which is commonly called Spanish fly. It is also known as the blister beetle because it is actually a major irritant if handled. It has an affinity with the urinary tract.

n o t e s • Cystitis – where there are highly uncomfortable, intense, burning-pains on urinating. • Evidence of burns or burning pains generally, as you would normally expect to get following sunburn, or burns from a hot pan.

MAG PHOS
Magnesia phosphorica

Magnesia phosphorica is one of the 12 tissue salts, as well as being a proven remedy. It is well known that it works directly in helping to ease tension in the nerves as well as in the muscles. It can therefore be considered as a very effective painkiller.

n o t e s • Violent, cramping and spasmodic pains, often in the abdominal area. • Pains better for warmth, gentle massage and doubling up.
• Can help with colic, period pains, sciatica, toothache and earache.

CHAMOMILLA
Matricaria chamomilla

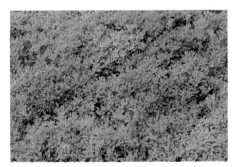

Chamomile is a member of the daisy family. It strongly affects the nervous system. It is one of the most important medicines for the treatment of children: Aconite, Belladonna and Chamomilla are together known as the "ABC" remedies.

n o t e s • Bad temper and irritability.
• Teething problems in angry babies.
• In cases of colic, the stools are usually offensive, slimy and green.
• Extreme sensitivity to pain.
• The child's temper is considerably improved on being rocked or carried.

MERCURIUS
Mercurius solubilis

The name of this remedy is sometimes abbreviated to Merc sol. It is prepared from the liquid metal mercury. It is used in acute septic states (infected areas) where the glands and their secretions are particularly affected.

n o t e s • Swollen and tender glands.
• Profuse sweating and increased thirst. • Breath, sweat and secretions can be offensive. • The tongue looks flabby, yellow and coated.
• Fevers blow hot and cold.
• Irritability and restlessness.

PHOSPHORUS
Phosphorus

Phosphorus is an important constituent of the body, particularly of the bones. It can be useful in acute situations. These include digestive problems, with immediate vomiting once the food is warmed in the stomach, and constant diarrhoea. Phosphorus can also help aid minor haemorrhages (i.e. nosebleeds). It also relieves the "spacey" feeling that lingers too long after an anaesthetic.

n o t e s • Suits people who are lively, open and friendly, but who are also occasionally nervous and anxious.

PHYTOLACCA
Phytolacca decandra

Phytolacca or poke-root is a well-known erect, unpleasant smelling plant that grows across the Northern Hemisphere, and also in South America. It is a glandular remedy that particularly affects the tonsils, and also the mammary glands. It is reckoned that Phytolacca is probably the most important remedy for helping in the treatment of mastitis.

n o t e s • Sore throats that look dark and angry. • Sore throats in which the pain feels like a hot ball. • Swollen, tender breasts with cracked nipples.

PULSATILLA
Pulsatilla nigricans

Pulsatilla is one of the most useful of acute remedies, as well as being a very important constitutional one. The remedy comes from the pasque flower and is also known as the weathercock remedy because it suits people whose moods and symptoms are constantly changing. For this reason, it is considered a wonderful remedy for small children.

n o t e s • Tendency to be weepy and clingy. • Suits people with gentle, sympathetic natures.• Yellow-green discharge from the eyes or nose.

RHUS TOX
Rhus toxicodendron

The remedy is prepared from poison ivy, native to North America. Its main use is in sprains, strains and swollen joints, but because of its itchy, rashy picture it can be a good remedy for illnesses such as chickenpox or shingles. It is also a useful remedy for acute rheumatism.

n o t e s • Extreme restlessness with a red, itchy rash. • Stiffness in the joints, which is eased by gentle motion. • The symptoms are far better for warmth, and considerably worse with cold, damp and over-exertion.

RUTA
Ruta graveolens

Ruta, or rue, is a much valued, highly attractive garden plant with blue-green leaves. It is also an ancient herbal remedy that has been often called the herb of grace. It acts particularly well on the joints, tendons, cartilages and periosteum (the membrane that covers the bones). It also has an affinity with the eyes.

n o t e s • Bruises to the bones. • Strains to the joints and connecting tissue, especially to the ankles and wrists. • The symptoms are worse for cold and damp and better for warmth.

SEPIA
Sepia officinalis

Sepia is a remedy prepared from the ink of the squid or cuttlefish. Normally its use should be left to the professional homeopath as it has a "big" picture (i.e. it can be used in many circumstances), but because of its affinity with the female reproductive system it can be helpful in some menstrual problems.

n o t e s • Suits tired, depressed, emotionally withdrawn people. • Morning sickness in pregnancy, which is worse for the smell of food. • Hot flushes during the menopause.

SILICA
Silicea

Silica is a mineral derived from flint. It is one of the 12 tissue salts, and its presence in the body aids the vital elimination of toxins. It can be used acutely in septic (infected) conditions to strengthen the body's resistance to continual infection, and also to help expel any foreign bodies such as splinters.

n o t e s • Suitable for symptoms that are slow to heal, or for people who feel the cold, or who lack stamina or vitality. • Small-scale infections that seem to be turning septic rather than healing.

SPONGIA
Spongia tosta

Spongia, as its name clearly indicates, is a remedy which is prepared from the lightly roasted skeleton part of the marine sponge. It actually works very well on the respiratory tract, and it is now generally considered to be one of homeopathy's major cough remedies. It is actually a significant and indeed important aid or remedy when it comes to treating croup in young children.

n o t e s • Dry spasmodic cough.
• The cough sounds like a saw being pulled through wood.

NUX VOMICA
Strychnos nux vomica

Nux vomica is prepared from the seeds of the poison nut tree of South-east Asia. It is a remedy that has many uses in both chronic and acute situations, and it is known to be very useful when the digestive system is involved.

n o t e s • Nausea or vomiting after a rich meal, when the food remains undigested like a load in the stomach.
• A feeling that if only you could vomit you would feel better. • An urge to pass a stool, but with unsatisfactory results. • Heartburn.

SYMPHYTUM
Symphytum officinale

The remedy is easily prepared from the common herb comfrey. It is also called knitbone, which indicates its main use in promoting the healing of broken bones. Use the remedy daily for several weeks after the bone has been set. Symphytum can also be used for many injuries to the eyeball such as, for example, getting a tennis ball directly in the eye.

n o t e s • Speeds up the knitting or fusing together of broken bones.
• Injuries to the eyeball, such as being hit by a hard object.

VALERIAN
Valeriana officinalis

Valerian is a well-known herb whose overuse in the 19th century caused insomnia and over-taxation of the nervous system to the point of hysteria. Because of the principle "like cures like", very tiny doses such as those used in homeopathy can cure these very same problems. Valerian is an important remedy for sleeplessness. Take one pill about one hour before bedtime. You should soon notice the improvement.

n o t e s • Especially useful when the mind feels like a "hamster on a wheel".

VERBASCUM
Verbascum thapsus

Verbascum is prepared from the great mullein, a common wayside herb. It is a highly regarded garden plant sending up marvellous stems. Homeopathically it is associated with earaches, and it is best used as an oil. The remedy is especially helpful for children, who tend to suffer from ear infections more often than adults. Place a few drops of the oil on a warmed teaspoon and gently insert into the ear, with the child lying on one side.

n o t e s • Earaches of all kinds, both in children and adults.

VIBURNUM OPULUS
Viburnum opulus

The guelder rose is widely distributed in woods and damp places throughout northern Europe and the US. It is a valued garden plant, especially in the form 'Roseum' which has large white flowers, giving rise to its common name, the snowball tree. It is also known as cramp bark and the homeopathic remedy, which is prepared from the bark, can be very helpful for period pains as well as for spasmodic cramps.

n o t e s • For aiding the treatment of severe cramping and muscle spasms.

ayurveda
ayurveda

ayurveda

Ayurveda is acknowledged as the traditional healing system of India. Thousands of years old, it has influenced many other healing systems around the world. In fact, it was already established before the births of Buddha and Christ, and some biblical stories clearly reflect the wisdom of the ancient Ayurvedic teachings.

There are many different branches to Ayurveda because it covers so many aspects of health and healing. They have been touched upon in the following pages, but the main emphasis is on diet and lifestyle, specifically tailored to the modern life.

Ayurvedic medicine is founded on the belief that all diseases stem from the digestive system and are caused either by poor digestion of food, which is the body's major source of nourishment, or by following an improper diet for your dosha (nature). Here you will find basic advice about suitable diets, as well as information about supportive treatments, including massage, exercise, colour, crystals, herbs and spices. There is also a list of common ailments that can be treated.

The following basic Ayurvedic approach will help you to develop some simple ways to keep yourself balanced in these days of increasing worry and stress. Identify your dosha, learn how to live in accordance with your own true nature, and discover how you can at last begin to heal your vikruti (current emotional, physical or mental health conditions) with the use of the best basic Ayurvedic methods.

what is ayurveda?

It may be little known – and remarkably few people seem to have heard of it – but Ayurveda is a highly respected, highly revered ancient form of learning which has an amazing amount to teach us. It brings peace of body and mind, important ways of seeing the world and your own place in the scheme of things, and highly practical, sensible ideas when it comes to medicine, diet and ways of staying calm and relaxed.

THE ORIGINS OF AYURVEDA

The origins of Ayurveda are uncertain. It is recounted that thousands of years ago, men of wisdom or rishis (meaning seers) as they are known in India, were saddened by the suffering of humanity. They knew that ill health and short lives allowed man little time to consider his spirituality and to commune with the divine – with God.

In the Himalayan mountains they prayed hard and meditated together, calling upon God to help them to relieve the plight of man, and God felt moved by compassion and gave them the essential teachings that would enlighten them in the ways of healing illness, and thereby alleviate and remove all suffering on the earth.

It is believed that these teachings are the Vedas, although this cannot be proven, due to the lack of historical records. A book called the *Atharva Veda* was one of the first detailed accounts of the system. From this, and perhaps other ancient writings, came

Indian sadhus, like the one shown here, tend to live a nomadic life, renouncing worldly goods, and devoting themselves to prayer.

the beginnings of Ayurvedic medicine, which has developed, changed and absorbed many other influences over hundreds of years to become what it is today. Due to the invasions of India over the years, and the subsequent suppression of many original Indian ways of life, several ancient texts have been lost or even destroyed, but enough have survived to ensure the active continuation of these highly valued, greatly respected teachings.

Ayurveda is now acknowledged as the traditional healing system of India. It comes from two Sanskrit words, *ayur*, meaning "life", and *veda*, meaning "knowing", and can be interpreted as meaning the "science of life". The oldest healing system to remain intact, it is very comprehensive and has influenced many healing systems around the world.

Ayurveda travelled out of India and influenced many other countries with its ageless wisdom about living in the light of truth.

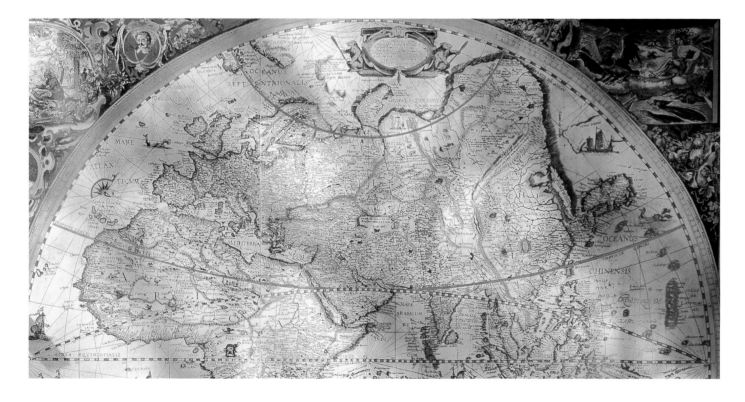

The influence of Ayurveda has spread far and wide. This is reflected in the different oils that are used. Many are made from plants that are found all over the world, not just India.

THE INFLUENCE OF AYURVEDA

For centuries after the end of the Vedic era, Ayurvedic medicine developed into a comprehensive healing system. Its philosophy and techniques soon spread far and wide to China, Arabia, Persia and Greece, gradually influencing Middle Eastern, Greek and Chinese methods of healing. It is well known that Ayurvedic practitioners reached the ancient city of Athens, and it can be noted that the traditional Greek folk medicine, based upon the bodily humours (characteristics), is significantly similar to Ayurveda. In turn, Greek medicine strongly influenced the subsequent development of what we call traditional or orthodox Western medicine. However, it is much too difficult to say exactly how much or to what degree the medical philosophy of Ayurveda was indeed influential, or even how much Ayurveda influenced current techniques.

Greek and European Medicine

The five elements in Chinese medicine appear to have come from Ayurveda. It is documented that the Indian medical system was brought to China by Indian Buddhist missionaries, many of whom were skilled Ayurvedic practitioners. The missionaries also travelled to South east Asia and Tibet, influencing the people of these lands. Tibetan medicine, for example, is an intricate mix of Ayurvedic practices and philosophy with a Tibetan Buddhist and shamanic influence.

WHAT IS AYURVEDIC MEDICINE?

The main aim of Ayurvedic medicine (which is only one branch of Ayurveda) is to improve health and longevity, leaving the individual free to contemplate matters of the spirit and to follow a spiritual path. This does not mean that you have to be spiritual or religious to benefit from Ayurvedic medicine; the system is very practical in its applications and deals with all kinds of health problems, without spirituality ever being mentioned. Its main focus is nutrition, supported primarily by the use of herbs, massage and aromatic oils, but there are many complementary branches as well.

Ayurvedic philosophy encourages those who practise it to eat the fruits and seeds of the earth, rather than take the life of animals. Since some animal products have in fact been included in this introductory guide, they should only ever be used in strict moderation. Let common sense and sensitivity be your guide.

The branches of Ayurvedic medicine include specific diets, surgery, jyotish (Vedic astrology), psychiatry and pancha karma (cleansing and detoxifying techniques). Yoga is not a branch of Ayurveda, but since it shares the same roots you will find that the two are often practised together. Yoga includes meditation, mantras (prayer chants), yantras (contemplation of geometric visual patterns) and hatha yoga (practices for bringing great harmony to the spirit, mind and body).

If you are actually much more interested in the many spiritual aspects of Ayurvedic teachings, then it is strongly recommended that you think very seriously about taking up yoga so that it becomes a regular part of your life.

Most people clearly benefit from meditation or yoga, which can help to illuminate the pathway to inner relaxation and peace.

the doshas

Instead of using modern psychology to group people into types, try using the ancient doshas. They pinpoint and identify three basic types of people, which in turn helps you to a greater self-awareness and to an appreciation of others. The doshas are also excellent ways of helping you to fine-tune and regulate your lifestyle, bringing greater peace and well-being. The doshas are not just terms, they are ways of actively improving your life.

THE SEASONS

There are three doshas (basic types of people, in terms of constitution) – vata, pitta and kapha. They are influenced by the rhythms of nature, seasonal change and the time of year. Autumn is a time of change when leaves turn brown and dry; vata is highest in the autumn and early winter, and at times of dry, cold and windy weather. Pitta is highest in late spring, throughout the summer and during times of heat and humidity. Kapha is highest in the winter months and during early spring, when the weather is frequently still cold and damp.

In Ayurvedic theory, the progress of a disease goes through several stages. There is accumulation (when it is increasing), followed by aggravation (when it is at its highest point and can cause problems). There is also decrease (when it is lessening) and a neutral time when it is passive (neither decreasing nor increasing). Use the questionnaire later in this chapter to discover your dosha, and see whether it is vata, pitta or kapha. People who are single types can refer to the dosha that scores the highest points on their questionnaire. Dual doshic types should vary their lifestyle to suit the seasonal changes, as shown in the dual doshas section.

Yoga can be a very helpful way of balancing both the body and mind. After a few classes you are free to practise by yourself.

YOUR BODY TYPE

This section clearly outlines how you can identify your dosha or body type. Dosha means "that which tends to go out of balance easily." Your dosha is in fact your bio-type or prakruti ("nature"). You are made up of a mixture of the five elements – ether, wind, fire, water and earth, and will display certain recognizable characteristics depending on your personality and nature.

As well as your prakruti, you may also have a vikruti, which is your current state of mental or physical health. This develops throughout your life and may actually differ from your prakruti. It is important that you treat your vikruti first (how you are now), then go back to living with your prakruti. For example, you may have developed arthritis or back trouble over a long period, or you may be suffering from a cold or skin rash which lasts a few days. Once you have have cleared your condition, maintain your prakruti using a preventative treatment, such as diet, massage, oils, colours and scents.

Levels of vata increase in the autumn when the weather is changeable. Surrounding yourself with flowers helps you relax.

Warming up/spring

pitta accumulating, kapha aggravated, vata neutral

Hot/summer

vata accumulating, pitta aggravated, kapha decreasing

Cooling/autumn

vata aggravated, pitta decreasing, kapha neutral

Cold/winter

vata decreasing, pitta neutral, kapha accumulating

Apart from the three single doshas, there are four combinations, making a total of seven differing constitutional types: vata, pitta, kapha, vata/pitta (or pitta/vata), pitta/kapha (or kapha/pitta), kapha/vata (or vata/kapha), and vata/pitta/kapha. These may be either out of balance or in a state of balance.

To discover your prakruti and vikruti, answer the questionnaire twice. Also ask other people who know you well to fill out the questionnaire for you, to give you as clear a picture of yourself as possible. The first time you fill out the questionnaire, you should concentrate upon your current condition – your vikruti – recording your answers based upon your present and recent health history.

You can discover your prakruti by answering the questionnaire a second time, this time with answers based upon your entire lifetime. Fill out the questionnaire with your complete history in mind. This will give you a better idea about the difference between your vikruti and your prakruti. Once the answers to the questionnaire have revealed both your vikruti and your prakruti (they may be the same, which is fine), the information here can be used to treat both. Follow whichever dosha scores most highly (vata, pitta or kapha).

ELEMENTAL ENERGIES

The elements are very important in Ayurveda. They descend from space (ether), down to air. Air descends into the fire element. Fire falls into the water element and water to earth, so that we move from the most rarefied elements (ether), to the most dense (earth). With this in mind, you will notice that the chart below follows a descending pattern of ether and air (vata), fire and water (pitta) and water and earth (kapha). Vata is a mixture of ether and air and is often translated as "wind". In the creation story of Ayurveda, vata leads the other doshas, because its combination of air and ether is actually the most rarefied. The elements move from the most refined down to the most dense. Consequently, if a vata is out of balance, the end result will be that the others will be out of balance as well.

Your age and the season of the year will also have an influence upon your doshic type. From childhood up to the teenage years you are influenced by kapha; from your teens to the age of 50 or 60 you tend to come under the pitta influence, and from 50 to 60 onwards you enter the vata phase of life.

Each dosha has a particular energetic principle which influences responses within the body. Everyone has all three doshas to an extent, but it is the ratio between each that is important, and that creates your individuality. Each dosha plays an important role in this equation and balancing act. For example, movement (vata) without the stability of kapha would simply end up in chaos, and the inactivity of kapha without activity and movement would quickly result in stagnation.

A kapha type (water and earth) will be intuitive, sensitive and will dislike change but will be good at holding things together.

Element	Dosha	Cosmic link	Principle	Influence
ether/air	vata	wind	change	activity/movement
fire/water	pitta	sun	conversion	metabolism/transformation
water/earth	kapha	moon	inertia	cohesion

You and Your Dosha

Working out exactly which dosha type you are is easily done, but before tackling the questionnaire on the opposite page, read the following notes very carefully. They put this huge wealth of information, and its references to skin types, lifestyle, and speech, into an objective framework, giving you a clearer perspective, helping you understand precisely what are called your humoral factors.

WHICH TYPE ARE YOU?

The questionnaire opposite is designed to help you to assess your basic ratio of humoral factors. From this you can determine which diet, colours, exercise routines, crystals, oils and scents are most likely to suit you. By referring to the sections on which you score the most points, you will identify whether you are a vata, pitta or kapha dosha, or what is called a combination type. Read the questions and, to discover your prakruti, tick those descriptions which apply to you in general terms. Allocate two ticks to the statement that you think is most applicable to you; use one tick for a description that could also possibly apply, but if a particular description does not apply to you, then leave it unticked.

Gems are used in Ayurveda only with a prescription from a jyotish (Vedic or Hindu astrologer), or from an Ayurvedic physician.

Revealing your Vikruti

As has already been explained, your current condition, or vikruti, may not be the same as your underlying constitution, or prakruti. If you wish to discover whether or not this is the case, go through the questions a second time, this time using crosses instead of ticks. To reveal your vikruti, answer the questions according to how you have been feeling in the more recent past, and how the descriptions relate to your current health or condition, including any illnesses or other changes, no matter how subtle, that you are currently experiencing.

When you are answering the questions, do make sure that you clearly focus either on your prakruti (your general state throughout life – ticks), or on your vikruti (current or recent state – crosses). To avoid any possible confusion, make sure that you finish with one set of answers before you start attempting to fill out and assess the questionnaire for a second time.

If you wish, you can answer the questionnaire a third time, separating questions about the mind from questions about the body. Use circles and squares to record your answers. This will indicate whether your body and mind are the same dosha. If they are different, follow the dietary advice for the mind. For example, if you have a kapha body and a pitta mind, follow the kapha eating and exercise plan, including the massage technique, and ensure that you have soothing colours and a calm environment.

"Vata", "Pitta", and "Kapha"

Following the questionnaire are three sections headed "Vata", "Pitta" and "Kapha". Having discovered your vikruti (condition) or prakruti (constitution), turn to the pages relevant to your predominant dosha for detailed advice on reducing any excess

Vatas need to learn how to be still because they tend to suffer from energy depletion, having the least amount of stamina.

(vikruti), or to see how you can maintain your true character (prakruti). When referring to the various sections, do please read the information very carefully before you begin to put it into practice. Please also note that when using Ayurvedic medicinal herbs, you should take them only for as long as you are experiencing any obvious symptoms. You must check that the herbs are suited to your basic doshic needs; do this quite frequently, monitoring yourself even on a weekly basis.

When you begin to use any of the Ayurvedic prescriptions and techniques, do not be tempted to try and elaborate on them. This will do far more harm than good. The effect of the prescriptions lies in the ratio of the individual ingredients. Change this even in the subtlest way and all the good work may well be undone. Ayurveda is extremely complex and precise. For example, there are lengthy guidelines about the specific crystals that may be used to make a crystal infusion for each individual dosha. It is advisable that you do not make other infusions unless you are qualified or highly experienced; since crystals and gems can have a very powerful effect.

Choose foods and herbs according to your doshic condition.

Discover your Dosha

Mark the questionnaire with either a √ (= your general constitution – prakruti) or x (= your current or recent state – vikruti).

	Vata	Pitta	Kapha
HEIGHT	Very short, or tall and thin	Medium	Tall or short and sturdy
MUSCULATURE	Thin, prominent tendons	Medium/firm	Plentiful/solid
BODILY FRAME	Light, narrow	Medium frame	Large/broad
WEIGHT	Light, hard to gain	Medium weight	Heavy, gains easily
SWEAT	Minimal	Profuse, especially when hot	Moderate
SKIN	Dry, cold	Soft, warm	Moist, cool, possibly oily
COMPLEXION	Darkish	Fair, pink, red, freckles	Pale, white
HAIR AMOUNT	Average amount	Early thinning and greying	Plentiful
TYPE OF HAIR	Dry, thin, dark, coarse	Fine, soft, red, fair	Thick, lustrous, brown
SIZE OF EYES	Small, narrow or sunken	Average	Large, prominent
TYPE OF EYES	Dark brown or grey, dull	Blue/grey/hazel, intense	Blue, brown, attractive
TEETH AND GUMS	Protruding, receding gums	Yellowish, gums bleed	White teeth, strong gums
SIZE OF TEETH	Small or large, irregular	Average	Large
PHYSICAL ACTIVITY	Moves quickly, active	Moderate pace, average	Slow pace, steady
ENDURANCE	Low	Good	Very good
STRENGTH	Poor	Good	Very good
TEMPERATURE	Dislikes cold, likes warmth	Likes coolness	Aversion to cool and damp
STOOLS	Tendency to constipation	Tendency to loose stools	Plentiful, slow elimination
LIFESTYLE	Variable, erratic	Busy, tends to achieve a lot	Steady, can skip meals
SLEEP	Light, interrupted, fitful	Sound, short	Deep, likes plenty
EMOTIONAL TENDENCY	Fearful, anxious, insecure	Fiery, angry, judgemental	Greedy, possessive
MENTAL ACTIVITY	Restless, lots of ideas	Sharp, precise, logical	Calm, steady, stable
MEMORY	Good recent memory	Sharp, generally good	Good long term
REACTION TO STRESS	Excites very easily	Quick temper	Not easily irritated
WORK	Creative	Intellectual	Caring
MOODS	Change quickly	Change slowly	Generally steady
SPEECH	Fast	Clear, sharp, precise	Deep, slow
RESTING PULSE			
WOMEN	Above 80	70-80	Below 70
MEN	Above 70	60-70	Below 60
Totals: *Please add up*	**Vata**	**Pitta**	**Kapha**

vata

Vata types are known to be rather restless, cool people, who certainly notice the cold. When you have excess levels of vata, fear, depression and nervousness become quite marked, significant traits, and with repressed emotions comes a definite weakening of the immune system. However, by adopting the appropriate lifestyle, and making one or two changes, you will create a better balance within yourself, and find that you achieve much more.

The vata body type is usually thin and narrow. Vatas do not gain weight easily and are often restless by nature, especially when they are busy and active. They have dry hair and cool skin and a tendency to feel the cold. Their levels of energy are erratic, and they have to be very careful not to exhaust themselves, leading to inconsistency. They may find it quite hard to relax, which can lead to an overactive mind and insomnia.

Vata symptoms will be changeable, being cold by nature and therefore worse in cold weather. Any pain will worsen during change. Vata people can suffer from wind, low back pain, arthritis and nerve disorders. Vata types, because of their individual restless nature, certainly require a regular intake of nourishment, and they should sit down to eat or drink at regular times. Careful exercise should always be taken in moderation, clearly maintaining a gentle, regular, well-worked out routine that will help to keep the mind focused, and in perfect harmony with the body.

Vata people should try to eat warming foods which are earthy and sweet, with the emphasis upon cooked foods, such as a bowl of dhal, rather than salads.

Elements: ether and air.
Climate: dry and cold.
Principle: movement.
Emotions: fearful, anxious, apprehensive, sensitive, timid, lacking confidence, slightly nervous, changeable.
Systems most affected by excess vata: the nervous system and also the colon.
Symptoms of excess vata: flatulence, back pain, problems with circulation, dry skin, outbreaks of arthritis, constipation, and nerve disorders.

In summer the vata quickly begins to accumulate as the heat of the sun begins to dry everything out. The best way to stop your skin from drying out too, so keeping it gently moist, is to use a top quality natural cream.

DIETARY TIPS

Vata people must always be quite careful, but not to the point that cooking suddenly becomes something of a difficult problem. The easy-to-follow, basic guidelines are as follows.

You must avoid all kinds of fried foods, no matter how tempting, and you should eat at regular intervals. Irregular huge meals are to be avoided at all costs. To reduce any excess vata, then follow the vata diet and recommendations in your eating and living plan. Always attempt to avoid any foods and other items that are not listed, as far as is possible. If animal products are a part of your diet, they should be used strictly in moderation.

HERBS AND SPICES

Almond essence, asafoetida (hing), basil leaves, bay leaves, cardamom pods, coriander (cilantro), fennel, fresh ginger, marjoram, mint, nutmeg, oregano, paprika, parsley, peppermint, spearmint, tarragon, thyme, turmeric and vanilla.

GRAINS AND SEEDS

Oats (cooked), pumpkin seeds, quinoa, rice (this includes all kinds and varieties), sesame seeds, sprouted wheat bread, sunflower seeds and wheat.

NUTS, MEAT & FISH

Almonds, brazil nuts, cashews, hazelnuts, macadamias, pecans, pine nuts, pistachios and walnuts. Beef, chicken, duck, eggs, sea fish, shrimps and turkey.

VEGETABLES

Artichokes, asparagus, beetroot, carrots, courgettes (zucchini), cucumber, daikon radish, green beans, leeks, okra, olives, onions (cooked), parsnips, pumpkins, radishes, spinach (cooked), swede (rutabagas), sweet potatoes, tomatoes (cooked), and fresh watercress.

FRUIT

Apricots, avocados, bananas, berries, cherries, fresh coconuts, dates, fresh figs, grapefruit, grapes, lemons, limes, mangoes, melons, oranges, peaches, pineapples, rhubarb and strawberries.

DAIRY PRODUCTS

Cow's milk, cottage cheese, goat's milk, goat's' cheese and soft cheese – all are to be taken sensibly, in moderation.

COOKING OILS

Unrefined sesame oil.

DRINKS

Apricot juice, carrot juice, ginger tea, grape juice, grapefruit juice, orange juice, hot dairy drinks, lemon balm tea, lemonade and peach juice.

AROMAS AND MASSAGE OILS

Vata people are unusual because they tend to benefit much more than either of the other two doshas from having a massage. Consequently they should consider massaging their feet, hands and head every morning, and have a regular massage at least once a week. The massage should become a regular, greatly appreciated part of your lifestyle.

Vata aromas are warm and sweet, and the most appropriate massage oil for the vata personality is gently warmed sesame oil. Bottles of sesame oil are widely available, and are generally of a high, well-perfumed standard. If that is impossible to obtain, any other oil (preferably virgin olive) will suffice. It can be perfumed by the addition of your favourite herb. Oil is good for vata types, and if your vata is seriously out of balance, increase the number of massages you have a week from one to as many as three. You will soon notice the enormous improvement.

When using essential oils, note they must be diluted. Do not put them directly on your skin or take them internally. In fact it is not advisable to use the same essential oil for more than two weeks; interchange your essential oils so that you do not create a toxic build-up, or overload of one fragrance. If you are pregnant or have a diagnosed medical condition, do not use any essential oil without consulting a qualified practitioner.

Warm, calming or earthy essential oils are the most suitable for vata. These include camphor (which can be an irritant, so do test yourself for sensitivity first), eucalyptus, ginger, sandalwood and jatamansi (a spikenard species from India).

vata massage

1 The correct vata massage should always be gentle.

2 Keep the actions firm, regular, soothing and relaxing.

3 Use flowing, continuous stroking movements.

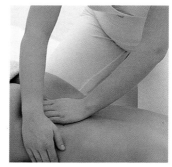

4 Oil and ease any areas displaying dry, tight skin.

COLOURS

Vata individuals generally benefit from most of the pastel colours, and from earthy colours that are gentle and warm to look at. They include ochres, browns and yellows.

Ochre

A warm, friendly and relaxing colour, ochre is good at drawing the energy down, right through the system, helping the vata individual to feel much more solid and steady.

Brown

A solid, reliable colour, brown helps to ground the vata type, stabilizing any tendency to flightiness. It is also good at holding the emotions in place; it consolidates and aids concentration.

Yellow

A warming, enlivening colour, yellow is linked to the mind and intellect. It helps to keep the vata mentality alert by focusing the mind, and calming any rising emotions.

Making a Colour Infusion

Begin by taking a piece of thin cotton or silk. The fabric should be warm yellow in colour, and sufficiently thin to allow the light through. Next, wrap it around a small transparent (not coloured) jar filled with spring water and leave it outside in the sunlight for four hours. Finally, remove the fabric. Note, vata infusions should not be stored in the fridge, but kept at room temperature.

This infusion will encourage a sense of warmth and well-being.

GEMS AND CRYSTALS

Gems and crystals have subtle healing qualities that can be utilized in Ayurvedic medicine. Their curious, well-known powers are taken seriously by the jyotish (Vedic astrologer), who can determine which gems or crystals you will need to use, depending on the circumstances of your life chart.

Topaz is a warm stone that traditionally dispels fear, making it an ideal stone for vata because it calms high emotions and anxiety. Wear topaz whenever you want to feel confident and in control. Amethyst is an appropriate crystal to wear when you want to balance vata. It soon promotes a fine clarity of mind and thought, and will help you to radiate harmony.

There may be times when it is advisable to remove all crystals – when you find circumstances in your life are changing for the worse. This indicates that your birth chart or constitution does not require the healing qualities of a particular crystal, or that it is highlighting an area of your birth chart in a negative way. Seek expert advice on replacements.

Cleaning Crystals and Crystal Infusions

Before making a crystal infusion, it is best to cleanse your crystal. In fact, crystals that are used for infusions should ideally be cleansed before and after each use. Once you have filled a bowl with spring water, dissolve a teaspoon of sea salt in it. The crystal sits in for up to about eight hours before being rinsed.

1 Place the crystal in the water and leave to stand for about four hours, or leave it overnight in the dark.

2 Rinse it in spring water, visualizing any residues that were being held in the crystal being washed away.

To make a crystal infusion, take the cleansed crystal and hold it in your hands, imagining that the crystal is full of peace and calm. Place the crystal in a clear glass bowl, cover it with spring water, and leave it in the sunlight for about four hours. Remove the crystal and bottle the spring water. You can now drink the infusion prior to any mentally demanding tasks. It will aid clarity of mind and help reduce any stress that might arise as a result of pressure. You can keep the infusion for just 24 hours, after which it should be discarded. Make sure you store the infusion away from domestic appliances and electrical equipment.

EXERCISE AND TONIC

Since vata is cold in nature it benefits from warmth and comfort. Make your own warming tonic drinks for cold windy days by combining ingredients from the vata eating plan. Be aware though that sugar weakens the immune system and vatas, with their tendency to stress (another immune suppressor), need to be particularly wary of sugary and refined foods, choosing naturally sweet-tasting foods, such as fruit, instead.

Vata people benefit from gentle, relaxing forms of exercise. Being the most easily exhausted of the various categories, they should be careful not to overdo things. Examples of suitable exercise include walking, yoga and slow swimming. In essence, it is not so much the form of exercise that you take, but rather the way in which you take it. With vata, the exercise routine should always be on the gentle side; with this in mind, vata types can undertake most sports and activities.

Yoga stretches will gradually and gently lengthen your muscles, and increase your flexibility. It has enormous all-round benefits. If you do not actively practise yoga as a form of exercise, you may well find that achieving a full or even half lotus for meditation is much too strenuous and difficult. If this is the case, do not try and force yourself. Instead, use a specifically designed meditation stool, or place some firm cushions on the floor beneath you. Push your bent knees on to the floor, then tuck your feet in towards you on the floor, forming a solid triangular base with your legs.

Fresh Ginger and Lemon Tea

This tea is remarkably quick and easy to make, and tastes absolutely delicious. It is also a marvellous tonic for a vata.

1 lemon	Spring water
A small slice of fresh ginger	Raw honey or fructose

1 Wash the lemon and then cut it into thin slices, leaving the peel on. Peel the piece of fresh ginger and slice it finely.
2 Place the lemon and ginger slices in a small teapot.
3 Add boiling spring water, then stir. Finally sweeten with honey or fructose, drink and enjoy.

pitta

Pitta people are generally quite well-balanced, well-proportioned, rounded types, admired by all, but they can suddenly become passionately focused and intense. At its most extreme this tendency leads to a high degree of intolerance and irritability. Consequently pitta types should keep well away from any foods that are known to be hot and spicy, and which might inflame them, and concentrate on meals that promote their more soothing side.

The pitta body type is usually of average build and nicely proportioned. Pittas like food and have a healthy appetite. The hair is usually straight, fine and fair, though dark-haired people can also be pitta types. People with red hair will automatically have some level of pitta within their nature. Like the fire element, their temperament can be quite intense, and when it manifests itself in excess this can lead to marked intolerance.

Pitta skin will have a tendency to be sensitive to the sun, and pitta types will need to be very careful how much time they spend in direct sunlight. The fiery nature of the sun will sometimes inflame the pitta person, leading to skin rashes, freckles and sunburn. Cool showers, cool environments and plenty of long cooling drinks (but not ice-cold ones) will help to alleviate any high temperatures and calm down pitta types.

People of this nature can be impatient, having highly active and alert minds. However, pitta people can also have a very good sense of humour and a warm personality.

Pitta people should always aim to eat food that is rather soothing. What they must do is avoid any foods that are considered hot and spicy. Ingredients such as fiery chillies are definitely off the menu.

Elements: fire and water.
Climate: hot and moist.
Principle: transformation.
Emotions: hate, anger, resentment, intolerance, impatience, irritability, indignation, jealousy, good humour, intelligence, alertness, open warm-heartedness.
Systems most affected by excess pitta: skin, metabolism, small intestines, eyes, liver, hair on the head.
Symptoms of excess pitta: skin disorders, acidity, sun-sensitivity, premature degrees of hair loss or loss of hair colour, outbreaks of diarrhoea.

Pitta types generally benefit from spending time away from fast, noisy, chaotic urban environments. They should seek out quiet, peaceful, well-shaded, naturally calming surroundings.

DIETARY TIPS

The pitta person should avoid all hot, spicy and sour foods, as they will aggravate this dosha; they should also avoid all fried foods. Since heated food will increase pitta within the system, pitta types should eat more raw than cooked foods. As a primarily vegetarian system, Ayurveda does not advocate the eating of animal products, especially for the pitta dosha, so although some meats and other animal products have been included in the following list, they should really be used in the strictest moderation. Let common sense always prevail.

HERBS AND SPICES

Aloe vera juice (totally avoid during a pregnancy), basil leaves, cinnamon, coriander (cilantro), cumin, dill, fennel, fresh ginger, hijiki, mint leaves, spearmint.

GRAINS AND SEEDS

Barley, basmati rice, flax seeds, psyllium seeds, rice cakes, sunflower seeds, wheat, wheat bran, white rice.

PROTEINS

Aduki beans, black beans, black-eyed beans, chick peas (garbanzos), kidney beans, lentils (red and brown), lima beans, mung beans, pinto beans, soya beans, split peas, tempeh and tofu. Chicken, freshwater fish, rabbit, turkey.

VEGETABLES

Artichokes, asparagus, broccoli, Brussels sprouts, butternut squash, cabbages, courgettes (zucchini), celery, cucumber, fennel, green beans and green peppers, Jerusalem artichokes, kale, leafy greens, leeks, lettuces, mushrooms, onions (cooked), parsnips, spinach (cooked). Eat most vegetables raw instead of cooked.

FRUIT

Apples, apricots, avocados, berries, cherries, dates, figs, mangoes, melons, oranges, pears, pineapples, plums, pomegranates, prunes, quinces, raisins, red grapes and watermelons. Always make sure that the fruits have fully ripened, and are very sweet and fresh.

DAIRY PRODUCTS

Cottage cheese, cow's milk, diluted yoghurt, ghee (clarified butter), goat's milk, mild soft cheeses and unsalted butter may all be taken but with a reasonable degree of moderation.

COOKING OILS

Olive oil, sunflower oil, soya and walnut oil. As with all dairy products, these oils should be used in moderation.

DRINKS

Apple juice, apricot juice, cool dairy drinks, grape juice, mango juice, mixed vegetable juice, soya milk, vegetable bouillon, elderflower tea, jasmine tea, spearmint tea and strawberry tea.

AROMAS AND MASSAGE OILS

Essential oils for pitta include honeysuckle, jasmine, sandalwood and vetiver. They must be diluted and should never be taken internally. Avoid a toxic build-up by interchanging the oils every two weeks. If you are pregnant or have a diagnosed medical condition, you must consult a qualified practitioner before attempting to use essential oils.

If possible go to an experienced masseur. They understand exactly how a massage should be given. In time you will pick up the basics and may be able to start giving others a gentle massage. The key to success is to take your time, and make sure that your partner is fully relaxed. There is no point in attempting a soft massage when they are in an agitated state, and are incapable of lying still for a couple of minutes, let alone 20. When applying the essential oils, it is important that you work with firm, consistent hand movements, totally avoiding any sudden changes of direction. Think of your hands as waves, sweeping in one long curving movement over a smooth beach. That said, do not go to the opposite extreme and be so frightened of touching or hurting the skin that you barely make any contact. The right degree of pressure is about the same as for a firm hairwash.

After the massage, do not expect to get up and rush out. That would immediately undermine all the good work. Instead, take your time, possibly even have a cat-nap, and only step back into everyday life when you are feeling absolutely ready. That way you will feel refreshed, calm and clear-headed. It also helps if you have a massage on a day that you know will be stress-free.

Pitta Massage

1 Start the massage in the middle of the back.

2 Use continuous, relaxing, deep, varied movements.

3 Be gentle on any areas of stiffness or soreness.

4 Continue with sweeping, slow movements.

COLOURS

If you are experiencing symptoms of excess pitta, such as irritability or impatience, or on occasions when you know that you are going to have a busy and active day ahead of you, balance your system by wearing natural fibres in cooling and calming colours, such as green, blue, violet or any quiet pastel shade.

Blue

Blue is a soothing, healing colour which is ideal for the active pitta type. It is linked to spiritual consciousness and helps the pitta to remain open and calm without being over-stimulated.

Green

Green, an integral colour of the natural world, brings harmonious feelings to the pitta personality, having the ability to soothe emotions and calm passionate feelings.

Violet

Violet is a refined colour that soothes and opens the mind, and increases awareness of spiritual issues.

Making a Colour Infusion

Take a piece of thin, translucent cotton or silk in violet or light blue. Wrap it around a small transparent (not coloured) bottle or jar filled with spring water. Leave it outside in dappled sunlight, not in direct sun, for approximately six hours. Finally, remove the fabric, and drink the infusion to encourage the wonderful sensation of inner peace and harmony.

A blue colour infusion will help to clear the system of a build-up of pressure.

GEMS AND CRYSTALS

When you want to reduce excess pitta, wear pearls or a mother-of-pearl ring set in silver upon the ring finger of your right hand. Pearls have the ability to reduce inflammatory conditions, including sudden passionate, heated emotions. Ideally, natural pearls should be worn, although cultured pearls are actually quite acceptable. The most harmonious day to put on your pearls is a Monday (the moon's day) during a new moon. However, do not wear pearls when you have a kapha condition, such as a cold. The moonstone has the ability to calm emotions and is soft and cooling, being feminine in orientation. It can certainly help to pacify the pitta personality.

You can also use stones, as shown right, to make a special infusion. It involves no more than placing the stone in a glass bowl that has been topped up with spring water. The key part of the process is standing the bowl and stone outside, preferably on a night when there is a full moon and a cloudless sky. The longer you can leave it standing out the better, three hours being about the minimum period for successful results.

When you bring in the bowl, pour the special water into a clean glass and drink before breakfast. If you can make standing this bowl outside at night a regular part of your routine, then you will soon notice the difference that drinking moonstone water makes. You will feel increasingly calm, relaxed, clear-headed, stable, grounded, and above all inwardly strong. Your confidence grows and grows. You will find that other people definitely notice, and become increasingly attracted towards you. Feeling more attractive actually gives you a new lease of life.

Making a Moonstone Infusion

1 Take a stone specimen that has already been cleansed.

2 Leave the bowl outside to stand under a full moon.

3 Remove the moonstone, and pour out the liquid.

4 Drink the moonstone infusion when you wake.

Orange and Elderflower Infusion

This infusion makes a light refreshing drink, ideal in summer.

1 large sweet orange	300ml/½ pint spring water
2 heads fresh elderflower	Fructose to taste
Fresh spearmint	

1 Wash the orange in spring water. Slice and put in a jug.
2 Add elderflower heads and spearmint; pour in spring water.
3 Leave for one hour, add fructose to taste, and drink.

EXERCISE AND TONIC

Cooling drinks made from fresh fruit and vegetable juices are ideal tonics for the pitta constitution.

Pittas require a moderate amount of exercise, which should involve some element of vigour and challenge – jogging, team sports and some of the gentler martial arts which do not stress sudden, fierce, aggressive movements. Pitta exercise should not overstimulate the body, and any exercise should be kept in line with an average amount of effort and challenge. You should avoid going to such extremes that your pitta nature gets carried away and you end up overdoing it. So, for example, doubles tennis is much better for you than singles, swimming is better than squash, and gentle jogging is much better for you than sudden sprinting. In the end, though, it is not so much what you do but how you do it that is deemed important.

This orange and elderflower infusion, left, is a light and delicate alternative to a cordial. Cordials are made by boiling all the ingredients together, which is not appropriate for pitta types because of the heat required in the cooking process. In fact, a general awareness of such techniques will help you make the right decisions in all aspects of your diet. Note that drinks are just as important as anything else you might have. They contribute greatly to our overall wellbeing.

kapha

Kapha types are restless, complex, interesting contradictions. You will also find that despite being quite athletic, they actually need plenty of motivation, without which they can easily become overweight. On the plus side, they are certainly highly sensitive, but in return they do need quite a lot of sensitive handling. All in all they are thoroughly reliable, methodical people, and with that extra energy input will always stay one step ahead.

The kapha body type is well built, with a tendency to weight problems, especially if an exercise programme is not followed to keep the kapha active and moving. Kapha people are naturally athletic but they do need motivation. They are generally very sensitive and emotional, and they do require understanding otherwise they tend to turn to food as an emotional support and stabilizer. They should always ensure that what they eat is suitable for their body type. Their hair will be thick, fine and wavy, their skin soft, smooth and sensuous, and their eyes large, trusting and attractive.

Kapha people are inclined to be slow and steady, methodical and pragmatic, with a real dislike of change. They make good managers though, because they like to be reliable and available. They act like an anchor in a business because they have an innate organizing ability. Note that bright, strong, striking colours will greatly help to reduce any excess kapha, and stimulate those who are feeling slow, sluggish and dull.

Kapha food should be light, dry, hot and stimulating. Always opt for cooked foods, such as hot and spicy vegetable curries, in preference to any kind of fresh salad.

Elements: water and earth.
Climate: cold and damp.
Principle: cohesion.
Emotions: stubbornness, greed, jealousy, possessiveness, lethargy, reliability and methodical behaviour, kindliness, motherliness.
Systems most affected by excess kapha: joints, lymphatics, body fluids and mucous membranes throughout the body.
Symptoms of excess kapha: congestion, bronchial/nasal discharge, sluggish digestion, nausea, slow mental responses, idleness, desire for sleep, excess weight, fluid retention.

Because kapha individuals have a tendency towards inertia, they need plenty of motivation. A good kick-start to the day is regular, early morning outdoor exercise, such as a brisk walk or a jog.

DIETARY TIPS

Kapha people should focus upon cooked food, but can have some salads occasionally. They should avoid fats and oils unless they are hot and spicy. Dairy products, sweet, sour and salty tastes and a high intake of wheat will also aggravate kapha. Although some meats and animal products have been included, they should always be used in moderation.

To reduce any excess levels of kapha (vikruti), or to maintain the right balance because you are a kapha dosha (prakruti), include the following items in your eating plan and try to avoid any foods that are not listed here.

HERBS AND SPICES

Asafoetida (hing), black or Indian pepper, chilli pepper, coriander leaves (cilantro), dry ginger, garlic, horseradish, mint leaves, mustard, parsley or any other hot spices.

GRAINS AND SEEDS

Barley, buckwheat, corn, couscous, oat bran, polenta, popcorn (plain), rye, sprouted wheat bread, toasted pumpkin seeds and occasional small quantities of toasted sunflower seeds.

BEANS AND PULSES

Aduki beans, black-eyed beans, chick peas (garbanzos), lima beans, pinto beans, red lentils, split peas and tempeh.

MEAT AND FISH

Eggs, freshwater fish, turkey, rabbit, shrimps and venison.

VEGETABLES

Artichokes, broccoli, Brussels sprouts, cabbage, carrots, cauliflower, celery, daikon radish, fennel, green beans, kale, leeks, lettuce, mushrooms, okra, onions, peas, peppers, radishes, spinach. Kapha vegetables should be cooked.

FRUITS

Apples, apricots, berries, cherries, peaches, pears, pomegranates and prunes.

COOKING OILS

Corn, almond or sunflower oil may be used in small quantities.

DRINKS

Fruit drinks should not contain sugar or additives. Recommended hot drinks include black tea, carrot juice, cranberry juice, grape juice, mango juice, mixed vegetable juice, nettle tea, passion flower tea, raspberry tea and occasional wine.

AROMAS AND MASSAGE OILS

Kapha individuals require minimal oil or none at all with massage, using instead a natural, unscented talcum powder which can be purchased from most health food stores. If an essential oil is used at all, the best ones for kapha individuals include eucalyptus, cinnamon, orange peel (since this can cause sun sensitivity, avoid strong sunlight after a massage with orange peel), ginger and myrrh. All of these oils are stimulating and it would be well advisable, after diluting approximately 7–10 drops of essential oil in 25ml/1fl oz carrier oil, to test an area of skin first to check for any possible sensitive reaction.

Unlike the sensitive gentleness of the pitta massage with its sweeping regular movements designed to relax, the kapha is actually quite fast and vigorous. You will notice that when having a massage the hands sweep over you firmly and energetically, keeping to a constant rhythm. If giving such a massage to a friend or partner, be aware that it can surprisingly be quite tiring. The aim is to kick-start and stimulate the metabolism that tends towards the sluggish.

Concentrate on the hip and groin areas to encourage lymphatic drainage, and also around the armpits to release any congestion. Finally, note as always that essential oils must be diluted and should not be taken internally. Do not to use the same essential oil for more than two weeks. If you are pregnant or have a diagnosed medical condition, do not use any essential oil without consulting a qualified practitioner. The risks are not worth taking.

Kapha Massage

1 Kapha massage needs to fairly vigorous and stimulating.

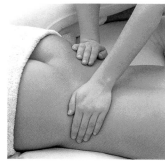

2 Use fast movements, using talcum powder.

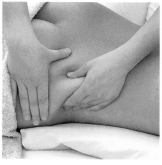

3 Use hip/groin massage to assist lymphatic drainage.

4 Another major lymph gland area is around the armpits.

COLOURS

Kapha individuals benefit from the warm and stimulating colours of the spectrum. Whenever you experience symptoms such as lethargy and sluggishness, which suggest excess kapha, or if you need to be particularly active, wear bright, invigorating, stimulating colours. You will quickly notice how effective they are, inspiring a change in your temperament.

Red

Red is the colour of blood and will increase circulation as well as being energizing and positive. It should be used sparingly to avoid over-stimulation of kapha, creating excess pitta.

Orange

Orange is a warming, nourishing colour which feeds the sexual organs, and its glowing colour helps to remove congestion.

Pink

Warm, comforting pinks gently stimulate kapha into activity. Being a softer colour than red, pink may be worn without ill-effects for significantly longer periods. A highly useful colour.

Making a Colour Infusion

Take a piece of thin cotton or silk. The fabric should be a warm pink and sufficiently translucent to allow the light to penetrate. Wrap it around a transparent (not coloured) small bottle containing spring water. Stand it in full sunlight or upon a windowsill with the window open so that the light can fall naturally upon the bottle. Leave it for about four hours. Remove the fabric and drink the contents of the bottle within 24 hours.

If possible, choose a fabric which has been dyed with natural dyes.

GEMS AND CRYSTALS

Lapis lazuli is a reliably suitable, highly useful crystal with which to reduce any excess levels of kapha. Known as the heavenly stone it will quickly help kapha individuals to increase their bodily vibrations, raising them from the level of the dense and slow to a much more refined and spiritual resonance. Lapis lazuli is a quite remarkable crystal, one that is well worth seeking out.

Crystal Infusion

Cleanse your lapis lazuli prior to making an infusion. Hold the lapis in your hands for a few moments, visualizing clarity and inspiration. Take your time to get this right. The crystal should now be ready for use. Place it in a clear glass bowl and cover it with spring water. Leave it outside in the sunlight for about four hours. The brighter and sunnier the sky, the better. Next, remove the crystal, and bottle the infused spring water. You can regularly drink small amounts of it throughout the day, as required, and this will certainly ensure a continued rising of your spirits towards inspired, enlivened action.

Make a lapis infusion to reduce excess kapha.

EXERCISE AND TONIC

Kapha types may well avoid this page because it suggests exercise! However, kapha people must address their natural aversion to physical activity. Exercise will make an amazing difference, cleansing excess kapha, and making valuable room for their inner beauty and radiance to shine right through.

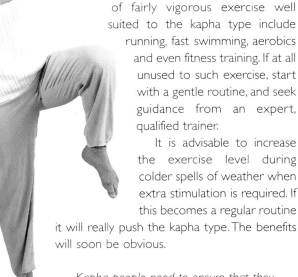

Since kapha individuals will tend to shy away from any vigorous exercise, a certain amount of self-discipline is required. Once a regular exercise routine is established, however, the kapha type will enjoy and benefit from the enlivened and energetic feeling that all activity and exercise brings. Examples of fairly vigorous exercise well suited to the kapha type include running, fast swimming, aerobics and even fitness training. If at all unused to such exercise, start with a gentle routine, and seek guidance from an expert, qualified trainer.

It is advisable to increase the exercise level during colder spells of weather when extra stimulation is required. If this becomes a regular routine it will really push the kapha type. The benefits will soon be obvious.

Kapha people need to ensure that they have vigorous exercise, such as aerobics.

Spiced Yogi Tea

Spiced yogi tea is a delicious, warming drink which will soon help to reduce any excess kapha and is perfect for warming up cold bones on a chilly winter's day.

2.5ml/½ tsp dry ginger
4 whole cardamom pods
5 cloves
A pinch of black pepper or pippali (Indian long pepper)

1 large cinnamon stick
600ml/1 pint/2½ cups spring water
30ml/2tbsp goat's milk or organic soya milk

1 Mix the spices together in a saucepan.
2 Add the spring water and boil off half the liquid.
3 Turn off the heat and add the goat's milk or soya milk.
4 Stir and strain the liquid. Serve hot.

dual doshas
In all relationships, at home and work, it will make a great difference if you can try to adopt the approaches recommended for your own particular dosha. The vata dosha may well need to work at being much more reliably consistent, with the pitta dosha aiming at far greater tolerance and patience. The rather possessive kapha dosha, on the other hand, should always put extra trust and flexibility right at the top of the list.

Vata/Pitta – Pitta/Vata

If, when you answered the questionnaire in the introduction, you found that you scored twice as many points on any one type as on the other two, this means that you will predominantly be that type. For example, a score of 30 points on kapha and 5 or 10 on the others would indicate that you are a kapha type. However, if there is a closer gap with perhaps 30 points for kapha and 20 for pitta then you are classified as a kapha/pitta type. If you are such a dual type, read the following essential information.

Vata/pitta is a combination of ether/air and fire/water elements. If you belong to this dual type, refer to both the vata and the pitta eating and living plans. Choose items from the pitta plan during the spring and summer months, and during outbreaks of hot, humid weather. Follow the vata plan during the autumn and winter months, and during any cold, dry spells. For example, pungent foods aggravate pitta but can actually help to calm vata (because vata is cold), which is why the plans need to be changed in accordance with the weather, your health and a wide range of other factors. It is really quite important that you keep

Vata/pitta – pitta/vata herbs include the different kinds of basil, coriander (cilantro), cumin seeds, fennel, mint, turmeric and vanilla pods.

a regular, accurate check on such factors, and modify your approach accordingly.

Eat your vegetables in season, and mostly cooked and flavoured with appropriate vata spices to minimize aggravation of vata and pitta. Only small amounts of bitter vegetables should be used. Among foods suitable for the vata/pitta type are broccoli, cauliflower, cucumber, endive, kale, onion (cooked), plantain, coconut, sweet oranges, apricots and other sweet fruits. Teas that are beneficial include elderflower, fennel, lemon balm and rosehip teas. Appropriate herbs and spices for vata/pitta – pitta/vata include fresh basil, caraway, cardamom, cumin, fennel, garam masala, spearmint and vanilla.

The nature of vata is change and when you are more familiar with the doshic influences that the climate has on you, you may be more flexible with the doshic recommendations. Remember, though, that you are influenced by everything touching your life.

Your lifestyle can be affected by your health. Pitta or vata doshas should find time to create a calming and restful ambience in which to relax and wind down.

If you belong to the vata/pitta type, eat plenty of sweet, ripe fruits, such as melons and oranges, when they are in season.

Pitta/Kapha – Kapha/Pitta

This is a combination of the fire, water and earth elements. If you belong to this dual type, follow the kapha eating and living plan during the winter months and during spells of cold, damp weather, and take note of the pitta plan during the summer months, and during hot, humid weather.

You should always choose foods that are pungent and astringent, such as onions, celery, lemons, dandelion, mustard greens and watercress, and eat fresh fruit and vegetables. All fruit juices should be diluted with water or milk. Suitable teas for the pitta/kapha – kapha/pitta type include bancha twig, blackberry, dandelion, jasmine, licorice (not to be used if you suffer from high blood pressure or oedema) and spearmint. The herbs, spices and flavourings that apply to the pitta/kapha type include coriander, dill leaves, fennel, kudzu, orange peel, parsley, rosewater, and sprigs of refreshing spearmint.

Vata/Kapha – Kapha/Vata

Vata/kapha is a combination of ether, air, water and earth. You should follow the kapha eating and living plan during the winter and spring months, and during cold, damp weather. You should stick to the vata plan during the autumn and summer months, and during any cold, dry windy spells.

Since the vata/kapha type is cold, you should therefore be encouraged to have plenty of pungent, hot and spicy foods. Chinese and Eastern cuisine is a "must". Good examples of suitable foods include artichokes, asparagus, mustard greens, parsnips, summer and winter squashes and watercress. Vegetables with seeds should be well cooked with the appropriate vata spices to minimize any possible aggravation.

It is equally important to eat plenty of fresh seasonal fruits, and they include apricots, berries, cherries, lemons, mangoes, peaches and strawberries. The vata/kapha type should be very careful to avoid a mono-diet of brown rice.

The herbs and spices for this particular type include allspice, anise, asafoetida (hing), basil, black pepper, basil, cinnamon, coriander, cumin, curry powder, garlic, nutmeg, poppy seeds, saffron and vanilla.

Tridosha

In very rare instances a person may score more or less equally for all three doshas, revealing themselves to be all three types, or what is known as "tridosha" (literally, three-doshas). If you are this interesting combination of three doshas you will require a specially formulated tridoshic diet and living plan. Since your make-up is more elaborate than for single types, your plan is accordingly more interesting and varied. The onus is on you, however, to closely follow the seasonal changes and modify the agenda as appropriate, making sensible, sensitive modifications. Being a tridosha involves quite a degree of self-discipline, and a clever ability to switch promptly between all three lifestyle plans.

Always eat according to the weather and to your personal circumstances. For example, on hot days, and during the spring and summer months, follow the pitta plan; on cold days and during the winter months, follow the kapha plan; and during the late summer and autumn, or on windy days or during spells of cold dry weather, follow the vata plan.

If you find that you fall into this highly unusual, remarkable category, it will certainly be worthwhile seeking out and consulting an Ayurvedic practitioner to find out more about what being a tridosha entails.

Pitta/kapha – kapha/pitta foods include curry leaves or powder, garam masala, mint, orange peel oil and rosewater.

ayurvedic treatments
ayurvedic treatments

ayurvedic treatments

The entire basis and the whole concept of Ayurvedic treatment is dietary; put bluntly, diet is exactly what it all leads back to – the tried and tested use and combination of specific foods. Fortunately, several excellent, imaginative Ayurvedic cookbooks with a wide range of tasty recipes have been published, and they are definitely well worth tracking down, collecting and studying if you want to learn more about Ayurvedic nutrition. They will make a great difference at meal times.

The following pages have been divided into several sections with the express purpose of outlining the basic characteristics of each type. This includes a wealth of vital information which forms the backbone, the foundation, and the essential core of the Ayurvedic approach. It deals with all kinds of related emotions, and the treatment systems closely associated with and most pertinent to each dosha. It also describes and explains the many symptoms of excess, together with a huge wealth of detail about what you should and should not be eating, which colours you really ought to be wearing, the scents and oils you should be using, the herbs and spices most beneficial to you, and the tonic recipes for each type, whether vata, pitta, or kapha.

In addition, there are key massage techniques, for example showing you how to follow the direction of the colon when massaging the stomach with brahmi oil, and which gem and crystal you should be working with in order to help you to reduce any excess levels in your dosha(s), thereby making sure they have a balanced, healthy relationship.

To the novice some of these ideas might seem slightly daunting, especially if you come from a background in which traditional forms of Western medicine have a stranglehold, but once they and the language in which they are expressed become familiar, you will see that the principles are actually very simple; they spell out some highly relevant advice. All you then have to do is to follow the right plan, whether you are trying to reduce an excess, or wish to build up and maintain the right balance in your system.

Once you become familiar with the many excellent Ayurvedic treatments, you can become slightly more adventurous. There is absolutely no reason why you should not start making up your own tonic recipes for your own body type. This is easily done by combining ingredients from the appropriate eating plan, and using recommended herbs and spices to enhance the healing.

the digestive system

One of the main cornerstones of Ayurvedic theory and medicine is that the gastro-intestinal tract (GI) is by far the most important and crucial part of the body because it is considered to be the focal point, or the principal seat, of the doshas. Vata is formed inside the colon, pitta in the small intestine, and kapha inside the stomach. In other words, this tract has extra dimensions not recognized by traditional medicine.

Constipation

Drink warm liquids; hot water is acceptable, but not chilled water. The best herbs for constipation are triphala and satisabgol (psyllium husks). (Do not use triphala if you are pregnant or suffering from ulcers of the GI.) Triphala is a combination of three herbal fruits, each of which has a rejuvenating effect in relation to one of the doshas. Satisabgol is a demulcent laxative. It is gentle and soothing and holds moisture in the colon, thus helping vata, which is known to be quite dry and cold. Use satisabgol with triphala; they complement each other well.

Gas, Bloating, Colic

These symptoms are usually related to constipation. Ideally food should pass through the system in 24 hours. If it is left for much longer the process of fermentation begins, which causes a build-up of gas. The traditional herbal remedy for this is hingvastak, a mix of asafoetida, pippali, ginger, black pepper, cumin, wild celery seeds and rock salt. Another traditional remedy is a massage with brahmi oil. It restores and relaxes the nervous system.

Eating a healthy vata diet can aid many vata problems associated with the gastro-intestinal tract.

Acidity/Heartburn

Sip aloe vera juice (without any citric acid added). Add fresh and dried coriander (cilantro), turmeric, saffron, coconut, fennel or peppermint to your diet. Shatavari (Asparagus racemosus), licorice (not to be used with high blood pressure or oedema) and amalaki are all used in traditional Ayurveda medicine in order to balance unwelcome levels of acidity.

Diarrhoea

Pitta diarrhoea is generally hot, and often yellowish and foul-smelling. Diarrhoea is mainly related to pitta but can sometimes be caused by other factors, such as high toxicity (ama), stress or emotional factors. Persistent symptoms must always be dealt with by an experienced, professional physician. If you have diarrhoea, avoid eating hot spices and carefully follow the pitta plan. Eat abstemiously if at all, drinking plenty of fluids. A simple straightforward diet of rice, split mung dhal and vegetables is most suitable for the pitta dosha, taken while symptoms last.

Persistent Hunger/Increased Appetite

In general, follow the pitta plan as outlined and use aloe vera juice as above. Increase relaxation, meditation and yoga. Also, have a long massage with brahmi oil. If strong symptoms persist, do please promptly consult your physician.

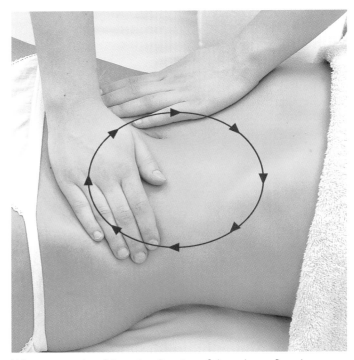

When massaging, follow the direction of the colon – from lower left, across the abdomen, up to the right and across to the left.

Nettle tea is very good at balancing the digestive system and can help to alleviate pitta conditions such as diarrhoea.

Nausea

Nausea can quite simply be defined as the strong sensation of needing to vomit. It might not actually result in vomiting, but produces a queasy, lingering feeling that needs to be quickly relieved. It certainly is not pleasant.

Ginger and cardamom tea is often very good at calming nausea. To make it, peel and thinly slice a piece of fresh ginger, add five cardamom pods and pour boiled spring water over them. Leave to stand for about five minutes, and then stir and drink while still refreshing and hot.

Ginger is also what is known as a carminative and a stimulant. This means that it has two key abilities, first to combat any intestinal bloating, and second to speed up processes in the GI so that balance is soon restored.

During the winter and spring seasons when kapha is seasonally high, dried ginger can be blended with some boiled spring water and a little fresh honey to help keep the digestive system active and moving. This also has the excellent effect of helping to reduce the possible risk of colds, coughs and flu, and any other winter bugs that might otherwise keep you confined to the bed or house for a number of days.

Cardamom (common in southern India as well as other tropical areas, and now freely available in supermarkets) can be used for kapha and vata digestive conditions. However, it can only be used in small amounts because it can quickly aggravate pitta, or bring about a high level of pitta excess.

As with all the recommended foods, herbs and spices, the purer the quality, the more beneficial they will be. Therefore, try to buy top quality, fresh organic herbs and spices whenever it is possible. You will immediately appreciate the difference.

The Doshas and the Gastro-intestinal Tract

Kapha

Typical kapha conditions of the GI include poor appetite – kapha tends to be low in agni (digestive fire), which can create a slow metabolism and weight gain; nausea; a build-up of mucus, leading to colds, sinus problems, coughs and flu; and poor circulation, resulting in a build-up of toxicity (ama). Follow the kapha plan and eat plenty of hot spices, such as chilli peppers, garlic, ginger and black pepper, until the condition clears, after which you should reduce your intake of hot spices. Herbs for kapha conditions of the GI include trikatu ("three hot things"), to be taken or added to meals. This contains pippali, ginger and black pepper. You should also have plenty of vigorous exercise.

Vata

Regular daily bowel movements are a sign of a healthy GI. Typical vata conditions of the GI include constipation, gas/flatulence, and tension – cramps or spasms, such as irritable bowel syndrome.

Pitta

Pitta digestion tends to be fast and "burns" food. This is made worse by anger or frustration. Begin a pitta-reducing diet and eat in a calm and relaxed way. Typical pitta conditions of the gastro-intestinal tract include acidity and heartburn, symptomized by belching and acid indigestion; diarrhoea or frequent loose bowel movements, and constant hunger, accompanied by consequent irritability.

Hot kapha dietary spices.

common problems

It is quite clear that the forms taken by various commonly occurring illnesses, and the appropriate remedies, will vary according to whether you have a vata, pitta or kapha dosha. The following sections therefore aim to give you individually a plan of action, setting out all the do's and do not's. Note that in the case of any persistent, or indeed serious illness, you must immediately contact a qualified professional expert.

Insomnia

Any vata-increasing influence can contribute to your insomnia, including regular travel, stress, an irregular lifestyle, and the excessive use of stimulants such as tea and coffee. The herbs used to treat vata-based insomnia are brahmi (Centella), jatamansi, ashwagandha (Withania somnifera) and nutmeg. Any good massage using brahmi oil will also produce considerable, quickly noticed benefits.

Insomnia in the pitta dosha is brought on by anger, jealousy, frustration, fever, excess sun or heat. Follow the pitta plan, which is cooling, and take brahmi, jatamansi, bhringaraj (Eclipta alba), shatavari and aloe vera juice. Massage brahmi oil into the head and feet. Again, this is marvellously refreshing.

As kapha types like to sleep and tend to be rather sleepy and sluggish, they rarely suffer from attacks of insomnia.

Headache/Migraine

Vata headaches cause extreme pain and are related to anxiety and tension. Relevant treatments include triphala to clear any congestion, jatamansi, brahmi and calamus.

Pitta headaches are associated with heat or burning sensations, flushed skin and a visual sensitivity to light. They are related to anger, frustration or irritability, and will be connected to the liver and gall bladder. Treatments are brahmi, turmeric and aloe vera juice. Kapha headaches are dull and heavy and can cause nausea. There may also be congestion, such as catarrh. Have a stimulating massage with minimal oil.

Juice from aloe vera plants can be used to combat sleeplessness.

Colds

A tendency to mucus production or catarrh/phlegm is unpleasant for the sufferer, and is usually the result of poor digestion of foods in the stomach which increases ama (toxicity) and kapha. In general, kapha is generally considered the most highly effective dosha.

Vata-type colds involve dry symptoms, such as a dry cough or dry throat. Herbs for vata coughs and colds are ginger, cumin, pippali, tulsi (holy basil, Ocimum sanctum), cloves and peppermint, licorice (not to be used with high blood pressure or oedema), shatavari and ashwagandha. Put one or two drops of sesame oil up each nostril, and then follow the vata plan until all the symptoms are seen to subside.

Pitta-type colds involve more heat, the face is usually red and there may even be a fever. The mucus is often yellow and can actually contain traces of blood. Herbs for tackling pitta coughs and colds include peppermint and various other mints, sandalwood, chrysanthemum and small quantities of tulsi (holy basil). Follow the pitta plan until your symptoms begin to subside.

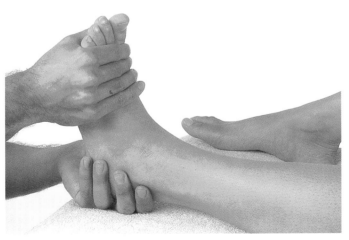

A foot massage with brahmi oil will often relieve insomnia.

Cardamom pods are beneficial to vata-type coughs.

Kapha colds are thick and mucusy, with a feeling of heaviness in the head and/or body. Avoid cold, damp weather and exposure to cold and damp conditions. Eliminate sugar, refined foods, meat and nuts, dairy products, bread, fats and oils from the diet and use plenty of hot spices. Drink a spiced tea of hot lemon, ginger and cinnamon with cloves or tulsi, sweetened with a little raw honey. Herbs for kapha colds are ginger, cinnamon, pippali, tulsi (holy basil), cloves and peppermint. Saunas and hot baths will help to increase the heat of the kapha person, but they should not be used in excess as this would actually increase the pitta too much. Follow the kapha plan until the symptoms subside.

Coughs

Vata coughs are dry and irritated with very little mucus, the chief symptom being a painful cough often accompanied by a dry mouth. Herbs and spices for the vata cough include licorice (do not use this if you have high blood pressure or oedema), shatavari, ashwagandha and cardamom. Follow the vata plan until the symptoms subside.

Pitta coughs are usually associated with a lot of phlegm. The chest is congested and very uncomfortable, but the mucus cannot be brought up properly. There is often fever or heat, combined with a burning sensation in the chest or throat. High fevers should be treated by a physician, and people suffering with asthma should consult their doctor immediately if a cough or cold leads to wheezing and difficult breathing. The best herbs for pitta coughs include peppermint, tulsi (holy basil) and sandalwood. Follow the pitta plan until the symptoms have completely subsided.

With kapha coughs, the patient usually brings up lots of phlegm, and suffers a loss of appetite combined with nausea. The chest is loaded with mucus, but this may not be coughed up because the kapha individual is likely to feel tired. Treatments for kapha coughs are raw honey, lemon, cloves and chyawanprash (a herbal jam). Follow the kapha plan until the symptoms subside, increasing your intake of hot spices, and do try to use trikatu powder. Also keep warm.

Skin Problems

These are often caused by internal conditions of toxicity (ama) and are mainly related to the pitta dosha. Vata skin problems will be dry and rough. Avoid letting the skin dry out. Herbal remedies for vata skin are triphala and satisabgol. Pitta skin problems will be red and swollen, often with a yellow head. Avoid sun, heat or hot baths, and increase your intake of salads. Follow the pitta plan and add turmeric, coriander and saffron to your diet. The remedies are manjishta (Rubia cordifolia), kutki (Picrohiza kurroa), turmeric and aloe vera juice. Kapha skin problems involve blood congestion which can cause the skin to form thick and mucusy whiteheads. Increase your level of exercise, and follow the kapha plan. Treatments should always include a small amount of calamus with some dry ginger and quantities of turmeric.

Urinary Infections

Excess cold water, tea, coffee, and alcoholic drinks will weaken the kidneys. Salt, sugar or foods that are rich in calcium, such as dairy products or spinach, will similarly tend to weaken and toxify the kidneys. The best kidney tonic to use in Ayurveda is shilajit, a mineral-rich compound from the Himalayan mountains, but avoid it if you suffer from kidney stones. Pregnant women, children or those on medication should consult an Ayurvedic practitioner before treatment.

Cystitis

In vata people, cystitis will tend to be less intense. Remedies are shilajit (to be avoided if you suffer from kidney stones) with bala (Sida cordifolia), ashwagandha and shatavari.

Cystitis is mainly a pitta condition because it burns and is hot. Follow the pitta plan, using plenty of coriander (cilantro) and avoiding hot spices. Remedies include aloe vera juice (not to be used in pregnancy), lime juice, coconut and sandalwood. Kapha-type cystitis is accompanied by congestion and mucus in the urinary tract. The treatments are cinnamon, trikatu combined with shilajit, gokshura and gokshurdi guggul.

It is worth having a supply of fresh mint and other herbs to hand for many of the common Ayurvedic treatments.

invigorating

healing   soothing

sensual

the power of touch

There are four key ways of demonstrating the power of touch, and the ways in which exciting

techniques can help cure all kinds of ailments, and best of all, keep you in first-rate condition.

The first is massage, which you can actually practise on yourself or a partner. The astonishing art of

aromatherapy shows how oils that have been carefully infused with various ingredients, taken

internally or used on the body, can greatly improve your health. Shiatsu, which in Japanese means

finger pressure, is the ancient art of knowing how to balance the yin and yang, and reflexology is the

amazing ability to read the body's signals in the feet, and by touch convert poor health into good.

massage

Do you come home at the end of the day with your neck and shoulders feeling as if they were set in concrete? Most of us almost unconsciously rub such tense, aching spots to get some instant relief; correctly performed, massage can have a wonderful effect, not just on the muscles themselves but on our whole sense of well-being. Touch is one of the most crucial, and yet often neglected, senses, and the need for human touch remains constant throughout life.

In the last 30 years, many studies have looked at the importance of touch for human development. Dr Saul Schanberg of Duke University in North Carolina, and Dr Tiffany Field from the University of Miami in Florida, have carried out detailed research on premature babies. Those babies who were gently stroked for 45 minutes a day were nearly 50 per cent heavier after 10 days than non-stroked babies, and they were also more active, alert and responsive.

In fact systematic, caring touch through massage has been shown to encourage the release of endorphins — chemicals that affect development in children, as well as emotional and physical well-being in adults. In addition a massage can be an effective treatment for a range of physical problems, and is a wonderfully relaxing experience. Many simple techniques can even be used at home to ease your own and a partner's tensions.

preparing for massage

It is quite possible to give a highly effective, spontaneous massage, but generally it is far better to prepare well in advance. This will certainly give you all the time you need to create the right atmosphere, and to check that you have exactly the right ingredients, everything from towels to oils. A really good massage should be a special occasion, and one that leaves you feeling relaxed, calm, gentle and well.

CREATING THE MOOD

Creating the right environment and space for treatment will definitely help make the massage an even more quietly relaxing and beneficial experience. Before you start, though, make sure that the room is pleasantly warm and that the massage room is sufficiently furnished for your partner to be completely comfortable. Make sure you have plenty of towels or a sheet handy to cover areas not being worked on – remember that if you are working on the floor, draughts can give exposed flesh some very unrelaxing goose-pimples. If you are using oil, place it in a convenient spot where you can reach it easily without the risk of knocking it over.

Preparing yourself is important too; physically this means removing watches and jewellery, trimming nails and wearing loose, comfortable clothing, ideally short-sleeved. Try to do a few stretches and take a few deep breaths to help you to feel calm; if you give a massage when you are tense yourself, this may be transmitted to your massage partner. This can work the other way round too, so feel prepared mentally to let go of any tensions that you feel coming from the other person's body, and avoid absorbing his or her stresses.

When using oil, pour it on to your own hands first to warm it up, never directly on to your partner. Cold oil will be extremely unsettling. The oil may be placed in a bowl, glass bottle or even a squeezy bottle for ease of use. Spread the oil slowly on to the body, and gradually begin.

Gently scented oils have long been a massage favourite.

MASSAGE OILS

The worldwide preference is for locally available oils, usually vegetable oils, to help the hands flow and glide over the skin. Olive oil, goose grease, goat butter and other ingredients have all been used successfully at various times; in parts of Africa a handful of oily dough is actually used to absorb dirt and toxins from the skin as the massage soothes and relaxes the muscles.

Some oils are far more pleasant and versatile than others, and have a beneficial effect on the skin in themselves. Probably the most useful oil, and the one most widely used in professional massage, is that of Sweet Almond. It is light, non-greasy and easily absorbed by the skin. Grapeseed oil seems to suit oily skins quite well; it is reasonably priced and probably more widely available.

Rather thicker, but still useful, is Soya oil. For dry skins a little Wheatgerm oil (but not if the person has a wheat allergy) or Avocado oil may be added. Nut oils such as Walnut are also rich but a bit sticky, and do not smell too good on the skin. Sunflower oil may be used for massage if nothing else is available, though it may give a slight hint of salad dressing! Olive oil can be used though that largely depends on how heavily flavoured it is; it is certainly a traditional favourite in Mediterranean countries. Finally, do not use mineral oils because they sit on the surface of the skin and tend to feel very greasy.

When giving a massage you can choose from a wide range of oils.

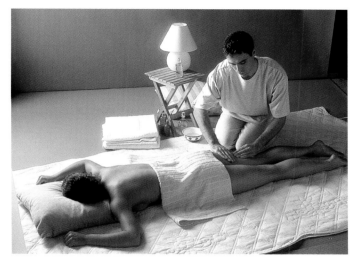

When giving a massage, always stay calm and relaxed because tense vibrations will promptly be picked up by your partner.

Essential Oils

As an alternative, try using essential oils which can be added to these base oils for two reasons – to add fragrance and to give extra therapeutic effects. These oils are highly concentrated and should always be treated with great respect. However, if you are in any doubt whatsoever, do not use them, and if any skin irritation does occur, wash off the offending oil immediately.

Most essential oils are now conveniently sold in dropper bottles, and it is absolutely imperative that they are only used in a diluted form on the skin. A generally safe level is considered to be 1 per cent, which is the equivalent of using just one drop of essential oil to 5ml/1 tsp of base oil. Never be tempted to try and use more than the recommended amount – this is actually counter-productive, doing more harm than good.

Adding essential oils to vegetable oils invariably works well because the latter can contribute their own health-giving properties. The best vegetable oils include Almond, which is high in vitamin D. Borage is an incredibly good source of GLA, and is frequently used to tackle eczema and psoriasis. If you need vitamin E, look no further than Jojoba oil, which has the added benefit of containing anti-bacterial agents which can help cure acne. Peachnut oil is also a good provider of vitamin E, and has the added bonus of toning up the skin, making it more elastic and supple. Try it as a facial massage.

All-purpose vegetable oils that are also worth using include Grapeseed. It suits all skin types, but being refined is best mixed with an enriching agent such as Almond oil. Safflower oil has the twin advantage of being inexpensive to buy and widely available, and it makes a very good base. So too does Sunflower oil, which is rich in vitamins and minerals.

As you get more skilled in the art of mixing oils, you will find that you can blend different essential oils together. When they are blended a particular chemical reaction occurs, creating a new compound. For example, by adding quantities of Lavender to Bergamot you can actually increase the sedative effect. However, if you add Lemon to Bergamot you increase its power to enhance and uplift. Mixing two essential oils in this way to alter effects subtly is known as synergy. It is an extremely useful means of letting you tackle several conditions simultaneously, especially your emotional and physical needs. With a bit of practice you will gradually learn exactly what ratio of oils you need, depending on your mood swings and current condition.

Getting the right scent is equally important. At first it seems quite bewildering. Will Almond oil or Sesame oil alone provide the best results, or should they be mixed, and in what quantities? By following established "recipes", you will gradually learn which oils mix best, and once you are confident at handling them you can start altering the quantities to suit your own specific needs. It is worth noting, though, that essential oils have been divided into three separate sections or "notes" to help you achieve the right balance when creating a scent. The three notes are called the top, middle and base, and theoretically a fine blend will contain one oil from each note.

The top notes are best described as fresh and immediately detectable because the oil evaporates at such a fast rate. The scent is immediately present. The core of the mix, the middle note, provides a deeper scent that wafts through, following the top note, and the base note adds a final, marvellous rich perfume. Be aware that you will need a higher quantity of top notes because the oils do evaporate so quickly. A sensible, general ratio would be 3 (top) – 2 (middle) – 2 (base).

For a generally relaxing massage blend, try essential oils of Lavender and Marjoram in equal amounts in a base vegetable oil. Both of these will help to release those tense, tired, over-stressed muscles, and will induce a general sense of well-being, followed by a warm, relaxed glow. They are highly effective. For a slightly more invigorating, uplifting blend, try essential oils of Bergamot and Geranium in your massage oil. Both have a refreshing effect on the whole system. To release tensions, and also to help increase the libido, try a dilution of an exotic, luxurious blend of essential oils of Rose and Sandalwood.

Use Bergamot oil with care – it can cause sensitivity to sunlight.

basic strokes

There are dozens of kinds of massage movements, each having a specific effect on the body. However, the pattern of each massage invariably follows certain fundamental principles. This crucially always begins with the initial contact; the confident, unhurried, relaxed way that you first touch your massage partner which lays the foundation for a long, soothing experience. It is well worth taking time to make sure you get this right.

1 Gliding strokes involves the use of the whole hand in smooth movements.

2 Apply even pressure as you move over the skin. Use plenty of oil.

GLIDING

A massage usually starts with slow, broad, relatively superficial movements, leading to deeper and perhaps more specific techniques on smaller areas of spasm or tension. If the person needs invigorating or toning up, then faster movements may be used, and finally more stretching or stroking movements to finish the massage session in a relaxed way. The first and last massage movements often consist of these gliding strokes.

CIRCLING

An allied form of movement is circling, where the hands move over large areas of muscle in a circular motion. Since tension within muscles can produce knotted areas which may need working along or across the length of the fibres, this circular action releases the knots before deeper movements are used.

Circling may be carried out with just one hand, or both hands can be used, one on top of the other, for greater depth and stability of action. Like the gliding motions, circling is essentially a slow, relaxing type of movement and should not be rushed.

1 A variation on simple circling uses both hands. As with all massage strokes, keep your own body comfortable and avoid tensing your hands or arms.

2 Take one hand around in a circle, then the other. This gradually builds up its own momentum and energy, and can be extremely calming and soothing.

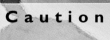

Caution

Do not attempt deep work if at all unsure of the effect, or if pain occurs. Underdo rather than overdo massage – effleurage and petrissage movements can make a complete and thoroughly relaxing massage.

3 The key to success is overlapping the hands so that they follow one another smoothly. Make this action as unforced and flowing as you can.

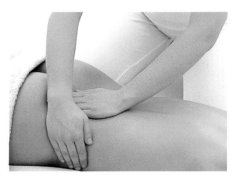

4 Gradually move the small and large circling movements of your hands up and down the back, from the base of the spine to near the neck.

WRINGING

Another important type of movement is wringing, where the action of one hand against the other creates a powerful squeezing action. When performed on the back, for example, the person's own spine acts as a kind of block against which the muscles can be wrung. This highly useful technique enables the speedy removal of any waste matter from muscles which are much too stiff and tense.

Do not be at all surprised by the mention of waste matter. All muscular activity actually produces potentially toxic waste materials, notably lactic acid. If the person also gets tense and stiff, these wastes are quickly trapped within the muscles, making them even stiffer with far more aching. Wringing is an extremely effective way of encouraging the removal of lactic acid and any other waste matter, which in turn allows new blood to flood in, bringing oxygen and fresh nutrients to individual cells.

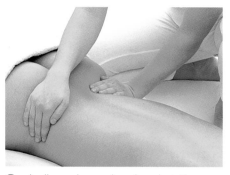

Gradually push one hand against the other in a wringing movement.

PRESSURE TECHNIQUES

As a massage treatment progresses, general techniques such as gliding and circling often change into more detailed and specific work on smaller areas of spasm. Professional massage therapists may move to even deeper work with firm pressure, using thumbs and fingers. Pressure is achieved by steadily leaning into the movement with the whole body, not by tensing your hands. Thinner people usually need lighter pressure.

1 The flat heel of the hand gives a broad, firm, no-nonsense effect.

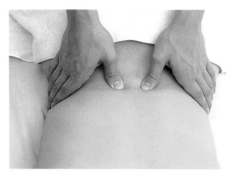

2 The thumbs can be used to exert the most precise kinds of pressure.

PERCUSSION

If someone has a generally sluggish system, or needs invigorating, then faster techniques can be useful. The term for these strokes is percussion, or tapotement. Unlike the other strokes that are described here, they need to be performed quickly, to stimulate the circulation under the skin, and to tone the associated muscles (pummelling with loose fists is excellent at toning larger muscles). One of the best known of these movements is hacking, in which the sides of the fingers are used to flick rhythmically up and down to create a slightly stinging sensation. Despite being the movement that most people think typifies a massage, it is not a major part of massage, but does have good results. Cupping is a similar stroke which helps bring blood to the area being massaged. It is used when treating medical conditions such as cystic fibrosis when a lot of thick, sticky mucus can build up in the lungs. Cupping on the back helps loosen this mucus.

Light hacking movements are excellent for stimulating the circulation.

KNEADING

After the recipient has been relaxed by steady stroking or gliding movements and any tense muscles start to release, a professional therapist may well begin to use deeper techniques to soften the knotted areas. The general term for many of these movements is petrissage, and they involve a firm, squeezing action to encourage all waste matter to be pumped out of the muscles, so allowing fresh, oxygenated blood to flow in.

1 Kneading with alternate hands helps to loosen any tense, knotted muscles.

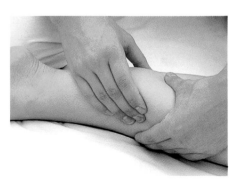

2 On smaller areas like the calves, use less pressure to avoid discomfort.

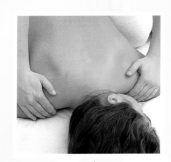

massage sequences
massage sequences

massage sequences

Probably the best way to improve and deepen a relationship is to increase caring physical contact, and massage is an ideal approach. The ability to ease tensions and deeply relax during a massage is very satisfying both for the giver and the receiver.

You can give massage to another person, or just to yourself, but whichever you choose, both are very valuable in therapeutic and emotional terms. Massage can help soothe aching and tired muscles, or it can help in releasing anxiety and tension stored in muscles.

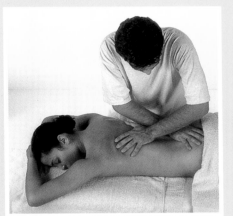

Massage does not have to be limited to yourself or your life partner; there are other members of the family, friends or colleagues who can all be helped in this way, and a better rapport will be developed with them too.

Being massaged by someone else does mean that you can let go of your muscles more completely, than if you are massaging yourself. Being massaged by another person does require a certain amount of trust, and if you are massaging a person you do not know too well, do be sensitive to this. Massage practitioners are well aware that they are being given permission to make a deep contact with their clients, which is quite a privilege.

When preparing for a massage, take a few moments to make sure that you have created the right environment. Check that the person is warm and comfortable, and that you have easy access to the part of the body needing massage. You can make a room more comfortable and relaxing by ensuring that no-one can see in from the outside, by darkening the room and by playing some gentle music. When giving a massage, remember to place everything that you might need close at hand, such as oils, talcum powder, cushions and extra towels.

Be aware that what is comfortable pressure for one person may feel like tickling or painful to another. So take care and tailor your massage to each person.

tense neck easer

Aching, tense, tired muscles are undoubtedly most usually experienced in the neck and shoulders. What is more, as you begin to get tired, your posture tends to sag and droop and the rounded shape makes your shoulders ache even more. Although it is actually most relaxing to lie down and have a long, deep massage, a self-massage can easily be done. It is extremely effective, does not take long, and leaves you feeling fine.

1 A simple movement is to shrug your shoulders, exaggerating the movement by lifting them up as far as possible and then letting them drop right down, and relaxing completely. This form of massage does not even involve using your hands.

2 One of the best massage techniques for removing any waste matter from tired muscles and getting fresh, oxygenated blood into them, is kneading. You can do this to yourself by firmly gripping your opposite shoulder with your hand and using a squeezing motion.

3 Take your time and move your right hand quite slowly along the top and back of the left shoulder, squeezing firmly several times. Now repeat the exercise exactly on the other shoulder, this time using your left hand.

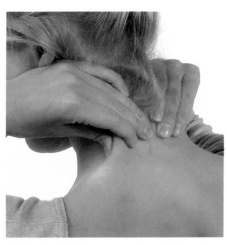

4 Next with the fingers of both hands, grip the back of your neck and squeeze slowly or rapidly in a circular motion. This very helpful technique will help you to relax all those muscles that lead up either side of the neck.

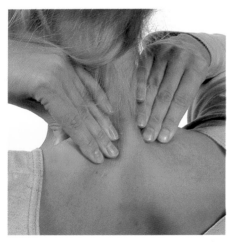

5 Slowly work up as far as the base of the skull, and then work right down again towards the shoulders.

6 To work more deeply into the neck, move the thumbs in a circular movement across the back of the neck, and then right up into the base of the skull. You will soon feel the bone as you start applying quite moderate pressure.

head revitalizer

Almost everyone at some time or another suffers from headaches. They can have a multitude of causes, such as spending too much time in front of a VDU, anxiety, insomnia, fatigue or sinus congestion. However, the most common cause is from tension after periods of stress. Use this simple self-massage sequence to help ease headaches, whatever their cause, and to increase vitality. It will also help you to focus your mind.

1 Use small, circling movements with the fingers, working steadily down from the forehead, then down around the temples and over your cheeks.

2 Use firm pressure and work slowly to ease tensions out of the facial muscles.

3 You can also use your fingers to gently and firmly press the area just under the eye socket, by your nose. Build up a satisfying regular rhythm.

4 Next, smooth firmly and satisfyingly around the arc of your eye socket immediately beneath your brow bone.

5 Work across the cheeks and along each side of the nose, then move on to the jaw line which is often tense. Try not to pull downwards on the skin. Instead, let the circling movements smooth away the stresses, and gently lift the face as you work. All these techniques can be used at any time of day.

Key Tips

• Headaches are very rarely symptoms of serious disorders. The pain comes from the membranes surrounding the brain, the scalp and the blood vessels.

• There are almost as many types as causes. The causes include a tension-tightening of the muscles from the neck up. This can stay localized or set up a chain reaction, with the pain passing into the head.

• Typical causes include hangovers, bad posture, excessive noise, too much sleep and lack of fresh air. It is also vital to have a regular intake of food.

• Some people might find that certain foods, such as red wine, can trigger attacks. The moment you feel the first signs of a headache, stop what you are doing and relax. The pain is better tackled now than later.

instant revitalizer
Do you find that you always run out of steam by eleven o'clock, or four o'clock? Have you got to be bright and alert for an early morning meeting, a long drive, picking up the kids or going out to a party where you need to impress? At any time of the day your energy can suddenly flag, without any warning. One moment you are fine, the next you are struggling. Give yourself an instant "wake-up" with this effective routine.

1 Do a kneading action on the arms, from the wrist to the shoulder and back again using a firm squeezing movement.

2 Knead more quickly than is normal in a massage. This technique will invigorate each arm and shoulder in turn.

3 Then rub firmly and swiftly up the outside of each arm which will gradually stimulate and improve your circulation.

4 Repeat in an upwards direction each time, which is good at encouraging the blood to flow back to the heart.

5 With the fingers and thumb of one hand, firmly squeeze the neck muscles using a relaxing, circular motion.

6 With the outside edge of the hands lightly hack on the front of each thigh, using a non-stop, rapid motion.

7 Do not try to karate-chop your thighs. Instead, you want the hands to spring up lightly from the muscles.

8 Next, rub the calves vigorously to loosen them and to get the blood moving. Do this with the leg bent.

9 Always work from the ankles to the knee, using alternate hands. Finally, stand and shake your whole body.

tonic for aching legs

Many people, such as sales assistants and indeed shoppers, teachers and hotel receptionists, spend far too long each day standing still, or barely moving. Such occupations create real problems for circulation in our legs, which can lead to tired, aching limbs, swollen ankles or even cramp. However, a quick self-massage at the end of the day can help reduce stiffness and sluggish blood flow. It is a wonderful, instant reviver.

1 Using both hands, knead one thigh at a time by squeezing between the fingers and thumb. Squeeze with each hand alternately for the best effect, working from the knee to the hip and back. Repeat on the other thigh.

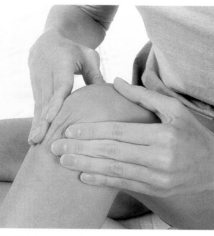

2 Right round the knees commence a similar kind of kneading action, but now use the fingers for a much lighter overall effect. Work in smaller circles.

3 Bend your leg, and if possible raise the foot on to a chair or ledge. With your thumbs, work on the back of each calf with a circular, kneading action.

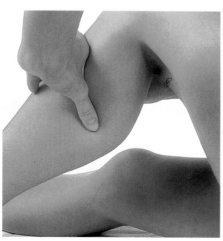

4 Repeat a few times, each time working from the ankle up the leg to the knee.

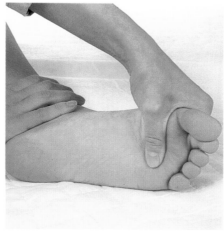

5 Squeeze the foot, loosening the muscles and then gently stretch your arch.

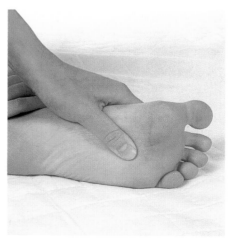

6 Use firm pressure with your thumb to stretch the foot. Repeat on the other foot.

headache and tension reliever

What is called the tension headache is probably the commonest result of getting stressed. Unfortunately, for some, this can become a daily occurrence and might lead to a migraine. But all this pain can be avoided by just a few minutes of soothing massage strokes which will eliminate the muscle spasms that lie behind such discomfort. It is even more relaxing if done by a partner.

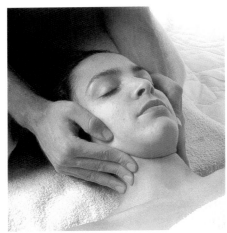

1 Gently using your fingertips, make a sequence of small alternating circles on the muscles to either side of the neck.

2 Continue circling, this time with both hands working around the side of the head and behind the ears.

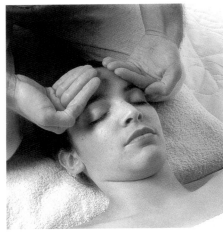

3 Smooth tension away from the temples with the backs or sides of your hands, in a gentle, stroking motion.

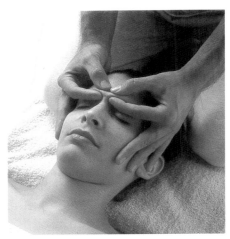

4 Gently pinch, and keep squeezing right along the line of the eyebrows, reducing pressure as you work outwards.

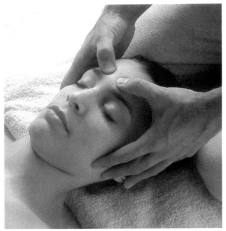

5 With your thumbs, use steady but firm pressure on the lower forehead, gradually working out from between the eyebrows.

6 Work across the brow to the hair line. This also covers many acupressure points, and will release any blocked energy in the area. It can also help to relieve sinus congestion.

arm and hand tonic

There is no doubt, the most over-worked, hard-pressed parts of the body are your hands and arms. No matter what your job, they simply do not stop – turning over pages, typing, holding, reaching, pointing, you name it. Consequently, they quite often end up feeling rather stiff and tense, yet a few deft massage techniques can easily reduce these uncomfortable feelings, leaving you feeling fresh again.

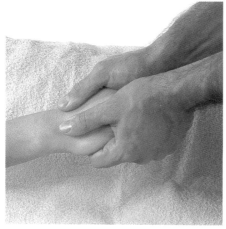

1 Kneel by your partner, who is lying face up. Hold your partner's hand, palm down, in both your hands and with your thumbs start to apply a steady stretching motion across the back of the hand.

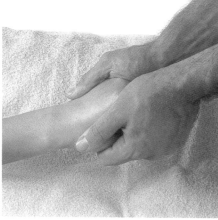

2 Repeat a few times, with a firm but comfortable pressure. Then turn the hand over and now, using your thumbs, begin smoothing and stretching the palm using a similar technique and action.

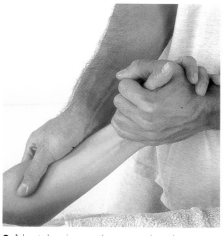

3 Next, begin gently squeezing the forearm. This too can get tense. Use your hand and thumb in order to work gradually down from the wrist, moving slowly on towards the elbow.

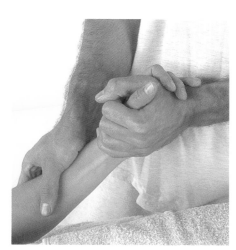

4 Repeat the motion. Move your hands quickly around the arm, not missing any area, making sure that you squeeze all the muscles that might be stiff.

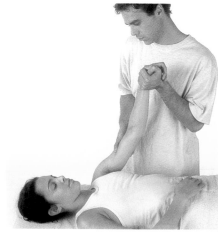

5 Lift the arm right up, not in any way forcefully, and then use a similar squeezing movement to work down the upper arm, from elbow to shoulder.

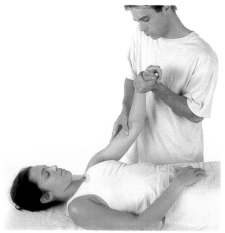

6 Repeat, working all around the arm. Swap hands if you find it necessary for a more comfortable action. Repeat all these movements on the other arm.

shoulder and neck reliever

The muscle that takes the main brunt of tension in the shoulder is the trapezius; it stands out on either side when you shrug your shoulders, and connects to the neck. Lifting heavy weights, excessive gardening and bending, for example, will tighten it, and when that happens you need help. Gentle kneading is one of the very best ways of relaxing it. This quick, effective massage will soon revive you.

1 This technique takes a little time to master but is well worth the effort. Place both hands on the far shoulder, and with alternate hands squeeze your fingers and thumb together. Do not pinch, but roll the fingers over the thumb. Repeat by moving to the other side, again working on the shoulder away from your body.

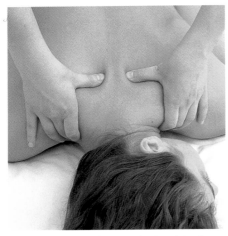

2 Having worked on each shoulder in turn, now work on both together. Place your thumbs on either side of the spine on the upper back, with the rest of each hand over each shoulder. Squeeze your fingers and thumbs together, rolling the flesh between them.

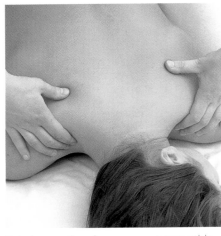

3 Let your thumbs move out smoothly across the shoulder muscles.

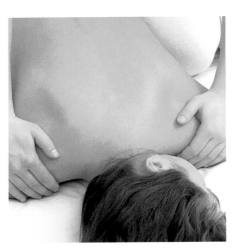

4 Release the pressure of the thumbs, and stretch the blades outwards using both your hands simultaneously.

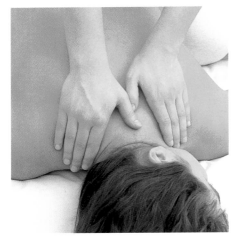

5 Now return both hands to the centre, and get the thumbs well in position to repeat this exercise.

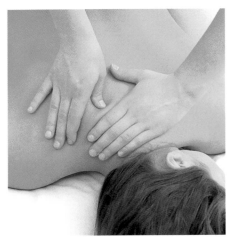

6 If the neck is very stiff, repeat the kneading exercise, applying slightly firmer pressure with the thumbs.

tension and backache reliever

The back is where most of our physical aches and pains are generally located; in fact more days are lost from work each year through back problems than from all other parts of the body combined. That is why it is a good place to massage, using broad, relaxing movements. Make sure that you keep your back in the best possible condition, treating it on a regular basis, not just when things go wrong.

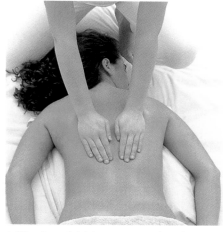

1 The best initial movement is called an effleurage. You begin by either sitting or kneeling at the head end; then place your hands on the back, with the thumbs close to, but not actually on, the spine. It is a comfortable position to find.

2 Steadily lean forward and glide your hands down the back, keeping a steady pressure all the way down.

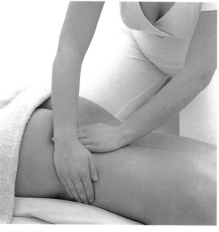

3 Kneeling at the side, place your hands on the other side of the back and move them steadily in a circular motion, using overlapping circles to work up and down the back. Move to the other side and repeat the circling technique.

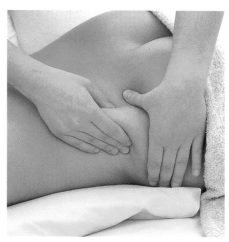

4 Place both hands on the opposite side of the back and use a firm squeezing motion with alternate hands, thereby creating a kneading effect.

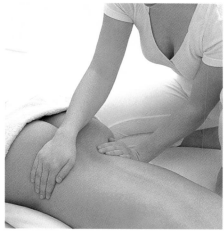

5 With one hand on the side of the back nearest you, and the other hand on the opposite side, push the hands towards and then past each other to reverse their position. Move up and down the back slowly and firmly, repeating this technique.

6 Place your hands centrally on the back and then push them away from each other, leaning forward to maintain an even pressure during this stretch.

lower back relaxer

One of the worst possible areas for tension is the lumbar part of the back, where it curves towards the pelvis. Continuous incorrect posture and lifting things without care – you should always bend from the knees and keep your back straight – are some of the causes that can aggravate lower back discomfort. If your partner suffers in any way from such twinges, a massage will stretch and relax the body.

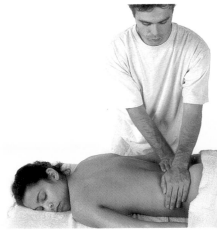

1 Standing or kneeling to the side, place your hands on the opposite side of your partner's back and pull them up towards you firmly; repeat on the other side.

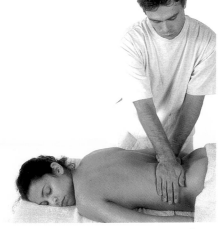

2 Overlap the hands to create an effect like bandaging, but much more soothing.

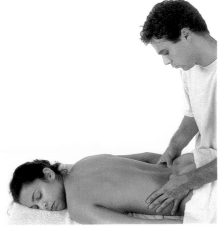

3 Using your thumbs, make circling movements over the lower back. Use a steady, even pressure, leaning with your body, but do not press on the spine.

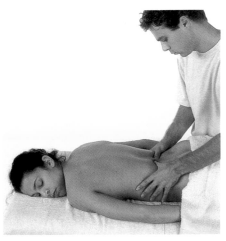

4 Stretch the lower back muscles by gliding the thumbs firmly up either side several times. Press in steadily with both thumbs just to either side of the spine, working gradually up it.

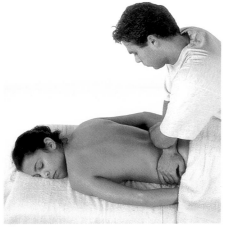

5 Stretch across the lower back with crossed hands moving away from each other to try and ease, and relax, any tense, taut muscles.

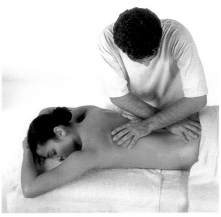

6 Finally, push the hands well apart and stretch the whole back.

Caution

Do not put pressure on the spine, and ease off if it feels at all uncomfortable.

instant foot revitalizer With really very little complaint,

your feet carry you around all day, sometimes for hours on end in the most dreadful heat. When you compare the size of your feet with the rest of you, it is not surprising that they sometimes rebel and feel sore. In fact the best way to relieve tired, aching feet is with a quick, ten-minute massage. It is amazing how quickly it can revive them, letting you get on with your life again.

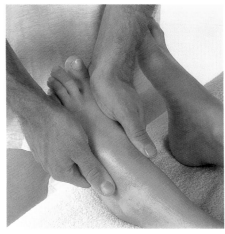

1 Hold the foot in your hands, with your thumbs on top and fingers underneath. Gently stretch across the top of the foot, trying to keep your fingers quite still while you keep moving your thumbs.

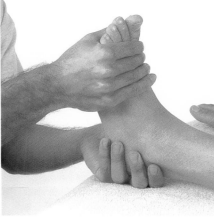

2 Flex the foot, pushing against the resistance to loosen the whole foot and ankle a little. Then gently extend the foot, stretching it as far as is comfortable.

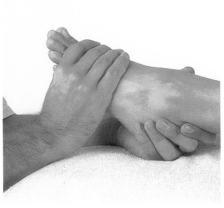

3 Now, twist the foot using a gentle wringing motion in both directions to stretch all the small muscles.

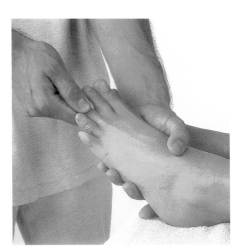

4 Firmly hold one of the toes, and then squeeze and pull it. Now repeat with every single toe.

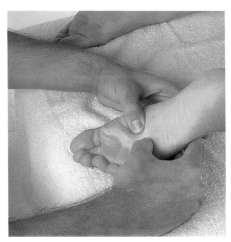

5 Circle over the sole firmly with your fingers, or thumbs if that feels much easier; make sure that you do not end up tickling your partner.

6 Support the foot with one hand, and stroke the upper side with the other hand. Smoothly stroke all the way from the toes up to the ankle. Repeat all the actions on the other foot.

tense abdomen reliever

Tension in the abdomen may reflect a degree of physical discomfort, such as indigestion, constipation or even menstrual cramp. However, the cause is just as likely to be emotional because many people hold their inner fears in this particular area. If you bottle up and cannot release or express your feelings, then abdominal spasms may occur. The following movements should ensure that such tensions soon go away.

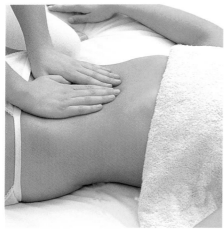

1 Begin by placing your hands gently on the abdomen. At this stage simply focus all your thoughts and energy on trying to pass good vibrations into your partner's body. You will be surprised by the results.

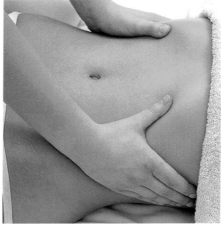

2 Next, spread each hand open, and slowly and gradually move each to the side of the abdomen. Repeat this two or three times, building up a slow, regular, soothing rhythm.

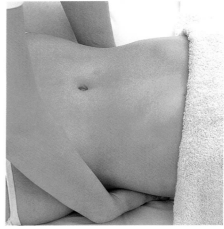

3 Kneeling by the side, now slide your hands under the back to meet at the spine. Lift the body gently to arch and stretch the back before pulling your hands out towards the hips.

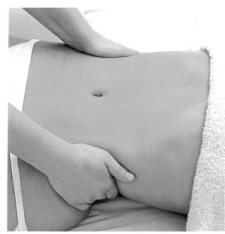

4 Firmly draw your hands out over the waist, and then gently glide them back to their original position to repeat the stroke a few times.

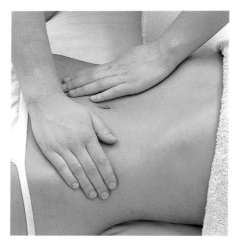

5 Placing your hands on the abdomen, move them around steadily in a clockwise direction (this follows the way in which the colon functions).

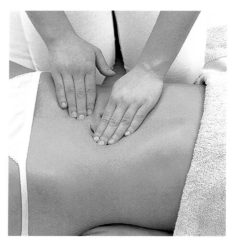

6 Finally, repeat the action, but this time working a little deeper by using your fingers, provided that there are no signs of any discomfort.

de-stress your colleagues

Massage is a highly versatile skill, and can be applied in many different situations, not least the office. How often have you heard one of your work colleagues complain of terrible tense, aching shoulders preventing them from doing any work? Now you can step in and do something about it. A five-minute massage is all it takes. It can be wonderfully effective, revitalizing and refreshing them.

1 Standing behind your seated colleague, place both your hands gently on the shoulders, thumbs towards you and fingers in the front.

2 Using your fingers, knead in small circles up and down the back of the neck. Support the head with your other hand while you are working on the neck.

3 Place your forearms over the shoulders, and then gradually press down with your body weight in order to squeeze and stretch the trapezius.

4 Move the forearms gradually outwards to cover the shoulders, maintaining a firm pressure all the time.

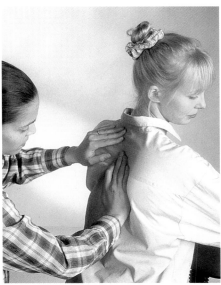

5 Allow your fingers to sink into the muscles around the shoulder blade. Repeat on the other side.

6 Place your hands on your partner's shoulder joints, and press back towards yourself to stretch the upper chest.

sensual massage

As well as releasing stresses and tensions from the muscles, massage is a wonderful way to enhance a relationship by increasing caring, sharing touch. If your relationship seems to have got into a rut, and sexual energy is low, why not revitalize yourselves with deep soothing massage strokes. To make the whole experience a real treat, make the room extra warm, and play some of your favourite, soothing music.

1 Place your hands to either side of the spine and glide them down the back, move out to the side, and then back again. Repeat several times.

2 With a gentle motion, stroke down the centre of the back with one hand following the other smoothly, as if you were stroking a cat.

3 As one hand lifts off at the pelvis, start again with the other hand at the neck.

4 Place both your hands on the upper back and stroke outwards in a fan shape.

5 Work down the back, including the buttocks, using a fanning action.

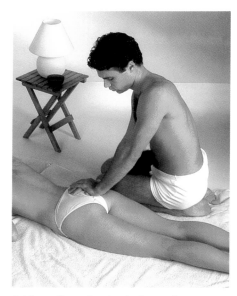

6 Use a firm, steady circling action on the buttocks.

7 Stroke up the back of the legs, with one hand after the other building up a smooth, continuous flowing motion.

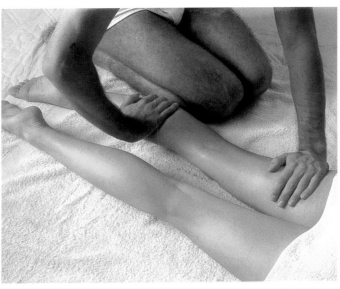

8 As one hand reaches the buttocks, start on the calf with the other hand to keep up that continuous steady rhythm.

9 Turn your partner over and stroke up the front of the legs; having the leg bent greatly helps the muscles to relax.

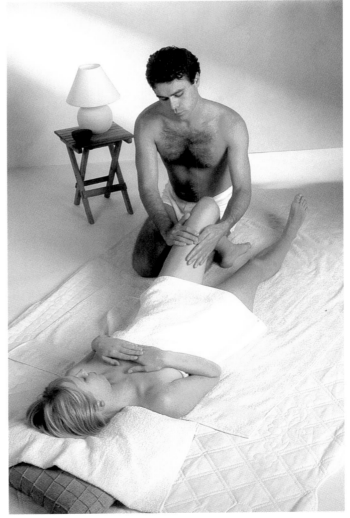

10 Continue the movement, using both hands to make stroking movements from the knees right up the thighs.

aromatherapy aromatherapy

aromatherapy

rapy

Do you have a favourite scent, one that evokes memories of wonderful times? The power of the sense of smell to arouse an emotional reaction confirms its ability to have an immediate effect on our systems; in fact smell is probably the most underrated of the senses, yet it has the most subtle significance in our lives. But how does it work?

Aromatic plants contain essential oils that have been used for centuries to relax, sedate, refresh and even stimulate. Each aromatic oil has its own individual combination of constituents, and they in turn can interact with your body's chemistry to have specific therapeutic effects.

In the early years of the 20th century, the French chemist René-Maurice Gattefosse was working in the laboratory of his family's perfumery business when he badly burnt his hand and lower arm. He plunged his hand into the nearest liquid, which was a jar of Lavender oil and discovered that this very quickly eased his pain, prevented scarring and promoted rapid healing. Gattefosse then set about investigating the precise therapeutic properties of essential oils, discovering that they were often more effective than isolated or synthetic compounds. He used the term aromatherapy in 1928 to describe the use of aromatic oils for treating physical or emotional problems. In the following pages the art of aromatherapy is mainly used to combat and overcome stress.

using oils
If you have never quite understood the art of aromatherapy, and are afraid that it involves all kinds of strange pieces of equipment, then you could not be more wrong. It actually involves a collection of small, highly attractive bottles that can be quite a feature, and maybe even a candle burner. That is all that it takes to become an aficionado. Once hooked, you will certainly never look back, and those oils will start improving your health.

BUYING AND KEEPING OILS

Aromatic essential oils can be used in various ways to restore good health. However, the oils are in fact concentrated substances, and need to be diluted for safety. A test massage with a weak dose will quickly reveal potential skin reactions. Also, seek medical advice before massaging a pregnant woman.

You will find that many companies now sell essential oils, and when buying them always make sure that they are pure and of a high quality (you get what you pay for in general). If possible, try to smell the sample bottle of the oil that you are buying, and make sure that it has a good, clean, non-synthetic perfume. Since essential oils are liable to deteriorate quite quickly as a direct result of sunlight, they should always be stored in a dark glass jar in a cool, dark place. Keep the lid firmly closed to prevent any evaporation. One good tip is always to buy small quantities, especially of citrus oil which deteriorates quickly.

Aromas are always tempered by an emotional reaction – a lasting memory of them from the past.

Creating Scents

When using essential oils at home, it is very helpful to have some basic equipment. A burner is an excellent way of vaporizing oils into the atmosphere. It consists of a candle in a simple, small, invariably terracotta, open-top container, and a bowl for the oil, which sits on top. When you want to simmer pot-pourri in a bowl, again all you need is a candle. Place it under the bowl and gently warm it until you can detect a delicious scent. This is an an excellent way of making a room much more fragrant. If you want a long-term scent, albeit one that is slightly fainter, use a ready-prepared commercial mix of dry pot-pourri. Place the bowls strategically round the house. They come in different perfumes and strengths.

Rose oil is a favourite for massage as it has such pleasant connotations. It will help even the most tense person relax.

HOW IT ALL BEGAN

When you take up aromatherapy, it is worth noting that it has a highly impressive history. People have been using scented products for thousands of years. Ancient written records dating back 3,000 years, in the case of the Indian Verdic manuscripts, describe in marvellous detail the use of aromatic oils. Egyptian papyri from 1500 BC, and biblical stories of the Jewish exodus from Egypt about 300 years later, also describe the widespread use of aromatic oils. Many were used in religious ceremonies and in rituals, but many were also used when having a massage, taking a bath, and for scenting the body and hair. To that extent, little has changed. Scented products have long been justifiably popular.

Aromatic Oils

These oils were probably first made by Arabic physicians in the 10th century AD. That much is definite, though it is now strongly argued by some that they were also used in the Indus valley, in the foothills of the Himalayas 5,000 years ago. Certainly, the Arabic use of concentrated, distilled oils – widely famed in the West as the "perfumes of Arabia" – did lead to a renaissance in the use of aromatic plants.

As distillation was taken up in the West, many more oils were extracted. There was also a gradual separation of the perfume side and more medical applications. Ironically, the former was the one that really provided the impetus for the development of aromatherapy. Today, it is enjoying a worldwide popularity rarely seen before. While aromatherapists now use specific essential oils for their physiological effects, there is no reason why they may not also be used for their relaxing properties. In fact, in today's turbulent, demanding world, that often seems to be their chief attraction. A calming, soothing, marvellously scented way of getting the body and mind back on track. Aromatherapy, with its long history, is guaranteed a long future.

A collection of oils quickly becomes an attractive feature.

Mixing Essential Oils for Massage

1 Before you begin, wash and dry your hands and make sure that all the utensils are clean and dry. Measure out about 10ml /2 tsp of your chosen vegetable oil. Next, carefully pour the vegetable oil into the blending bowl.

2 Add the essential oil, never rushing things, always with great care, one drop at a time. Mix gently using a clean, dry cocktail stick or perhaps even a toothpick. Make sure that the children are well away before doing this.

how aromatherapy can be used

Aromatherapy is surprisingly varied in its uses. It can help with all kinds of problems, and what can make it such a regular part of your life is that it can also tackle everyday aches and pains. It is also marvellous for coping with poor circulation and headaches, and those long, hard days at work which result in a tired, sore back. Treat oils with respect, and they will soon perk you up.

MASSAGE

Massage is a wonderful way to use essential oils, suitably diluted in a good base oil, for your partner or family. Always try to use soft, thick towels to cover any areas of the body that you are not massaging, and make sure that the room is kept warm, perhaps with an additional portable heater. Do not undermine the effect of the massage by draughty, cold conditions.

Also note that while essential oils are wonderful natural remedies they are highly concentrated and must therefore be used with care and caution. You should consequently only take essential oils internally if they have been professionally prescribed for you, and always use essential oils in a diluted form – normally 1 per cent for massage and just 5 drops in a bath or for a steam inhalation. You should also be extra careful with anyone who has asthma or epilepsy, and if anyone does experience any kind of adverse reaction, use common sense and stop using the oils immediately. A quick test beforehand will usually reveal possible problems.

BATHS

Imagine soaking in a hot bath, enveloped in a delicious scent of exotic flowers, feeling all the day's tensions drop away . . . well, that can easily become a reality with aromatherapy. The oils seem to capture the essence of the plant, and can effortlessly transport you to pine-scented forests, refreshing orange groves or even magical, oriental spice markets.

When using oils in the bath, pour in 5 drops just before you get in. The oils form a thin film on the surface of the water which, aided by the relaxing warmth of the water, will be partly absorbed by your skin as you breathe in the scent, producing an immediate psychological and physiological effect.

Morning and Evening Baths

For a refreshing, uplifting bath in the mornings, try a blend of 3 drops Bergamot and 2 drops Geranium essential oils. To relax and unwind after a long day, make a blend of 3 drops Lavender and 2 drops Ylang Ylang. For tired, tense muscles when you have been overdoing it, have a long soak in a deep, warm bath to which you have added approximately 3 drops Marjoram and 2 drops Chamomile essential oils.

Gently rubbing the body all over with a loofa greatly increases the effect of an aromatherapy bath.

Hand and Footbaths

The circulation to our extremities can be greatly affected by levels of tension and stress, among other factors, and the warmth of the water quickly helps the blood vessels to dilate. This can be very helpful when treating tension headaches and even painful migraines, when the blood vessels in the head are frequently engorged with blood. When you are using essential oils to make a hand or even a footbath, you should two-thirds fill a large bowl with warm, but not too hot, water and then carefully add and stir in 3–4 drops of your favourite oil.

Excess Heat when Hot and Tired

For hot, aching feet or hands, use a mixture of 2 drops peppermint and 2 drops lemon. To boost your circulation try the following: add 2 drops Lavender and 2 drops Marjoram oils. This is also extremely good for those who suffer from poor circulation and tense, cold extremities.

A relaxing bath in the evening promotes enhanced sleep.

STEAM INHALATIONS

Colds and sinus problems may all too easily cause congestion, but we can also feel blocked up and unable to breathe freely as a result of all kinds of tension levels. Using a steam inhalation warms and moistens the membranes, and the use of essential oils also helps to open and relax the airways. Just boil a kettle, pour the water into a bowl, add the oils and inhale deeply. It makes a simple but highly effective cure.

If you suffer from nasal congestion, and have that extremely irritating, stuffed-up feeling, possibly combined with tiredness, do try using 3 drops Eucalyptus and 2 drops Peppermint. Just mix them in a large bowl filled with steaming water; it should make a marvellous remedy. For those who have that tight, tense feeling in their chest which makes breathing rather uncomfortable, try to relax your airways using just 4 drops Lavender, and 3 drops Frankincense.

For respiratory complaints in particular, steam inhalations have long been considered very helpful remedies.

SCENTED ROOMS

Aromatherapy has many applications in the home or office including the creation of an aromatic environment which has wide-ranging beneficial effects.

Pot-pourri

It is possible to scent a room by making a simmering pot-pourri. Place a mixture of scented flowers and leaves (without any fixatives or additives) in a bowl of water and heat gently from below – a candle may well be sufficient. Unlike dry pot-pourri, the simmering variety does not last for long but gives off a much stronger aroma. Try making your own blends; add about 1 cupful of dried material to 1.2 litres/2 pints/5 cups water.

For a sleep-enhancing pot-pourri use ½ cup Lime flowers, ¼ cup Chamomile flowers, 1 tbsp Sweet Marjoram and 1 tbsp Lavender flowers. For a more refreshing, uplifting blend try ½ cup Lemon Verbena leaves, ¼ cup Jasmine flowers, 2 tbsp Lemon peel and 1 tsp Coriander seeds.

A wonderfully fragrant bowl of potpourri.

Essential Oil Burners

Most oils can be used with a burner. The basic principle is very simple: a small dish to hold a few drops of essential oil, with some type of gentle heat underneath, often in the form of a candle. The heat needs to be fairly low in order to allow slow evaporation of the oil and a longer-lasting scent.

If you want to fumigate a room, then try adding 3–4 drops of oils such as Pine, Eucalyptus or Juniper to a burner. In order to help you keep really sharp and alert, a couple of drops of Peppermint or Rosemary may work wonders, while 2–3 drops of Ylang Ylang or Lavender will have the opposite effect and soon help you to wind down at the end of a long, tiring, difficult day.

It is well worth visiting a specialist shop with a wide range of such burners. Chose an attractive one that makes an interesting feature; the Oriental kind often have interesting ornamental styles. They also make good presents – the whole kit, with oils, makes a marvellous surprise Christmas present, one that will get someone quickly hooked on the subject.

Bowl of Hot Water

Adding a couple of drops of an essential oil to a bowl of hot water is a pleasant way to give fragrance to a room or office. Try to use an attractive bowl and make sure that it is placed well out of reach of any children. Use an oil that is a big favourite, as it will release its scent for some time when used in this way. For mornings, Bergamot, Mandarin or Lemon would be uplifting. Later in the day you may wish to use Rose or Jasmine.

Other Scented Products

Essential oils are quite often included in a wide variety of excellent gift items. They range from candles to incense sticks and cones. It is quite important, though, that you check the natural essential oil that is being used to scent these products. You may well find that they actually repeat scents that you are already using, which can produce an excessively strong aroma.

therapeutic recipes
therapeutic recipes

therapeutic recipes

One of the great delights of taking up the ancient art of aromatherapy is discovering the many exciting ways in which oils can be blended to create a wide range of enhanced therapeutic effects, with new fragrances to soothe the senses at the same time.

On the following pages you will find scores of all kinds of ideas for using different combinations of oils; they have been specially selected for their healing properties, and also because they provide an array of exquisite aromas. However, since the sense of smell is very individual and highly subjective, do not feel that you have to like certain aromas. Above all, do not feel that the not-so-good has to be enjoyed. It does not. If you find that you dislike a particular combination then feel free to make your own blends, bearing in mind the actions of the oils and the dilution rates that were described earlier.

The key to success is quite simple. Always try to ensure that you buy good quality essential oils, with a pure scent that comes from the natural, unadulterated extract. There are no rules about what you should like. The best way to proceed is by trusting your nose. If something has what might be called the ooh-ah factor, an aroma that is totally arresting rather than subtle almost to the point of not being present, but without being fiercely competitive and dominating your senses, then feel free to enjoy it.

For each of the blends suggested in this section, the number of drops of oils given should be diluted for massage purposes in 20ml/4 tsp of a base vegetable oil such as sweet Almond oil. When creating a steam inhalation, use the number of drops given in a large bowl holding about 1 litre/1¾ pints/4 cups hot water, and for a compress add the specified number of oil drops to a bowl holding 250ml/8fl oz/1 cup hot water. Also remember that when creating a mix about which you are slightly unsure, make a tiny dose to check that it is what you want. It is prudent to proceed by caution.

stress soothers
Sadly, stress is now playing far too large a part in all our lives, and while we cannot always avoid the causes, we can at least dispel its effects on us. All you need to do is set aside just a few minutes at the end of the day when you can be quiet and relax. Then, using a variety of soothing, relaxing therapeutic measures, such as a marvellous, long, slow rhythmic massage, you will end up feeling totally invigorated and refreshed.

STRESS RELIEVERS

Stress, or rather our inability to cope with an excess amount of it, is one of the biggest health problems today. Lifestyles seem to include so many varied and often conflicting demands that it is not surprising that most of us feel stressed at times, sometimes constantly. We all react to excess stress in different ways, perhaps through anxiety, depression or exhaustion, but we can all certainly benefit from the wonderfully balancing and stress-calming effects provided by aromatic oils.

Our bodies are geared to cope with a stressful situation by producing various hormones that trigger off a series of physiological actions in the body; they are known collectively as the "fight or flight" syndrome, and serve to place the body in a state of alert in a potentially dangerous situation. Extra blood is shunted to the muscles, and the heart rate speeds up while the digestion slows down. These responses are appropriate when we are faced with a physical threat, but can nowadays be triggered by quite different kinds of stress and end up placing a strain on our bodies without fulfilling any useful need.

In order to help reduce the impact of stress on the whole system, it is necessary to find ways both to avoid getting over-stressed in the first instance, and of letting go of the changes that occur internally under stress. Aromatherapy can be a great help in each case, especially during and immediately after a long relaxing massage, because the oils will help to keep you calm.

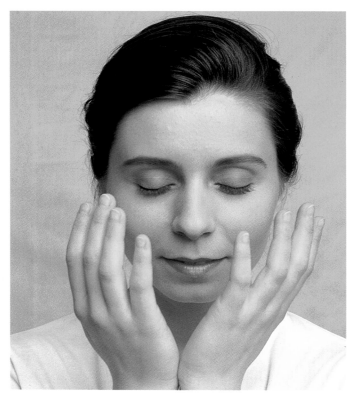

It should not take you long to discover which particular essential oils work best for you as an individual.

1 Ideally have the person lying down with the head in your lap or on a cushion. With your fingertips, gently begin smoothing the essential oil into the face.

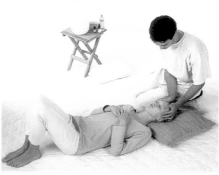

2 Using your thumbs, one after the other, stroke tension gently and carefully away from the centre of the forehead.

ANXIETY CALMERS

When people are described as being "uptight", that is often exactly what they are: tense muscles in the face and neck are a sure sign of anxiety. You can release that tension with a face massage, using gentle, soothing strokes on the temples and forehead especially. This is very good as an evening treat, calming away the day's cares and worries.

Use just a few drops of oil because most people do not like having a greasy feeling on the face. Make up a blend of 4 drops Lavender and 2 drops Ylang Ylang in a light oil such as Sweet Almond.

MUSCULAR ACHES

When you are under any kind of difficult stress for any length of time, your body promptly reacts by becoming and staying permanently tense. Clearly this is not good for you. It can make quite specific muscles, or indeed all of your muscles, ache and feel overwhelmingly tired and sluggish, leaden and heavy.

In order to relieve this all too familiar list of thoroughly unwanted symptoms, and also to start releasing the underlying tension, use essential oils in what is called a massage blend.

As the massage movements begin to work on the aching muscles at surface and deeper levels, the oils begin to be absorbed. In time they too get to work and start tackling the inner tension. Such treatment is in itself quite refreshing.

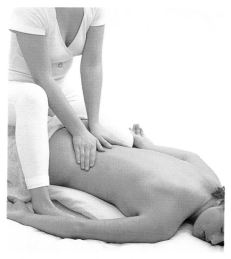

1 Rest your hands on the lower back to either side of the spine. Lean your weight into your hands and stroke up the back towards the head. Mould your hands to the body as they glide firmly along.

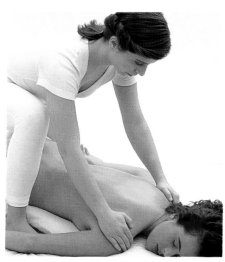

2 As your hands reach the top of the back, fan them out towards the shoulders in a long, smooth, flowing, ceaseless motion.

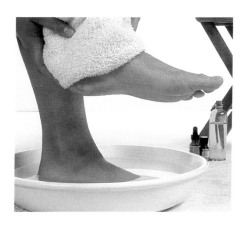

BLOOD PRESSURE

It should be emphasized that anyone with very high blood pressure should first seek expert medical (or professional) treatment. You should not even think about trying to tackle such a condition yourself without accurate guidance. However, in much milder, far less dangerous or acute cases, which are almost entirely related to anxiety and tension, you can help get temporary relief by using essential oils.

Begin by giving yourself or your partner a special treat – a marvellous soothing footbath. For such a bath you should fill a large bowl three-quarters full with hot water. Then carefully add 2 drops Rose, 2 drops Ylang Ylang and 3 drops Lavender. Using a clean, new wooden kitchen spoon, specially reserved for the job, mix everything in, and let stand for a couple of minutes. Then let the feet sink into the water and soak for at least five well-earned, relaxing minutes.

COLIC

Colic is the term that is used to describe spasmodic bouts of cramping pain, building up in intensity until it finally reaches a peak, before abating and returning a short while later.

The causes can range from an obstructing stone, for which professional medical treatment is required, to intestinal gas. The latter is extremely common in babies, and it may strike adults as a result of high tension levels. Fortunately, you can easily aid the adult condition by having a short gentle massage that will also leave you feeling calm and gently relaxed. It only takes about ten minutes.

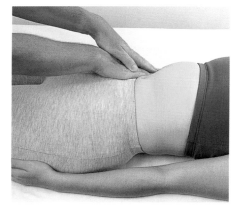

1 Starting in the lower right-hand corner, steadily and firmly press in using both your hands, but taking care not to cause any discomfort.

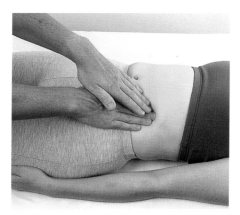

2 Slowly move the hands in a clockwise direction around the abdomen. Keep making continuous small circles to massage the colon.

reducing anxiety

One of the worst problems of anxiety is that it can end up causing headaches. To some people they are but a mild inconvenience, others might find that they slow them down, but in severe cases they can be totally debilitating. The sooner you act, especially if you tend to have major attacks, the more likely you are to be fine. One of the best remedies is a soothing head massage – it can work wonders in reducing the pain.

HEADACHE EASERS

Tension headaches are quite a common feature in most people's lives. In fact they are often completely unavoidable, caused by anything from long tedious slavish hours on a computer to bringing up unruly small children.

Whatever the cause, try and stop what you are doing at the first available opportunity, and take a break. Impractical though it sounds, it is the only way to stop the massive build-up of a nasty headache.

Try to draw the curtains, and to create a deep, dark relaxing astmosphere shut off from the outside world. Besides the massage described on the right, see if you can find time to make yourself a wonderful warm compress. If the head feels at all hot, then try using an oil infused with 4 drops of Peppermint. Another option is 4 drops of Chamomile.

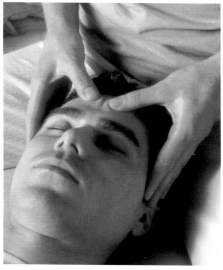

I Ease tension headaches by massaging oils gently into the forehead. With your thumbs, use steady but gentle pressure to stroke the forehead. Repeat this technique for several minutes.

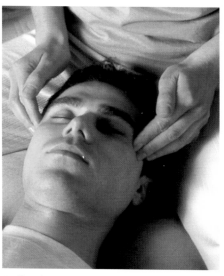

2 Gently massage the temples with the fingers to release tension and stress.

I Use small circling movements just under the bony edge of the skull.

2 Now gently squeeze the neck muscles in a slow, rhythmic way.

MIGRAINE EASERS

One of the most complex of health problems, migraines are nature's way of shutting us down when life has been too demanding. The triggers that spark off a migraine attack are highly individual, and professional treatment is really needed to try to understand the causes for each person. Since many migraine sufferers have a heightened sense of smell at the onset of the attack they may find any aroma intolerable, so do use oils sparingly and sensitively.

At the earliest stage of a migraine attack, try using a blend of 2 drops Rosemary, I drop Marjoram and I drop Clary Sage, diluted in a massage oil and very gently massaged into the temples and forehead.

BREATHING ENHANCERS

"Breathe" . . . how often have we said this to ourselves when we are tense and stressed? Although breathing occurs without our conscious control, it can be affected to quite a considerable extent as we start to tense up, with a tightening of the chest muscles, which restricts any lung expansion.

The tightening feeling in the chest can be extremely uncomfortable, and you should most certainly seek expert medical advice at the first onset if it appears on the left-hand side of the body. Assuming that it is nothing too serious, though, your first consideration is to make sure that you start to relax, and begin breathing deeply and regularly. Take your time, and do not rush this. It is important that you regulate your controlled breathing sensibly.

Once you are happy that you have taken every step to calm down, shutting out whatever the cause might be, you can try the following steam inhalation. The key to success is making an aromatic blend. This is best done by taking a bowl of steaming water and adding 3 drops Benzoin, 2 drops Marjoram and 2 drops Eucalyptus. Mix them all together, leave to stand for a couple of minutes, and then with a covering towel placed over your head, begin inhaling deeply. You will soon notice the beneficial effects.

As the oils vaporize, inhale the steam deeply. If you hold a towel over your head this will slow down the evaporation.

MILD SHOCK SOOTHERS

You bump your head, trip over the cat, fall down the stairs, or stand on the upturned end of a garden rake so that it suddenly smacks you viciously on the head. In fact garden injuries are among the commonest, and most dangerous kind. As in the case of the rake, they can leave you absolutely taken aback, shocked and stunned. You might well feel a little weak and giddy, and need to sit down for a few minutes. At these times, essential oils can be a remarkably useful first-aid help, quickly bringing us right back to our senses.

The quickest, and by far the simplest way to benefit from aromatherapy in instances of mild shock, is to put an open bottle of either Lavender or Clary Sage oil under the injured person's nose and let them sniff the aroma directly. Of course you cannot always have such an oil on the spot, and it is therefore well worth having the pre-made "Rescue Remedy" ready to hand for such an occasion. Another extremely good remedy involves putting a couple of oil drops on a tissue, holding it under the nose and inhaling deeply for just a few minutes.

If, however, you suspect that the injured person is in severe shock, then do not try to treat them at home. Seek medical advice immediately. Such shock is caused by a sudden reduction in blood flow which, in extreme cases, can lead to collapse. The symptoms to look out for include fast, shallow intakes of breath, cold damp skin, a weak pulse, dizziness and even fainting.

tummy problems
Stomach problems might sound slight and comical, but they certainly are not when you are the sufferer. They can be completely debilitating, easily ruin a night out, make a long journey impossible, or disrupt that highly crucial meeting at work. Knowing how to deal with them promptly, however, can quickly revolutionize your life. Take any of the measures described and explained below, and you will find that you never look back.

DIGESTIVE SETTLERS

Nervousness often shows itself in an upset stomach, or abdominal spasm. It has been said that our digestive organs also digest stress, and too often they end up storing emotions, causing all manner of discomfort and indigestion.

The key is to teach our bodies to let go of any such worries, and aromatherapy can help a great deal. One of the easiest ways to use oils in this context is to make a hot compress and then place it over the abdomen, keeping the area warm for about ten minutes. Begin by filling a bowl of hot water with either 2 drops Orange and 3 drops Peppermint, or 3 drops Chamomile and 2 drops Orange. Then soak a flannel in the hot water. Place the compress over the abdomen and relax.

TRAVEL CALMERS

They say that travel broadens the mind; unfortunately, for some people it does quite the opposite. It contracts the mind and condenses it into a compact series of dark, inescapable worries — will the car break down? Is this plane safe? Will I be sick? Will I come though this in one piece, and alive? Once you are on the conveyer belt of anxiety and possible problems, it simply does not stop.

If you are indeed such a poor traveller, try using one of the following essential oils to calm the mind and stomach. They will let you enjoy the delights of new horizons freely without being stressed by how to reach them. The simplest way to use essential oils is to put a couple of drops on to a tissue or handkerchief, and smell them frequently. Useful oils are Peppermint, Mandarin or Neroli.

I Put a couple of drops of essential oil on a tissue, and keep it freely available so that you can reach for it when you wish.

2 To use, hold the tissue under the nose and lean the head slightly forward. Inhale two or three times.

women's health
While for many it used to be a case of grin and bear any problems, and suffer in silence, widespread help is fortunately now available. In extreme cases you should, of course, always consult your doctor, but for more minor conditions there are all kinds of different, soothing massages you can have. They should certainly reduce the impact of too much discomfort, and make sure that normal life is not too greatly disrupted.

PMT SOOTHERS

For many women the days leading up to a period can be fraught with mood swings, irritability and other symptoms. Sometimes they feel guilty that they are snapping, and this adds to the general sense of irritability. One feeds upon the other. While in particularly difficult cases professional help can be sought, in more low level cases there is much that you can do to help yourelf.

Try this satisfying blend of oils using 3 drops Rose, 3 drops Jasmine and 2 drops Clary Sage to a bath. Then get in and lie back, allowing the tension to soak away. Alternatively use this mixture to make a massage oil, and rub it gently into the abdomen for a relaxing, soothing, long-lasting effect. In fact you may find this so comforting it becomes a habit.

1 Slowly and firmly massage the abdomen with your hands. Rub in increasing and then decreasing circles, so that you can actually feel the discomfort slowly diminish and then vanish.

2 You can try moving your hands first in a clockwise, then anti-clockwise direction. It may be more beneficial if your partner helps give the massage. This should help make him more understanding.

MENSTRUAL PAIN RELIEVERS

Painful periods can be due to a number of reasons, but tension will certainly add to muscle spasm and cramping pains. There is nothing more infuriating and frustrating than having a gnawing, cramping painful period just when you have reached a crucially important stage at work, or are planning a major day out.

If there is no organic or structural cause of the discomfort, try using essential oils as part of your routine. They can be applied in one of two key ways, either as a hot compress over the lower abdomen, or while having a deliciously long and soothing bath. Some oils actually have a reputation for improving the menstrual cycle in other ways; seek advice from a professional aromatherapist if you would like to find out more about such long-term treatments.

To make a compress, use 1 drop of Rose, Geranium and Clary Sage oils. Alternatively, a fairly hot bath with 3 drops Rose, 3 drops Geranium and 2 drops Clary Sage will relax cramped muscles.

A long bath with a few drops of oil will help you to relax and soon soothe away any discomfort.

mood changing recipes

It is all too easy to get dragged down by the ever-increasing, remorseless demands made on you. There never seems to be a moment when you can be quiet and alone, and recharge your batteries. Everything seems stacked against you. But just take a little time out with these oils and you can quickly change your mood, getting rid of the blues and giving yourself a wonderful, refreshing pick-me-up.

UPLIFTING OILS

There are unfortunately times in all our lives when we get depressed to some extent, whether due to a specific event or an accumulation of chronic tiredness. As part of a programme of recuperation and restoring your vitality, aromatherapy can certainly be very effective in lifting the mood and giving a boost to your overall energy levels.

For a strong, but relatively short-lived effect, try 4 drops Bergamot and 2 drops Neroli in the bath, ideally first thing in the morning when you are still feeling quite well and relaxed. Do not leave it until too late in the day when the effects of tiredness and stress have taken a strong hold. Aromatherapy stands a far better chance right now of working, and what is more, when it does work it will set you up for the day, giving you renewed confidence. Incidentally, after the bath, gently pat the skin with a soft towel. Do not rub yourself too vigorously.

A gentler effect, which should also pervade the atmosphere all day long, involves using Bergamot or Neroli oils in an essential oil burner. You will probably only need just one drop of each oil at a time, repeating the process as many times as you like.

REVITALIZING OILS

In today's high pressure world, "high pressure" is exactly what it is all about. We are all expected to pack two lifestyles into one. Mother and worker, father and possibly chief provider. Nobody gets the right amount of time to themselves to boost their energy levels, or become quietly absorbed in reading or listening to music, etc. The end result of trying to juggle too many demands is that nearly all of us reach a state of "brain fag", when mental fatigue and exhaustion grind us to a halt.

Rather than reach for the coffee, or worse still alcohol, which far from being a relaxant is actually well known for depressing the central nervous system, try using these revitalizing oils. They will give you an instant, revitalizing pick-me-up and make you feel wonderfully more alert.

You can use 1–2 drops of Rosemary or Peppermint oil in a burner. Alternatively, add 3 drops Rosemary and 2 drops Peppermint to a bowl of steaming water, or use 4 drops of either oils on their own. Give the oils plenty of time to evaporate into the room, and breathe freely. Make sure you then spend some time quietly relaxing, taking in the full benefits of these oils.

INVIGORATING OILS

Chronic tension all too often leads to a feeling of inescapable exhaustion, when we just totally run out of steam. At these demoralizing, difficult times we need a sudden boost, and many oils have a tremendous tonic effect, restoring vitality but without in any way over-stimulating. As a group, the citrus oils are excellent for this purpose, ranging from the more soothing Mandarin to the highly refreshing Lemon oil.

Have a warm, but not too hot bath, with 4 drops Mandarin and 2 drops Orange or 4 drops Neroli and 2 drops Lemon. Alternatively, just add a couple of drops of any of these oils to a bowl full of steaming water. Then sit down calmly, and gently begin inhaling. This will soon help you clear away the tiredness and lift your spirits again.

This kind of steam inhalation is a valuable and simple way to receive the benefits of essential oils when either time or circumstance prevents a massage or indeed a bath.

SENSUAL OILS

Tension, anxiety, worry, depression, and loss of confidence and self-belief – these are just some of the many factors that can adversely affect your sexual energy and performance. Sometimes this leads into a no-escape negative spiral of anxiety about sex, leading to less enjoyment, and so on.

The best answer is not to get dragged down, feeling ever more anxious and depressed, until the problem becomes seemingly insurmountable, but to take a little time out of your hectic life. Be together with your partner and have fun; add to your sensual pleasure with an intimate massage session, using one of these excellent blends to release tensions and allow your natural sexual energy to respond freely.

Use whichever of these blends – 5 drops Rose and 5 drops Sandalwood or 4 drops Jasmine and 4 drops Ylang Ylang – appeals to you both, and include in a massage oil. Use gentle, stroking movements all over the back, buttocks, legs and front.

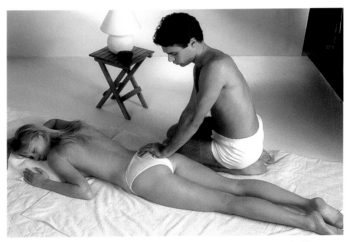

Massage gently all over the body with a light, caring touch. The secret is taking your time, getting the atmosphere right and making sure you choose the right moment.

SLEEP ENHANCERS

Worries can go round and round inside our heads, usually just as we are trying to get to sleep. Worse, they strike in the middle of the night and get blown out of all proportion. The resulting disturbed and restless night leaves us more prone to stress and anxiety, and a vicious cycle can be created. Help break into this cycle with a pleasantly hot and relaxing evening bath. Many oils can be useful – just having a fragrance that you enjoy will help you to unwind after a long day.

Add oils to an evening bath to aid relaxation and sleep. A couple of blends that relax without over-sedating are 4 drops Rose and 3 drops Sandalwood or 5 drops Lavender and 3 drops Ylang Ylang. Incorporate aromatherapy preparations into your daily bathing routine.

the oils

The more you study and learn about oils, the better you will be at making up your own mixtures or recipes to tackle your own highly individual needs. It is not as difficult and demanding as you might think. Just take your time and quietly browse through the following descriptions, and you will quickly see how oils are capable of overcoming a wide range of problems. They will make a wonderful addition to your lifestyle.

THE KEY PLANTS

Essential oils may be extracted from exotic plants such as Sandalwood or Ylang Ylang, or from the more common plants such as Lavender and Chamomile, but each one has its own characteristics and properties. Try to get used to a few oils at first, understand their different effects, and enjoy their fragrance!

Essential oils are in fact concentrated substances; while the skin of citrus fruits such as Lemon or Orange may yield a fair amount of oil, flowers such as roses only contain tiny amounts of the precious essence – about 5,000 roses may be needed to obtain 5ml/1 tsp of what is called a pure essential oil. Such a concentration really emphasizes the importance of only using drop doses of the oils in a suitable dilution, because a little goes a long way.

Oils are extracted from many different plant parts. Each contains powerful healing properties. Nature provides an abundance of therapeutic compounds to help us regain our health.

SANDALWOOD
(Santalum album)

Probably the oldest perfume in history, known to have been used for over 4,000 years. Sandalwood has a heavy scent, and often appeals to men as much as to women. It has a relaxing, antidepressant effect on the nervous system, and where depression causes sexual inhibitions and problems, Sandalwood can be the answer – a genuine aphrodisiac.

CHAMOMILE
(Matricaria recutita [German] or Chamaemelum nobile [Roman])

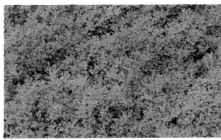

Roman and German Chamomile are both used to obtain essential oils with very similar properties. Chamomile is relaxing and antispasmodic, helping to relieve tension headaches, nervous digestive problems or insomnia, for instance.

BENZOIN
(Styrax benzoin)

This Asiatic tree produces a gum which is usually dissolved in a solvent to produce the "oil". It has a wonderful fragrance of vanilla, and is widely used in various kinds of inhalation mixtures. It is good at relaxing the airways, and it can be used whenever tension levels lead to an uncomfortable tight chest or cause restricted breathing.

GERANIUM
(Pelargonium graveolens)

The Rose-scented Geranium has very useful properties, not least being its ability to bring a blend together, to make a more harmonious scent. Geranium has a refreshing, antidepressant quality, good for nervous tension and exhaustion.

YLANG YLANG
(Cananga odorata var. genuina)

This tropical tree, native to Indonesia, produces an intensely sweet essential oil that has a sedative yet antidepressant action. It is very good for a range of symptoms such as excessive tension, insomnia, panic attacks, anxiety and depression. It also has a good reputation as an aphrodisiac, through its ability to reduce stress levels.

PEPPERMINT
(Mentha piperita)

This oil is another classic ingredient in inhalations for relieving catarrh, although commercial menthol (a major part of the oil) may be used with good results. Peppermint's many known analgesic and antispasmodic effects make it very useful for rubbing on the temples in order to ease any tension headaches; ideally dilute a drop in a little base cream or oil before you begin applying.

JASMINE
(Jasminum officinale)

One of the most wonderful aromas, Jasmine has a relaxing, euphoric effect, and can greatly lift the mood when there is debility, depression and listlessness. Use in the bath or in massage oils, or use Jasmine flower water for oily skin.

EUCALYPTUS
(Eucalyptus globulus)

One of the finest oils for respiratory complaints, found in most commercial inhalants. Well diluted (never use more than 1 per cent) in a base vegetable oil, it can be applied to the forehead to help relieve a hot, tense headache.

LAVENDER
(Lavandula angustifolia)

One of the most well-known scents, Lavender has been used for centuries to refresh and add fragrance to the home, and as a remedy for many stress-related ailments. It is especially useful for helping to relieve tension headaches, or for nervous digestive upsets; use in a massage oil or in the bath for a deeply relaxing and calming experience. The finest oil is produced from the true Lavender (Lavandula angustifolia), and is one of the most versatile of all oils. Its uses range from first-aid treatment of burns, to stress reduction.

ROSEMARY
(Rosmarinus officinalis)

With its highly penetrating, stimulating aroma, Rosemary has been used for many centuries to help relieve nervous exhaustion, various tension headaches and migraines. It is also known to improve the circulation to the brain, and is an excellent oil for overcoming mental fatigue and debility. **Caution** Do not use in pregnancy without seeking professional advice.

MARJORAM
(Origanum marjorana)

Marjoram has a calming and warming effect, and is good for both cold, tight muscles and for cold, tense people who might suffer from headaches, migraines and insomnia. Use in massage blends for rubbing into tired and aching muscles, or in the bath, especially in the evening to help obtain a good night's sleep. **Caution** Do not use in pregnancy without seeking professional advice.

PINE
(Pinus sylvestris)

There are a few species of Pine that produce oils, notably the American Long-leaf Pine which is a commercial source of oil of turpentine. However, the Pine oil used in aromatherapy generally comes from the Scots Pine. It helps to clear the air passages when used as an inhalation, and is also good for relieving fatigue. Tired, aching muscles can be eased with massage using diluted Pine oil.

CLARY SAGE
(Salvia sclarea)

This oil gives a definite euphoric uplift to the brain; do not use too much, however, as you can be left feeling very spacey! Like Ylang Ylang and Jasmine, its antidepressant and relaxing qualities have contributed to its reputation as an aphrodisiac. **Caution** Do not use in pregnancy without seeking professional advice.

ROSE
(Rosa x damascena, centifolia)

Rose is probably the most famous of all oils. There is probably more symbolism attached to roses than any other flower. Several kinds have been used to extract the oil, notably the Damask Rose and the Cabbage Rose. Each one is slightly different, but the overall actions are sedating, calming and anti-inflammatory. Not surprisingly, Rose oil has a wide reputation as an aphrodisiac, and where anxiety is a factor, it may be very beneficial. Use in the bath for a sensual, unwinding experience, or add to a base massage oil to soothe muscular and nervous tension.

BERGAMOT
(Citrus bergamia)

The peel of the ripe fruit yields an oil that is mild and gentle. It is the most effective antidepressant oil of all, best used at the start of the day. Its leaves give the distinctive aroma and flavour to Earl Grey tea. The oil can be used on a burner for generally lifting the atmosphere. Do not use on the skin in bright sunlight, as it increases photosensitivity.

LEMON
(Citrus limon)

Possibly the most cleansing and antiseptic of the citrus oils, useful for boosting the immune system and in skin care. It is also very good at helping to refresh and clarify the thinking process.

GRAPEFRUIT
(Citrus x paradisi)

Oil of Grapefruit is very helpful in the digestion of fatty foods and helps to combat cellulite and congested pores. It has an uplifting effect and will soothe headaches and nervous exhaustion.

shiatsu

T ouch is the essence of shiatsu. We all need to be touched in some form, and shiatsu gives you a wonderful opportunity to fulfil this need in a loving and caring way. The nurturing touch of shiatsu helps trigger the vital self-healing process within each of us.

Shiatsu is a physical therapy aimed at treating your condition through the application of touch, as well as helping you to learn how to heal yourself. The treatment approach and philosophy is similar to acupuncture in its usage of the meridians (energy channels) and tsubo (pressure points) but shiatsu does not call for needles.

"Shiatsu" is a Japanese word meaning finger pressure. The application of pressure is the underlying principle of shiatsu. Different stretching techniques and corrective exercises may also be part of the treatment with the intention of creating balance in the body, both physically and energetically.

It is easy to learn the basic principles of shiatsu; it is also enjoyable and makes you feel good. You are taking responsibility for your own health, and taking care of yourself which is very important because it empowers you to create changes when required. In shiatsu we take a holistic approach and look at the whole person – body, mind and spirit – in trying to find out where the imbalances and causes of stress actually lie.

meridian health

It is always very exciting to hear and learn about radically different interpretations of how the body and mind work. While you may not agree with every last precise detail, they do, as in the case of shiatsu, provide a large number of marvellous insights into how we can manage and regulate our lives. One really beneficial result is knowing how to eliminate stress, enabling you to stay young, vibrant and healthy.

COPING WITH STRESS

Stress upsets both your mental and physical well-being, and every one of us has felt its grasp at one time or another. Stress is well known to all shiatsu practitioners and is recognized as one of the major factors affecting health in our modern society. It is a normal part of life; in fact, a certain level of stress is actually considered quite good for us. Some people seem to be able to thrive on it, yet for others the same degree of pressure can quite simply be too much.

The increasing, cumulative impact of events sometimes means that, eventually, we can not cope. The pressure becomes overpowering and we begin to react to the stress in different ways. These reactions will affect our health and well-being and may interfere with our jobs and social lives in a significant, negative way. The body reacts to a stressor with first a diminished, then an increased, level of resistance. This is usually

A well-balanced diet, with plenty of daily fruit and vegetables, is essential for excellent health.

called the "fight or flight" reaction, which means that the body is instinctively ready to stand and confront, or escape. But stress, with all its different symptoms, is a sure sign that we have lost the wonderful sense of balance in our lives. Human beings have a marvellous natural system for maintaining balance, and the body is always striving to achieve this state of inner harmony. It is this balancing adaptive energy that is tested by stress, and which is constantly under challenge.

Coping with stress can be made easier by asking for help and support from family and friends. Talking to someone helps you to see a problem more clearly. It puts it into a sharper, wider perspective. Far better than just talking, however, having someone give you a long and gentle shiatsu treatment will relax your body and mind, and bring back a marvellous sense of general well-being. It is the ultimate experience when it comes to winding down.

A BALANCED LIFESTYLE

You can improve your general health and well-being, and your battery of defences, by understanding exactly what causes you stress, and by learning how to avoid it or even how to adapt to it. There are basically two key aspects to stress reduction: lifestyle modification and relaxation.

Lifestyle modification could mean changing your job and reassessing your goals in life, or simply adapting a more open attitude to what you are doing. Having a sense of control over events lessens their stressful impact. There is no point in trying to over-reach yourself. Ambition is good, but not when it leaves you constantly floundering with a marked sense of failure and desperation. Give yourself a chance.

Daily relaxation represents the most important element of maintaining health and vitality. Deep relaxation is not the same as sleep, and to gain full benefit from it, it is important not to fall asleep while you are relaxing. Giving or receiving a shiatsu treatment will relax your whole body and mind, and you will feel totally refreshed and energized afterwards.

The back-up treatment involves eating a well-balanced diet rich in fibres, grains and fresh vegetables. Cut down on sugar and

salt as well as coffee, tea and carbonated soft drinks. Water and quality fruit juice are so much better for you. A certain amount of physical exercise is also necessary if you want to maintain your health and vitality. A pleasant, brisk 20-minute walk in the fresh air every day will stimulate and balance the energy within. Never attempt any kind of exercise that is too difficult or demanding.

Fight or Flight Response

- The brain registers danger and sends messages along the nerves to different muscles and organs to react accordingly (nervous/muscular system).
- The heart beats faster, pumping out blood to muscles and areas in need and you start to sweat (circulatory system).
- The breathing rhythm changes; you start to breathe faster due to more air being drawn in through the bronchial tubes as they expand (respiratory system).
- The digestion slows down (digestive system).
- Increased production of certain hormones, such as adrenaline and noradrenaline (hormonal system).

Organs – Meridians

The balanced functioning of our body is controlled by 12 vital internal organs. In Oriental medicine the organs have a wider meaning than in the West, based on their physiological and energetic function. Each has a different quality of energetic movement and responsibility and is linked to a meridian, or energy channel, named according to the internal organ it affects. The meridians run in pairs either side of the body, and they ensure the successful nurturing of energy, known as Chi.

Tsubo – Pressure Points

Along each meridian are a varying number of tsubo, or pressure points. They are points along the meridian where the energy is thought to be flowing near the surface of the body and therefore more accessible for treatment. There are more than 700 tsubo in your body, and they are numbered in sequence according to which meridian they are on. The first point on the kidney meridian, for example, will be Kidney 1 (KID 1). The points reflect the internal functioning of the body.

Lungs (LU):

• Take in air and vital Chi during respiration to refine and distribute it around the body. A fundamental process for building up resistance against external intrusions.
• Elimination of gases through exhalation.
• Openness, emotional stability, enthusiasm and a fulsome positive approach.

Large Intestine (LI):

• Helps the function of the lungs. Processes food substances and eliminates what is unnecessary.
• The ability to "let go". Elimination.

Spleen (SP):

• Corresponds to the function of the pancreas in Western terms and governs all organs secreting digestive enzymes. It also relates to reproductive glands in women and is a controlling factor in the immune system.
• Maintains the health of the flesh, the connective soft tissue and the muscle tissue.
• Self-image is strongly affected by the spleen function, as is the desire to help others. Self-confidence.

Stomach (ST):

• It is responsible for "receiving and ripening" ingested food and all fluids.
• Information for mental and physical nourishment.
• Groundedness, centredness, self-confidence and reliability.

Heart (HT):

• It governs blood and blood vessels as well as the circulatory system.
• Houses the mind and our emotions.
• Joy, calmness and communication.

Small Intestine (SI):

• The quality of the blood and tissue reflects the condition of the small intestine, and anxiety, emotional excitement or nervous shock can adversely affect the small intestine energy.
• Emotional stability and calmness.

Kidneys (KID):

• The kidneys include the function of the adrenals, controlling the whole of the hormonal system.
• Provides and stores essential Chi for all other organs and governs birth, growth, reproduction and development; the reproductive system.
• Nourishes the spine, bones and the brain; the nervous system.
• Vitality, direction, courage and will power.

Bladder (BL):

• Purification and regulation.
• Nourishes the spine.
• Courage and the ability to move forward confidently in life.

Heart Governor (HG):

• Protector of the heart and closely related to emotional responses.
• Related to central circulation.
• Relationships with others; protection of others.

Triple Heater (TH):

• Transports energy, blood and heat to the peripheral parts of the body; circulatory system.
• Helpfulness and emotional interaction.

Liver (LIV):

• Stores blood and nutrients which are subsequently distributed throughout the body. Ensures free flow of Chi throughout the body.
• Governs the muscular and digestive systems.
• Creativity and ideas; good planning and organization.

Gall Bladder (GB):

• Stores bile produced by the liver and distributes it in the small intestine; digestive system.
• Practical application of ideas and decision-making.

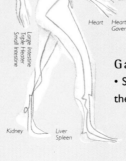

  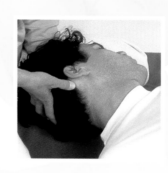 

treatments
treatments
treatments

Giving and receiving shiatsu is both extremely enjoyable and relaxing, and a wonderful way of spending time with another person. Before you begin, however, you must consider a few key points. First, consider your own health and condition. How are you feeling? Never try to give a shiatsu treatment if you are feeling in any way tired or depressed, or even intoxicated, have a contagious disease, or for any reason do not feel quite up to the task in hand. You must be fully alert, and able to concentrate. Your partner will quickly pick up the fact that your heart is not in it.

Before giving treatment you must also check that the environment is clean, warm and totally comforting. In fact it is well worth spending quite a bit of time getting this side of the treatment right. You do not want the excellent effects of shiatsu being undermined by the likes of a small, hot, airless room with the radio playing pop music. What you do want is calm, relaxing music, perhaps even a tape of bird song or early morning church bells, and soft muted lighting instead of a fierce glare. As for clothes, wear a loose fitting, airy, comfortable garment, possibly one made of cotton, and avoid eating any heavy meals for two hours before giving the treatment. Such detailed consideration is essential for a good session.

The next crucial step involves taking just a few moments to prepare yourself and your partner. Sitting in the Seiza position (that is, on your knees), to your partner's right-hand side, place your hand on the sacrum, as shown. Sit quietly, gradually begin to regulate your breathing, empty your mind until you feel totally quiet and at one with your partner, and focus on how they feel right now. Shiatsu practitioners always have excellent empathy.

The final point to note is that when giving treatment, sometimes your touch needs to be very light, and at other times it should be firm for deep tissue work. Try using your hands as an extension of your heart, and remember to be sensitive to your partner's needs at all times.

doin exercises

The term "Doîn" literally means self-massage, and involves a combination of different techniques to improve the circulation and flow of Chi throughout the whole body. The following exercises can be used not only to revitalize your tired muscles and low spirits, but also to relieve a stiff, tense body and a stressed mind. Starting your day with a Doîn session will quickly awaken your body and mind. You will soon notice the benefits.

THE PREPARATION

Prepare yourself by gently shaking all your limbs, and body. Shake your arms and hands to help release any tension in your upper body. Now gently shake your legs and feet as well. Place your feet shoulder-width apart and unlock your knees. Straighten your back to allow a better energy flow, relax your shoulders and then close your eyes. Take a minute to focus internally, and get in touch with how you and your body are feeling before starting the Doîn routine.

Note that when doing this exercise it is vitally important that you become aware of any areas that might be in any discomfort, and that you try completely to empty your mind of any disturbing or distracting thoughts. It takes time to learn how to do the latter, and you will eventually succeed. What counts in the end is that you do not let tension ruin the effects of the Doîn.

The Best Way to Complete

After having worked through your whole body as described in the following pages, stand up and gently shake out again. Now place your feet shoulder-width apart and bend your knees slightly. Imagine a string passing through your spine, from the tail bone to the top of your head. Stretch the string and feel your spine straighten up to allow for better Chi flow. Close your eyes for a moment and see how you feel after your Doîn session. Try to remember how you felt at the beginning and compare that with the sensation you have now. Open your eyes again and to complete your session, practise breathing deeply.

You can do this Doîn exercise as often as time permits. Ideally it should become a part of your daily routine, being practised early in the morning and again perhaps later in the evening. You will quickly notice and appreciate the benefits.

NECK

1 Using one hand, place the palm across the back of your neck and firmly massage in a squeezing motion. This will increase the flow of blood and Chi to the area, release stagnation, and remove waste products such as lactic acid.

2 With your thumbs, gently apply pressure to the point at the base of the skull, directing the pressure upwards against the skull.

3 Use your fingers and rub across the muscle fibres at the base of the skull. This technique will release the muscles and tendons in the area, and also help to relieve headaches and any level of pain in the shoulder.

HEAD AND FACE

1 Open your eyes and make a loose fist with both hands. Keep your wrists relaxed and tap the top of your head.

2 Slowly work your way all around the head, covering the sides, front and back. This exercise will wake up your brain and stimulate blood circulation.

3 Pull your fingers through your hair, stimulating the bladder and gall bladder meridians on the top and side.

4 Place your fingers on your forehead, and apply a little pressure and stroke out from the centre to the temples.

5 Bring your fingers up to your temples. Drop your elbows, and massage your temples, using circular movements.

6 Massage down the sides of your face until you reach your jaw.

7 Squeeze along the jawbone, working outwards from the centre. This is a very good technique for trying to relax.

8 Using your index finger and thumb, squeeze your eyebrows starting from the centre line and move slowly and laterally.

9 Bring your thumbs to the inside of the eyebrows (point BL2). Allow the weight of your head to rest on your thumbs.

10 With your index finger and thumb, pinch the bridge of your nose and the corners of your eyes.

11 Apply your thumbs to the sides of your nose. Breathe in as you stroke down the side of your nose.

Key Tips

The above routine is particularly good if you feel a cold coming on, or have one already. Although DoIn exercises are specifically designed for self-help, they can just as easily be carried out by another person, particularly if you are feeling too lethargic to do it yourself. The above routine will ease discomfort and speed recovery.

SHOULDERS, ARMS AND HANDS

1 Lift up your shoulders up and breathe in. Breathe out, letting your shoulders drop and relax. Repeat.

2 Support your left elbow and with a loose fist you can begin tapping across your shoulder.

3 Press your middle finger into the shoulder's highest point, known as point GBL21, the "Shoulder Well". **Caution** Sometimes used in childbirth to speed up labour; do not use during pregnancy.

4 Straighten your arm, open your palm and tap down the inside of your arm from the shoulder to the open hand. Good for the heart meridians.

5 Turn your arm over and tap up the back of your arm, from the hand to the shoulders. This technique stimulates the meridians for the intestines. Repeat three times.

6 Use your left thumb to work through your right hand, gently massaging the centre of your palm to relieve general tension and revitalize you spiritually.

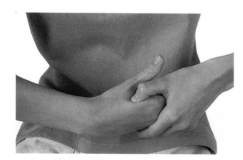

7 Stimulate the "Great Eliminator" on the large intestine meridian, in the web between the index finger and the thumb. **Caution** Sometimes used in childbirth to speed up labour; do not use during pregnancy.

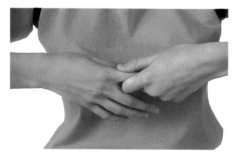

8 Carefully squeeze and massage the joints of each finger using your index finger and thumb. Repeat as often as you find it necessary.

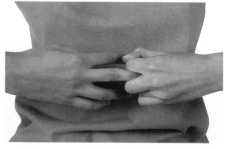

9 Pulling out the fingers will stimulate the starting and end points of all the meridians. This is a great way to release any stress and tension in your hands.

CHEST, ABDOMEN AND LOWER BACK

1 Open up your chest, and using either a loose fist or flat hands for comfort, tap across your chest, above and around the breasts. This will stimulate your lungs and strengthen your respiratory system.

2 Take a deep breath in as you open your chest again; then on the out breath tap your chest and make a deep resounding "Ahhh…" sound.

3 Proceed down towards your abdomen, and with open hands tap round your abdomen, clockwise, for about a minute.

4 Place one hand on top of the other, and then make exactly the same circular motion around your abdomen for about another minute.

5 Place your hands on your back, just below your ribcage. Start to rub the area until you feel some warmth. This will stimulate your kidney energy.

6 Place one hand on your knee. Using the back of your other hand, tap across your sacrum bone at the base of the spine. It activates the nervous system.

LEGS AND FEET

1 Tap down the backs of your legs from your buttocks to your heels, following the flow of energy. Tap up the inside of your legs, stimulating your liver.

2 Sit down on the floor, and measure four finger widths down from the knee-cap on the outside of your leg. Place your thumb on the point ST36 and press. Good for tired legs.

3 On the dorsal part of your foot, between the big toe and the second toe is LIV3, "Big Rush". Good against cramp. **Caution** Do not use this particular point during pregnancy.

system calmers with a partner

If you notice that your partner looks listless, is feeling at all tired and stressed, is experiencing any tension in the upper body, or suffers from shallow, rapid breathing, the following treatment will be very beneficial. It will aid relaxation and promote much deeper breathing, facilitating a more efficient energy distribution to all parts of the body. The treatment is quickly and easily given.

I To prepare for treatment, kneel by your partner's side and place your hand at the base of the spine. Concentrate on how your partner feels. Then place your palms on either side of your partner's spine. Crouch down if it feels easier.

2 Ask your partner to breathe in; on the out-breath lean into your hands and apply pressure to your partner's back. Ease the pressure to allow your partner to breathe in again. Move your hands down and press on the next exhalation.

3 Start at the top of the back between the shoulder blades. Work your way down towards the sacrum. Repeat three times. Always keep your elbows straight, and use your body weight as you work.

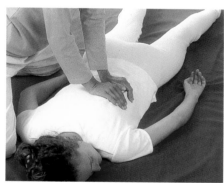

4 Kneel at 90 degrees to your partner, place your palms in the valley (on the opposite side of the spine) formed by the spinous processes (spinal bumps) and the broad muscles running on either side of the spine. Rock the body with the heels of your hands. As you rock, you can move your hands down the back, one following the other. The rocking should be continuous and rhythmic. Repeat three times. Do both sides, working from the opposite side of the body.

5 This technique allows you to focus specifically upon the spinal column. You still need to rock; however, this time the spinous processes are gripped between the fingers and the thumbs. Applying a positive (firm) contact, gradually work the hands along the full length of the spine, moving it from side to side. This action is good for loosening the muscles and stimulating the nervous system.

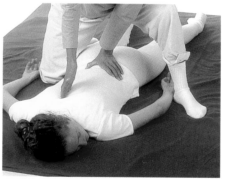

6 Place your left hand on your partner's sacrum. Using the edge of your right hand like a knife, perform a sawing action down either side of the spine. Work both sides alternately, repeating the sequence three times.

7 Run your hands along the spine to feel the undulations of the spinous processes. Bring your thumbs sideways, two fingers' breadth from the dip between the two spinous processes. Apply perpendicular pressure.

8 Put one hand on top of the other and place your hands on your partner's sacrum. Apply pressure to the sacrum, focusing all your energy into the base of the spine.

9 Turn around to face your partner, spread your knees and, using the fleshy part of your forearm in a penetrating and rolling action, apply pressure across the buttocks. Stay on the same side to work both buttocks.

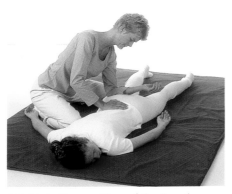

10 Note the position of the "mother hand", and keep the hands relaxed as you roll your forearm right across the surface of the buttocks.

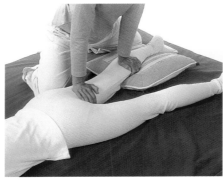

11 Adjust your position so that you can move down the leg. One hand remains on the sacrum or is placed on the back of the thigh. Starting from the back of the thigh, gradually work down the leg, applying pressure with your thumb. Support your partner's lower leg with a cushion beneath the shin.

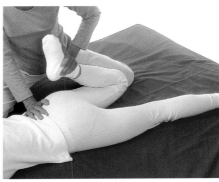

12 Take hold of your partner's ankle and bend the leg towards the buttock. Adjust your position to allow you to use your body weight to achieve the stretch. Now move yourself all the way down to the feet. With both hands, take a firm hold of the ankle, lean back and stretch out the leg to its full length.

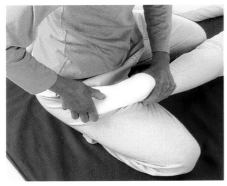

13 Place your partner's foot in your lap and using your thumb apply pressure to Kid I, "Gushing Spring", one-third of the distance from the base of the second toe to the base of the heel.

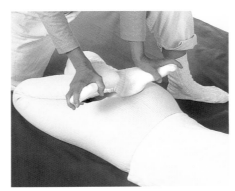

14 Cross your partner's ankles and bring them slowly towards the buttocks. Do this stretch twice, the first time placing the more flexible leg in front (nearest to the buttocks), then reverse the position.

15 Stand up and walk on the soles of your partner's feet using your heels. Have the feet turned inwards and apply pressure to the soles but with no weight at all on the toes.

nervous system calmers: self-help

Stress can have quite a significant and dramatic effect on the nervous system, and badly affect a wide range of functions, including breathing. One excellent way to get you back on track is to balance the energy in the bladder channel through the following exercises and the shiatsu treatment of the back. Both techniques are tailor-made to calm your nervous system.

1 Stand with your feet shoulder-width apart and knees bent. Keep your back straight. Let your arms hang loose at your sides. Swing them from side to side.

2 Swinging your arms will create a twist in your spine, gradually loosening up the joints between the lumbar vertebrae and allowing for better flexible movement.

3 Bring your arms a bit higher up so that you now feel the twist in the middle part of your back. This will loosen up the thoracic vertebrae and the diaphragm.

4 With your feet wider than shoulder-width apart place your hands on your legs, above your knees, and straighten your back. Sway back and look up.

5 Bend your arms and slowly bring your upper body down towards the floor. Keep looking at the ceiling until you no longer see it. Relax the head downwards.

6 Pull your abdominal muscles in and slowly roll up your spine allowing the head to come up last. Lift your head and straighten your spine. Return to the sway back and repeat the whole movement about ten times.

7 Stay in the same position as for the last step of the previous sequence.

8 Breathe in and, on the exhalation, drop the left shoulder down as shown. Keep your elbows gently locked and look up to the ceiling over your right shoulder. Feel the twist in your spine.

9 Take another deep breath in, return to the starting position and drop your right shoulder down as you exhale. Repeat another three or four times on each side. Finish by coming back to the starting position. Relax your upper body forward. Move your feet closer together and slowly roll up your spine, until you come to a relaxed standing position.

10 To treat your back further in case of pain and tension, or whenever you feel in need of general relaxation, try using tennis balls as extra help. Put two tennis balls into a sock and knot the top. Lower yourself on to the tennis balls, which should be placed on either side of the spine. This is where your bladder meridian is located. Start from the area between your shoulders, or anywhere where you feel any pain and discomfort.

11 Breathe deeply and allow your back to sink on to the balls. The balls will mould themselves to the contours of your back and stimulate your bladder energy. Keep the balls in one place until you feel the muscles relax and then slowly roll the balls to the next area "in need". Work this area in the same way, using your breath to enhance the relaxation. Give yourself 10–15 minutes, working down the whole spine. Afterwards your spine will feel open and relaxed against the floor. You will have a sensation of warmth down your back.

12 When you have finished these spinal exercises it is good to lie down on the floor and relax with your lower legs resting on a chair. This relaxes the lumbar area of your back and realigns the whole spine. Close your eyes, allow your breathing to slow down and feel the energy moving from the top of your spine down to the sacrum like a wave. Stay in this position for 10–15 minutes.

This relaxation exercise works directly on the nervous system, calming it down, and you can use the exercise at any time when you feel stressed.

breathing enhancers with partner Correct

breathing is the first, fundamental technique that keeps us going. Surprisingly, when things get stressful we do not always breathe as we should. Deep, relaxing inhaling is replaced by short shallow gasps for air, and the whole body quickly suffers. The following techniques are aimed at the upper part of the body, helping you feel calm, relaxed and well in control again.

1 Place one hand underneath your partner's back in the area opposite the solar plexus and the other hand on top covering the area just below the sternum (breastbone). Focus into the area between your hands and encourage your partner to do the same. Feel the Chi from the breath of your partner reach this space, slowly allowing it to open and expand. You will gradually feel the tension go and the muscles relax to allow a deeper and more relaxed breathing.

2 Cross your arms over and place the palms of your hands on your partner's shoulders. Ask your partner to breathe in and on the out-breath bring your body weight over your hands, stimulating the first point of the lung meridian and gently opening the chest. Repeat this three times.

3 Keep your left hand on the shoulder and take a firm hold of your partner's hand with your right hand. Lift the arm from the floor, shake it out, and then finally allow it to relax again.

4 Firmly hold on to the thumb and give the arm and the lung meridian a good revitalizing stretch. You can repeat this technique several times.

5 Place your partner's arm at a 45-degree angle to the body. Use one of your hands to support the shoulder while the other hand palms along the arm to the hand. Stay on the thumb side of the arm to activate the energy in the lung meridian.

6 Continue all the way down to the thumb (end point of the lung channel). Avoid applying any direct heavy pressure over the elbow joint.

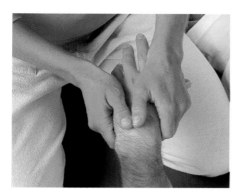

7 Using your thumbs, massage the whole of the dorsal side of your partner's hand.

8 Loosen up the wrist joint by slowly rotating the hand.

9 Open up the palm of the hand and gently massage. Apply pressure to the point in the centre of the palm, called "Palace of Anxiety". A very good point for calming and releasing tension.

10 Find point LI4 which is located in the web between the index finger and thumb. Stimulating this point with gentle pressure from your thumb will relieve headaches and help clear any mucous congestion taking place in the lungs.

11 Hold your partner's arm by the wrist and support the shoulder with your other hand. Step forward and rotate the arm into an overhead stretch. Before you step forward, you need to apply pressure to the supporting hand at the shoulder. Maintaining this pressure ensures a strong stretch. Step back, allowing the arm to return to the starting position.

12 Place both hands on top of your knees and stretch the arms by leaning backwards. Let go of the arm you have treated and move over to the other side. Repeat the whole sequence working on the other arm.

13 Stand behind your partner. Take hold of the hands, gripping around the thumbs, and as you both exhale, lift up from your knees and lean backwards until your partner feels the stretch.

14 Kneel down behind your partner and ask them to clasp the hands behind the neck. Bring your arms in front of your partner's arms, and on the out-breath gently open up the elbows to the sides.

15 Bring one knee up to support your partner's lower back. Take hold of the lower arms, and on the out-breath bring the elbows towards each other behind your partner's back.

self-help breathing enhancers

The lung energy controls our intake of fresh air and Chi from the external environment. However, when your stress levels are high for a period the bronchial tubes expand to let in more air and the end result is that we tend to "over-breathe", or hyperventilate. By working on the lung meridian and practising these breathing exercises, you will facilitate deeper, more satisfying breathing.

1 Link your index finger and thumb on both hands. Step forward with your right foot and reach to the ceiling. Step back, relax the arms and repeat with your left foot. Repeat 3 or 4 times on each side.

2 Stand with your feet apart. Lift your arms to the sides with elbows bent, and make loose fists. Take a deep breath in, opening your chest by bringing your arms back as far as is possible.

3 On the exhalation, cross your arms over in front of you and relax your head down. Keep your knees bent, press back the area in between your shoulder blades. Repeat four or five times.

4 Stand with your feet shoulder-width apart and knees bent, and spread your feet slightly apart so that your toes point out. Hook your thumbs together behind your back, and inhale as you look up.

5 On the exhalation, bend forward and stretch your arms over your head. Breath in and feel the stretch along the back of your legs, back and arms, Slowly exhale. Stay down and repeat twice more.

6 Lie down with a rolled-up towel along your spine, allowing the head to drop back on to the floor or a pillow. Place your fingers along your ribs, gently pressing as you breathe out.

immune system revivers

The immune system includes your spleen, thymus gland and lymph nodes. It is responsible for moving proteins and fats around the body, and is also responsible for filtering body fluids, producing white blood cells and immunity. However, periods of stress will weaken your immune system and leave you prone to infections. These simple shiatsu techniques will help awaken your immune and lymphatic systems.

1 Ask your partner to lie down on the back with legs straight. Place your palms over the soles of your partner's feet. Intermittently rock the feet towards the head in a rhythmic motion of about two movements per second for 3-4 minutes.

2 Bend your partner's leg and move yourself up to the side. Hold the leg just below the knee. Slowly rotate the hip joint, moving from the centre of yourself. Keep a fixed distance between your chest and your partner's knee.

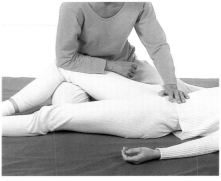

3 Place your partner's foot against the opposite inside ankle so that the leg is bent, exposing the inside leg. Ask your partner to inhale and gently use your forearm to stretch open the spleen meridian on the out-breath.

4 Support the lower leg with a cushion and, starting from the inside of your partner's big toe, use your thumb to apply perpendicular pressure along the medial part of the foot.

5 At the top of the shin bone on the medial side of the leg is SP9, another powerful point on the spleen meridian. Press this point to treat abdominal and menstrual pain, or local pain in the knee.

6 Rotate the leg you have worked on and then bend the other leg as well. Come to a standing position, bring your feet close to your partner's hips for support and gently bring the knees to the chest. Ease up on the stretch and rotate both legs. Move over to the other side, stretch out the treated leg and repeat the sequence for the other leg.

working on the digestive system
The stomach and spleen energy channels are associated with the highly important functions of ingestion and digestion of food. In traditional Chinese medicine, the stomach corresponds to the entire digestive tract, from the mouth to the small intestine, and it creates Chi energy. The following exercises are aimed at fine-tuning and improving the health of your digestive system.

1 Sit in the Seiza position at your partner's side. Take a few moments of stillness to "tune in" and observe. Be aware of any tension and note the breathing rate: fast and shallow indicates tension; slow and deep shows relaxation.

Trace the borderlines of your partner's *Hara* (vital body centre). Start at the ribcage just below the breastbone and move slowly out to the pelvis.

2 Using two hands, one on top of the other, apply finger-pad pressure in a clockwise movement around the Hara, as shown. Where you find tension, apply gradually deeper pressure to dissolve it.

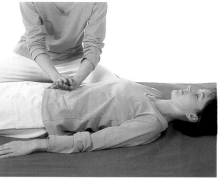

3 With one hand on top of the other, make a rocking and pushing type motion like rolling dough, from one side to the other, and pull back using the heel of the hand. Repeat for relaxation.

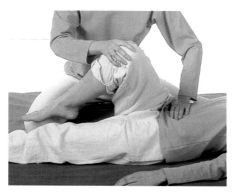

4 One hand holds the right leg just below the knee. Move from your centre, using your whole body, not just your arm muscles, to rotate your partner's leg. Keep a fixed distance between your chest and your partner's knee to ensure a balanced rotation of the hip.

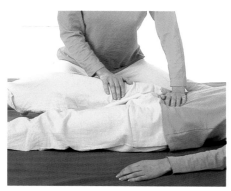

5 Stretch your partner's leg out, and place your knee underneath your partner's knee for support or use a pillow. Apply palm pressure along the outside frontal edge of the leg following the stomach meridian. Start from the top of the thigh and work to the foot. Repeat three or four times.

6 Stimulate ST36, "Leg Three Miles", using thumb pressure. The point is located four fingers' width below the knee-cap on the outside of the shin-bone. The name refers to this point's remarkable effect. It has been used since ancient times to build up endurance.

circulatory system enhancers

The heart organ, the heart and heart governor channels are the central focuses for regulating circulation, according to traditional Chinese medicine. However, heart energy can be surprisingly weakened in several circumstances. One excellent way of tackling the problem is by using wonderfully specialized shiatsu techniques. Dual functional, they will help calm the mind and cure such problems.

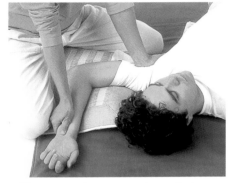

1 To expose the energy channel, place your partner's arm with the hand above the head, palm facing upwards. Support your partner's elbow with a cushion, and kneel in an open Seiza position. To improve the blood circulation to the skin generally and to the peripheries in particular, give yourself a daily body scrub. Use a dry loofah, skin brush, rough face cloth or even a towel.

2 To balance the energy in the heart meridian, sit on the floor, bend your knees and bring the soles of your feet together in front of you. Hold on to your ankles and straighten your spine. Inhale and lean forwards, keeping your back as straight as possible. Breathe out as you bring your head towards your feet and your elbows in front of your legs. Open up the axilla (armpit) and relax.

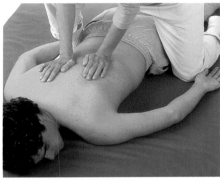

3 Use both palms in a technique known as palm rubbing to apply pressure quite firmly and rub down either side of the spine.

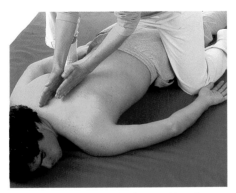

4 To rub, use the little finger side of your hands and vigorously rub down either side of the spine a few times until the area begins to redden.

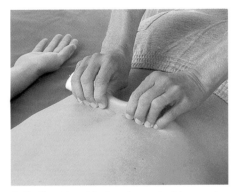

5 Rolling the skin involves pinching and taking hold of the skin on the lower part of the spine (lumbar area). Lift the tissue and gradually "roll" it up the spine. Repeat three or four times. Then roll the skin from the spine, the centre line, out towards the sides to the back.

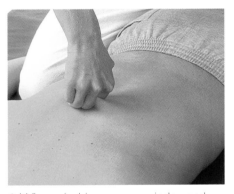

6 When pinching, use your index and middle fingers to pinch and take hold of the tissue. Twist and lift the skin at the same time. Work within your partner's pain threshold. Cover the whole back using this technique. You will see the area redden as the circulation improves.

tension relievers

Surprising though it may sound, when you are under stress your centre of gravity tends to lurch and shift from the abdominal area up to the chest, causing tension levels in the neck, shoulders and face. It often also results in a feeling of great heaviness on your shoulders. Imagine how wonderful it would be to have someone who could touch these tender areas sympathetically, providing instant, soothing, long-lasting relief.

1 Sit down in the Seiza position at your partner's head. Place your hands on the shoulders and tune in. Be aware of the breathing and state of relaxation before you start. Ask your partner to breathe in, and on the exhalation apply a bit of pressure to the shoulders by leaning into your arms. Repeat a few times. This encourages relaxation.

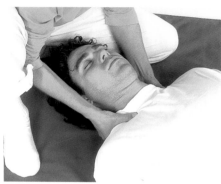

2 With your fingers underneath and thumbs on top, gently and firmly massage the shoulders using a kneading action. Feel the tension in the muscles relaxing and the tissue gradually softening up.

3 Move your hands to the neck. With your thumbs on the side and fingers underneath, stretch out the neck by gently pulling away. Repeat a few times until you feel the neck muscles relax.

4 Now, gently lift your partner's head off the floor and firmly squeeze the muscles of the neck. Do be careful not to squeeze too hard, causing possible discomfort.

5 Turn the head to one side and support it with one hand. Use the finger pads of your other hand to "rub" across the muscle fibres. Treat the other side of the head in the same way.

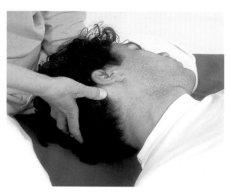

6 With your partner's head turned to the side, press the points along the base of the skull. Start at the ear and work towards the spine. Turn the head and treat the other side in the same way.

7 Rub the scalp using your fingertips, and then run your fingers firmly through the hair. Repeat several times.

8 Turn your partner's head to one side and support it by placing one hand under the skull. Tell your partner to breathe deeply.

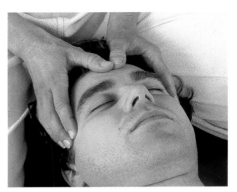

9 Start treating the face by placing your thumbs gently on the midline of your partner's forehead, with your fingertips to the side.

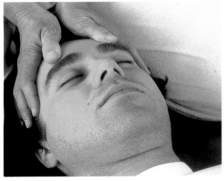

10 Apply a bit of pressure and stroke your thumbs out towards the temples. Repeat three or four times. This will ease tension in the head.

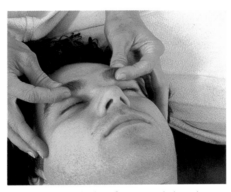

11 Use your index finger and thumb to squeeze your partner's eyebrows. Work from the centre out to the sides. Repeat a few times to clear sinus problems.

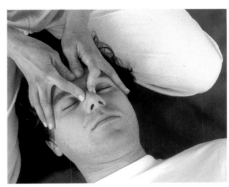

12 Using your index fingers, stroke along the side of the nose to help clear nasal congestion. Come all the way up to the bridge of the nose.

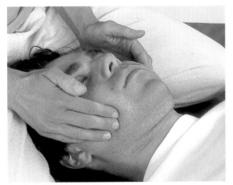

13 Massage the side of your partner's face, moving down to the jaw. This treatment will relax the whole body.

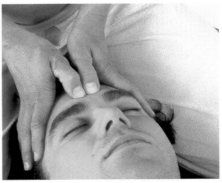

14 Come back to the starting point at your partner's forehead. Apply some pressure and stroke out to the sides.

Key Tips

When giving tension relievers, try to take a little time fully relaxing yourselves. Commence the techniques from a position of well-being and strength. Listen to some calming music, make sure that the room is warm and dry, and when you are feeling entirely comfortable, begin. Since this is an intimate kind of massage, it is also important that the subject feels completely at ease with you. A little deep breathing before the first exercise will help induce a marvellous, soothing feeling of harmony. It will certainly make all the difference. Afterwards, you may begin.

reflexology

reflexology reflexology

Using our hands to release and alleviate tension in our bodies is something that we do instinctively. When you bang your shin it is an automatic response to hold your hurt leg or rub it better. You are thus releasing the disturbed energy from the traumatized part of your body through contact with the undisturbed energy of your hands. In effect you are re-balancing the traumatized part to restore it to its natural state of well-being, with harmony between the flow of energy, circulation and muscle tension.

Our hands have been a means of caring, comfort and giving since we first ceased to need them to walk on, and started to use them for focused, specialized activities. They are the tools of many natural therapies. In reflexology you can use them, specifically your fingers, to apply pressure-point therapy to certain key points, usually on the feet, although often on the hands. There are reflex points elsewhere, notably on the head, but these are used far less frequently.

The word "reflex" means to reflect. Pressure points on your feet and hands reflect all the parts of your body, both external and internal: organs and glands as well as limbs, torso and head. Each point actually reflects the activity of another part of the body. By learning to read the right signs and act accordingly, it is therefore possible to effect a wide range of cures.

how reflexology works
Reflexology acts on parts of the body by stimulating the corresponding reflexes with compression techniques applied with the fingers. Where there is inhibited functioning we find congestion in the form of deposits that have not been cleared away by the venous circulation and the lymph. Both feet together hold the reflexes to the whole body. The part that corresponds to the spine runs along the instep of each foot.

Head and Neck
Your head is represented on the toes; to be more precise, the right side of your head lies on the right big toe and the left side on the left big toe. In addition to the whole head being fully represented on the two big toes, the eight other toes hold the reflexes to specific parts of your head for fine tuning.

Your neck reflex is actually found in the "necks" of all the toes: if you find tension in one area of your neck, you will find tension or discomfort, or be able to feel congestion, in the corresponding areas of your toes. The correspondence between the head and toes may be initially difficult to understand because you have only one head while you have ten toes (or two sides to your head and five toes on either side). However, reflexology is a long-lived, well-known art, and you will quickly come to appreciate these close connections.

Gently working on the spinal reflex which in fact runs right along the instep of each foot.

Torso and Spine
It is much easier to comprehend how the torso is reflected in or fits on to the body of the feet once you have grasped the concept of your two feet together representing your whole body. The key to such understanding lies in the fact that the spinal line runs right down and along the insteps of your feet, where they finally meet if you put them firmly together. In your feet the whole of you comes together.

Chest
The ball of each foot represents one side of your chest. So in the balls of your feet, and on the same area on the top of your feet, lie the reflexes to your lungs, air passages, heart, thymus gland, breast, shoulders and everything contained in your chest. The whole area is bounded by your diaphragm, the important reflex that lies across the base of the ball of each foot.

Abdomen
In your instep, where your feet are not weight-bearing and are therefore not padded like the ball, you will find contained all the reflexes to your abdominal organs – those concerned with digestion and those dealing with the maintenance and well-being of life. This crucial area is clearly bounded by the diaphragm line above, and also by the heel line that lies below.

Pelvis
The whole of your heel all around your foot contains the reflexes to your pelvic area: they lie on the sole and the sides of your heel and also across the top of your ankle.

Limbs
The limbs are clearly represented on the outer edge of your foot but also, and most particularly, on the corresponding upper or lower limb. There is no part of the foot that actually resembles the limbs. The arms and legs, however, follow the same basic structure, and as such each limb holds and contains the reflexes to the other limb on the same side. Shoulders reflect hips and vice versa. Elbows and knees, wrists and ankles and hands and feet are related in the same way. These are known to practising, experienced reflexologists as the cross reflexes.

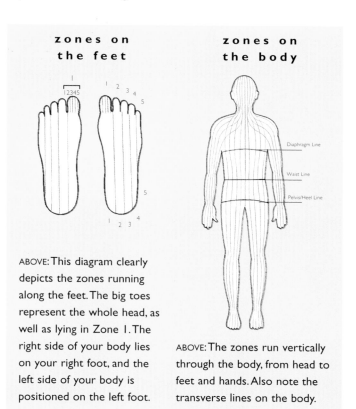

zones on the feet

zones on the body

ABOVE: This diagram clearly depicts the zones running along the feet. The big toes represent the whole head, as well as lying in Zone 1. The right side of your body lies on your right foot, and the left side of your body is positioned on the left foot.

ABOVE: The zones run vertically through the body, from head to feet and hands. Also note the transverse lines on the body.

the benefits of reflexology

Reflexology works quite simply, and in a highly effective, efficient way. It manages to relax and overcome any build up of excess tension in the muscles. Consequently, during a treatment, all parts of the feet will be stimulated and the significant dual effect is to relax your muscles and also to increase the efficiency of the circulation to all parts of the body. You will quickly notice the effects.

REFLEXOLOGY AND YOU

Working along holistic principles, reflexology takes into account body, mind and spirit as they are all interrelated. Whatever happens to you will affect all levels of your being, whether you notice or not. If you feel under pressure or are stressed, the effect on your body will be detrimental, as your muscles remain tense and taut, constricting the circulation and nerves, and compromising their functioning. Similarly, if you have a physical mishap, your feelings will be affected by the degree of pain you experience, the way in which the accident happened, and the effect it has on you afterwards.

Through working the hands (or feet) you are working the whole body.

Although you are working mostly on the feet in reflexology, you are affecting the whole of the body, both inside and out, through the treatment. This is achieved by working the reflexes to the internal organs and glands as well as to the surface of the body. It appears that you can have a more far-reaching effect by working the reflexes than by working directly on the corresponding body part. Such referral treatment, as it is sometimes called, is highly effective.

Pain in the back, for instance, may be due to the onset of structural problems in which the bones are actually out of place and misaligned, and should be checked by an osteopath, cranial osteopath or chiropractor. If the pain results from muscular problems, or if manipulation has already been done but muscular strain remains, the next step is to identify the muscles involved and then begin work to relieve the situation with massage and reflexology. As a follow-up treatment it is highly effective.

Massage has an immediate and profoundly relieving effect, but the pain and discomfort is likely to recur when the effects of the massage have worn off. Benefits resulting from working the reflexes to the relevant area of the back will be more long term than those produced by working directly on the muscles themselves. This is because through the reflexes you are stimulating the body from within, rather than exercising and soothing the muscles from without. Stimulating the reflex to a troubled area will promote healing. Reflexology uses both massage and specific stimulation of the reflexes to gain lasting relief.

Always wash your feet before any treatment to refresh the skin.

What Treatments Involve

Reflexology is not just a foot massage, but this technique is certainly incorporated. Sweeping whole hand movements on the whole foot will relax the entire person and prepare the feet for reflex work. During the working of the reflexes, massage soothes and relaxes the area where congestion or discomfort is to be found. It actively links the treatment together into a continuous, flowing whole, and manages to relax and stimulate the whole of the body while various individual parts are being treated specifically. Equally beneficial is the use of whole hand massage movements which is used to complete a reflexology treatment, and to give a feeling of well-being to the entire person before ending the session.

A reflexology session can be both relaxing and stimulating for the patient. As muscle tensions are relaxed, and the nerve supply freed from constriction, the body slips into a deep state of relaxation. At the same time, the circulation is being stimulated to bring nutrients to all parts of the body, and to remove waste products that interfere with the healthy functioning of the parts and the whole. Energy is able to flow more freely around the body, and feelings of total well-being result.

giving reflexology

Anyone new to reflexology will immediately notice a marvellous difference in the way treatment is given. Instead of being seen as an assembly of parts with one or two needing a quick overhaul, the whole body is considered, and the whole is carefully fine-tuned to get you back into shape. It is the recognition of the way in which every part of the body interracts with another that makes reflexology such a success.

THE HOLISTIC APPROACH

Reflexology works on the whole of the body, stimulating the reflexes to the internal organs, glands and body parts, as well as massaging the outside of the body. Through working on your feet as a whole, healing is stimulated throughout the body rather than just in one part that may well be influenced, or have influence on, other parts or systems. This is what makes the holistic approach of natural medicine so completely effective.

When you have a problem, natural therapies do not address you as a machine - repairing or replacing the part that does not work, but treat you in your entirety to deal with the cause of the problem, rather than merely alleviating the symptoms locally. If you have a raging toothache you may be able to relieve it by taking painkillers, but you will not make the abscess to go away unless you deal with the poison that gave rise to it in the first place.

Make sure that your partner is comfortable, with pillows under their head, neck and knees for support.

Locating the Problem

If you develop a headache you may or may not know its cause. Where in your body is the trouble seated? Does it come from tension in your neck or lower down your spine, from digestive disturbance, or even from held-in tension in your legs? Many headaches have such roots even though we do not notice the beginning of the trouble until the pounding in our head attracts our attention. Recurrent headaches happen because their causes have not been recognized and dealt with.

If you massage the reflexes to the head you might give temporary relief, but you will probably not cure the headache. Stimulating a related reflex, however, is effective. You will only find it if you work the whole foot, and do not spot-work for one symptom.

The feet must be where you can comfortably reach them.

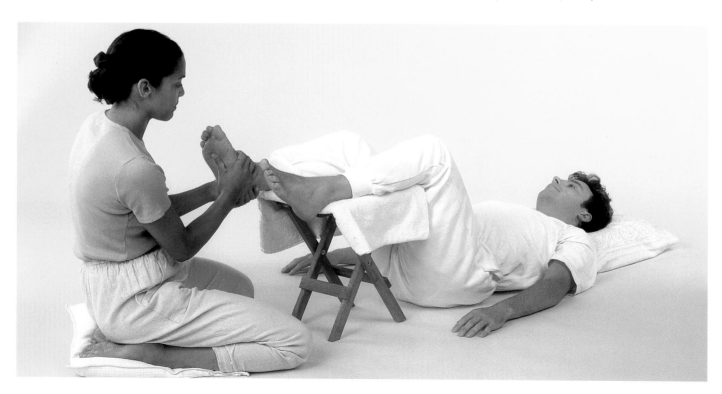

basic techniques

Make sure that the room you are going to use is warm and quiet without any interruptions from telephones, faxes, pagers, you name it, with people coming and going. Once you have created the right conditions you can proceed with the basic techniques for the hands and feet. They make an excellent introduction. Once mastered you will quickly pick up reflexology's movements. They are straightforward and highly effective.

HAND AND FOOT TREATMENTS

1 To thumbwalk, hold your two thumbs straight up and bend one at a time at the first joint. Repeat several times.

2 The therapeutic movement is on the firm downward press with your thumb bent. Use one hand only.

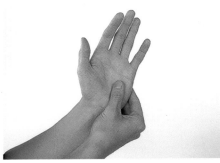

3 Slide forward as you straighten your thumb. The technique is sometimes called caterpillar walking.

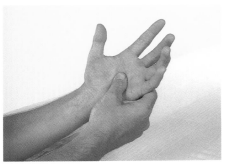

4 To rotate, place your thumb on part of your hand and gently rotate it on the spot. Try exerting a little more pressure.

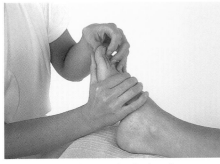

5 To fingerwalk, use the index finger. The technique is as for thumbwalking but using one or more fingers.

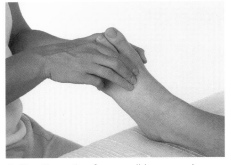

6 Continue the fingerwalking exercise, but this time keep the three middle fingers together.

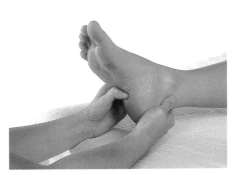

7 To pinpoint, use your thumb and fingers. Move them together and apart, like a pincer, then press in the thumb.

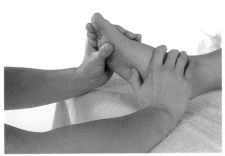

8 To hold and support, use one hand to hold the foot securely. This will help you give more sensitive treatment.

Getting Relaxed

Make sure that you find a comfortable position for the person whose feet you are going to treat. They may be lying on a sofa, with cushions to support their back, head and neck in one corner, and their feet at the opposite end so that you can reach them easily. If they are sitting in an armchair, find an upright chair or stool of a suitable height and support their legs with a cushion. Be sure you sit comfortably too.

warm-up foot massage

It is always of great benefit to the patient if their feet are massaged right at the beginning of a reflexology treatment. This gives them time to get used to your touch, and to leave behind the cares of the day. Their overall mood is extremely important, and you should do your best to make sure that they are feeling relaxed. Give another massage at the end of the reflex work, and then at the end of the session.

THE FIRST STEPS

Massage prepares the feet for reflex work: it warms and relaxes the tissues, accustoms the receiver to your touch and soothes and relaxes the whole body. Massage will also loosen tensions in the muscles and stimulate the blood supply to and around the feet. Consequently, when the reflex points are worked the tissues will not be strained, and they will respond fully. Do not miss out this stage, as it is extremely important.

During treatment use plenty of massage to link the movement from one reflex area to the next, to soothe and relax the foot in between working the reflex points, which may produce sensations of tenderness, and use it where any tenderness or discomfort is found.

Oil and Massage Treatments

When you have covered all the reflex points, end with a massage on both feet to instil a sense of deep relaxation. Use 2–3 drops of essential oils mixed in with some almond oil. Do not use the oil beforehand because once on your hands it will counter any accurate hand reflexology movements.

When it comes to massage movements, note that there is no one set sequence. The prime object is to fit movements together in a way that is customized to your individual needs. They should feel good to you and to the person you are working on. The first few movements are good as an introduction, and you should always rotate the ankles as this frees up the blood and nerve supply through the ankle to the foot.

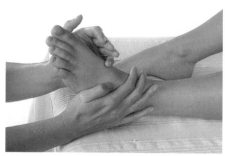

1 Stroking movements, or effleurage, are just as they sound, sweeping and soothing, and are good all over the foot. Add wherever appropriate.

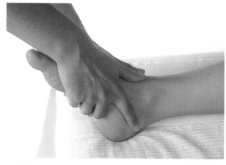

2 To make spreading movements on the top of the foot, draw your thumbs off sideways, keeping your fingers still.

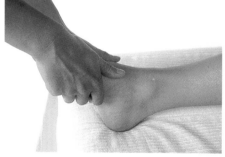

3 Repeat the first movement, gradually working your way down the foot with each subsequent repetition.

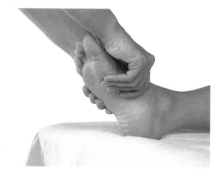

4 To cover the sole of the foot, start in the same position as before, but this time draw your fingers off sideways, keeping your thumbs still.

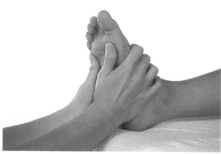

5 Finally, massage into the ball of the foot with your thumbs.

6 To knead, use a movement like kneading dough and work into the sole of the foot using the lower section of your fingers.

7 To rotate the ankle, rotate the foot clockwise several times, feeling gently as you proceed so that you do not force stiff ankles, but you do manage to exercise the joint.

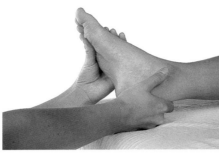

8 Repeat the ankle rotation, but this time in an anti-clockwise direction.

9 To make vigorous, fast movements, massage both sides of the foot, running your hands freely up and down the whole length of the foot. Repeat this technique several times.

10 With your hands in the same starting position, this time move them alternately up and down from the top to the sole of the foot so that the foot tips from side to side. Do take great care not to twist the ankle.

11 With your hands palms up on either side of the foot, move them quickly to and fro, to exercise and loosen the ankle. When this movement is done correctly, the foot will waggle around.

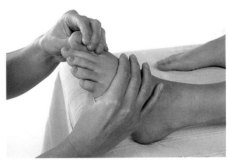

12 To rotate the toes, begin with the big toe, holding it securely but not too tightly and gently rotate. Repeat this movement carefully with each toe.

13 To relax the diaphragm, hold the foot and bring it down on to the thumb of your other hand, and lift it off again. Next, move your thumb one step to the side and repeat the movement.

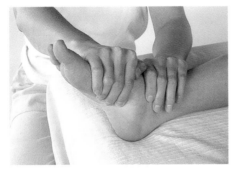

14 To make a spinal twist, the hand on the ankle remains still while the other, lower hand moves to and fro across the top of the foot, round the instep and finally back again. Repeat several times.

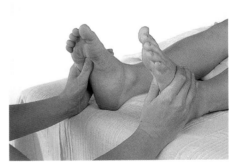

15 For good breathing and to relax the solar plexus reflex, place your thumbs in the natural dent. As your partner breathes in, press in with your thumbs and as they breathe out, release them.

reflexology routines
reflexology routines

reflexology routines

The following pages are a clear step-by-step illustration of the full reflexology routine, which should be performed on your partner before you begin treating specific problems. In fact, the full routine covers most key parts of the body, and includes the spine, toes, chest, abdomen, pelvis and limbs. Depending on how it is given, it can be an invigorating or relaxing beginning to a treatment.

To see how all these parts of the body are reflected and simultaneously contained in your hands and feet, look at the detailed charts shown at the end of this chapter. It is immediately clear that both hands and feet are much more than themselves; they have become highly detailed referral points, in essence being like blueprints to all parts of the body. It obviously takes time to remember the exact wherabouts of all these areas, and to feel confident that you are treating the lungs alone and not, say, the adjacent stomach or even the spleen. Part of the art of reflexology is sensitivity and pinpoint accuracy.

In order to guarantee such accuracy it is important that your hands are not covered with any essential oils or they will glide and slide everywhere, which is not what you want. Also note that though this routine runs before more detailed work, it is not something that can or should be rushed. Besides fully toning up your partner, and making sure that their body is fully tuned in and responsive to what is happening, the routine is an excellent way of helping them relax. It gears up the body for what is to come. Interestingly, many patients claim that this is the high point of the treatment; and it can certainly be highly effective.

When you start giving such treatment there is invariably a stop-start feel to it as you have to remember precisely what to do next. The joy of working with an experienced practitioner is that one routine seamlessly and effortlessly flows into the next, and your body quickly learns to yield itself up to the continuous waves of well-being that the routine soon imparts.

the full reflexology routine

The following step-by-step illustration of the full reflexology routine should be performed on your partner before moving to treat specific problem areas. Always try to treat the areas of the body in exactly the same order as outlined here, from the spine to the limbs. Just occasionally, as a help, fine lines have been drawn on the photographs to highlight the important reflex points.

1 To treat the spine, thumbwalk up and down the spinal lline as shown here. Repeat several times.

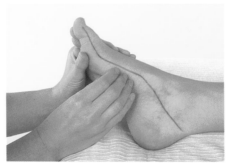

2 Use the three middle fingers to fingerwalk across the spine/instep in stages, from big toe to heel.

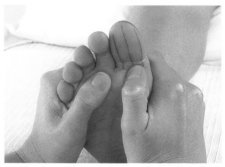

3 To treat the head and neck, work up the back of the big toe, thumbwalking in three lines to cover the whole area.

4 Use your index finger to fingerwalk down the front of the big toe again in three lines. Next, work up the side of the big toe with your thumb.

5 For the other side of the toe, approach from the back and tuck your thumb between this toe and the second one. Now thumbwalk the side of neck.

6 Change hands and, using your other thumb, approach from the front and tuck it in between the big toe and second toe again. Work up this side to the top.

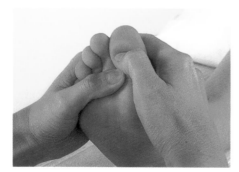

7 Find the centre of the whorls of the big toe print and position your hand for pinpointing the pituitary reflex. Press gently at first, as it can be tender.

8 Work around the neck of the big toe in two semi-circles: thumbwalk the back part first of all.

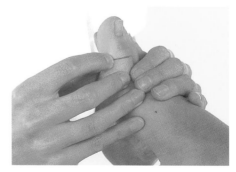

9 Fingerwalk right around the front of the big toe, but this time using your index finger.

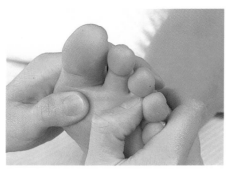

10 For the smaller toes, follow exactly the same routine as for the big toe. These toes can be covered in one line to each surface. Thumbwalk up the back. Fingerwalk down the front.

11 Thumbwalk up one side of the toe. Always approach the side from the front. Next, change hands and then gradually work up the other side of the same toe.

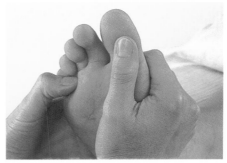

12 Finally, commence thumbwalking the ridge under the little toes. Repeat several times, then culminate this routine.

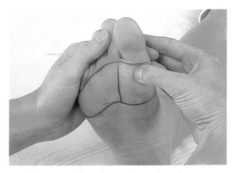

13 To treat the chest, thumbwalk horizontally in from the instep under the big toe, starting just next to the neck. Repeat just below the first line, bordering on it. Continue thumbwalking lines like this until you have covered the ball under the big toe down to the diaphragm line.

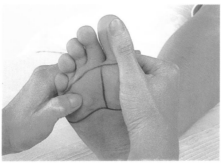

14 Thumbwalk horizontally in from the outside of the foot under the little toes, starting just below the ridge. Cover the whole of this area in the same way as described in step 13.

15 Next, work carefully along the diaphragm line under the big toe, and follow the natural line up between the big and second toes to the actual base of the toes.

16 Work along the diaphragm line from the outside of the foot, and when you finally meet the line between the big and the second toes you can continue up this line to the base of the toes.

17 Starting from just under the big toe, thumbwalk the whole diaphragm line.

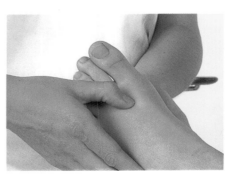

18 When on the top of the foot, you may now commence thumbwalking right along each individual channel that exists between the bones which lead up to the toes.

19 The last step involves using the three middle fingers together to fingerwalk the whole of the top of the foot. You should work from the base of the toes right up the foot.

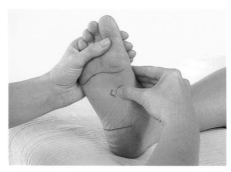

20 To treat the abdomen, thumbwalk from the medial edge, under the big toe, to the outer edge in horizontal lines as you did for the chest, each line bordering the previous one.

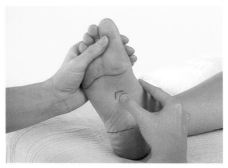

21 Next thumbwalk in diagonal lines covering the same area, as described in the previous step.

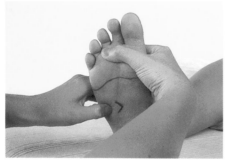

22 Now swiftly change hands and thumbwalk in horizontal lines. You should now be working from the outside of the foot towards the inner (medial) edge, as previously shown.

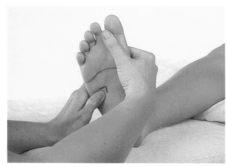

23 Employing the same thumb, begin thumbwalking in diagonal lines and gradually work from the outside towards the inner edge, covering the whole area, as before.

24 While referring to the foot chart, gently begin rotating the reflex to the adrenal glands, pushing in under the tendon running down from the big toe.

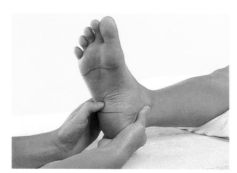

25 Work along what is called the ileo-caecal valve reflex, using the inner corner of your thumb to pinpoint it.

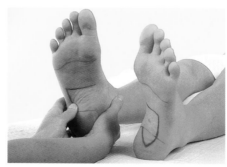

26 Thumbwalk the path of the colon, starting on the right foot at the bottom of the colon line.

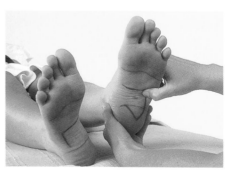

27 Continue on to the left foot, but change from the left hand to right hand at the point above.

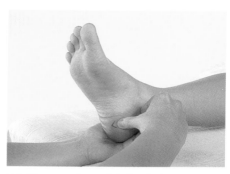

28 To treat the pelvis, begin by thumbwalking the heel across the sole in horizontal, overlapping lines. Note that this can actually be quite hard work.

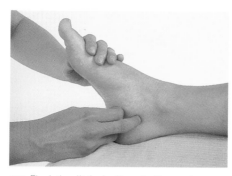

29 Find the little hollow halfway along a diagonal line between the centre of the ankle bone and the right angle of the heel on the inside of the foot, and rotate this point with your middle fingertip. Do not apply too much pressure.

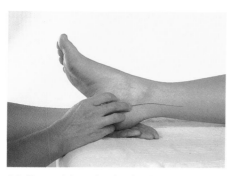

30 From this point, begin the fingerwalking movement using the same finger, going up the line running behind the ankle and up the leg.

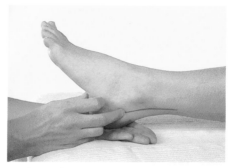

31 Now find the point described in step 2, but on the outside of the foot. Rotate it with the middle finger of your other hand and then fingerwalk up the outside of the ankle and leg, just as you did on the inside.

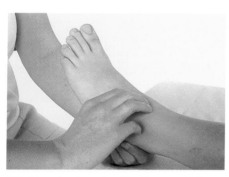

32 Now begin using the three middle fingers, and start fingerwalking right across the top of the ankle.

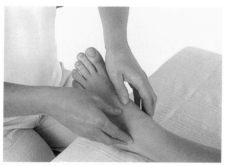

33 Continue the fingerwalking movement, going right round the ankle bone, using the same fingertips.

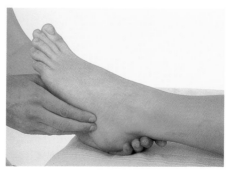

34 Finally, refer to the foot charts to find the hip/knee reflex, and work it by fingerwalking two fingers together.

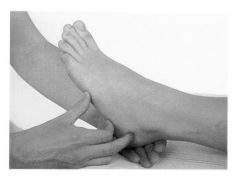

35 To treat the limbs, work the outside of the foot, then begin massaging the relevant cross reflex.

Key Tips

Although the routine is described for one foot only. Remember to treat the other foot too. Start with the right foot, as here, then when you have completed the routine, move to the left foot and duplicate what you have done (reversing hands and movements as appropriate to the shape of the left foot). It is always a good idea to start with general foot massage and to incorporate some soothing massage movements into the routine.

tension releasers

We collect far too much tension in our necks. If you are not aware of how much neck tension can accumulate, put your hands to either side of your neck and begin to massage gently. If it feels in any way tight or uncomfortable you may benefit from this sequence as your partner carefully works your feet. When the neck muscles are tense and tight they may lead to pain, noises in the ears, and tired eyes. These releasers will cure that.

NECK AND SHOULDER TENSION

1 Treat neck tension by thumbwalking up and round the side of the big toe, then up the necks of all toes.

2 Thumbwalk right along the ridge immediately under the toes. Make sure that you are right on top of this ridge.

Self-help

Thumbwalk along the base of your fingers, and repeat several times.

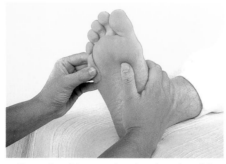

3 Ease shoulder tension by thumbwalking along the line of the shoulders in horizontal, overlapping lines.

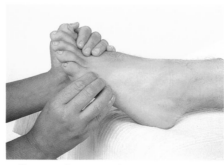

4 Fingerwalk across the same area on the top of the foot with three fingers. Fingerwalk around the mid-back (from the little toe to halfway down the foot).

5 To relax the diaphragm, position your thumb on the diaphragm line. Hold the foot, bring it down on to the thumb and lift it off again. Repeat across the foot.

6 Ease whiplash injuries by thumbwalking between the big and second toes.

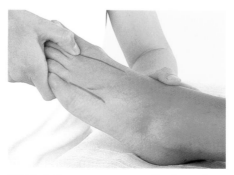

7 Work the same area on the top of the feet with your thumb.

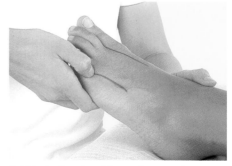

8 Work the shoulder reflex on the top and the bottom of the feet.

BACKACHE RELIEVERS

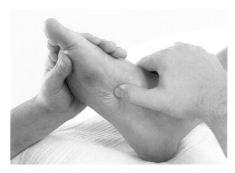

1 Thumbwalk up and down the spine, gently supporting the outer edge of the foot as you work.

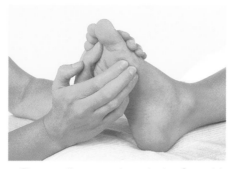

2 Fingerwalk across the spinal reflex with three fingers together, right down the instep in stripes.

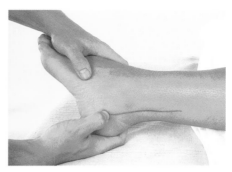

3 Thumbwalk up the helper reflexes for the lower back, behind the ankle bones on either side.

RELIEVING REPETITIVE STRAIN

1 Thumbwalk up the back and sides of the second and third toes for the eye reflex. This will also relieve neck tension.

2 Work the shoulder reflexes thoroughly by using the thumbwalking technique. Then fingerwalk across the same area on the top of the foot, with the three middle fingers together.

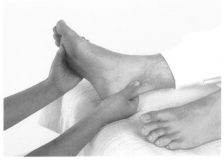

3 Rotate the ankles to ease any aching wrists and to stimulate the healing process within the joints.

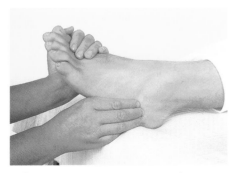

4 For the penultimate step, work across and down the outer foot on both feet to relax shoulders, arms, legs and knees.

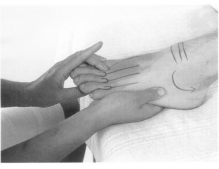

5 Work the lymph system on both feet. Fingerwalk down the lines from the toes to the ankle. Then work round the ankle.

Self-help

Use the detailed hand chart on page 175 when trying to locate the relevant reflex on your hands to give temporary, quick relief for your particular problem. The key point to remember at all times when dealing with repetitive strain is that there is no one particular sequence of movements that guarantees special help. It is completely up to you to work out exactly which part of your body is suffering from the strain. You must then set about locating the relevant reflex on the charts. Then proceed with the treatment.

stress and pain relievers

Excessive stress lies somewhere behind most troubles and illness. If your adrenalin runs at a high level for long periods, with little chance of appropriate action, your adrenal glands will become depleted. Your breathing will also become too rapid or will be restricted and shallow, and your digestion will be upset or strained in some way. When this happens, you know it is time to act and start curing yourself.

RELIEVING GENERAL STRESS

1 Relax the diaphragm by bringing the foot down on to the thumb of your other hand, and then lifting off again. Repeat, moving your thumb to the outside.

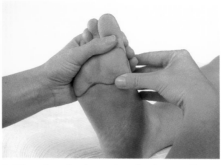

2 Thumbwalk along the diaphragm line. Tension collects in the diaphragm, causing tightness. When the diaphragm is relaxed the abdominal organs are stimulated.

3 Work the lung reflexes on the chest area so that once the diaphragm is relaxed, breathing can be increased. This will help with relaxation.

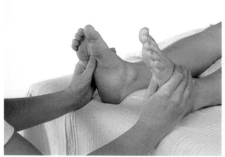

4 With both feet together put your thumbs in the diaphragm line. Press in on the in-breath, and release on the out.

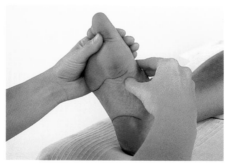

5 Thumbwalk the stomach area and the whole of the instep, which is the abdominal area. This will help digestion.

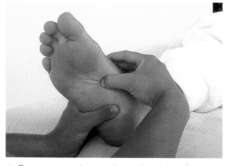

6 Rotate gently on the adrenal reflex.

7 Work the neck reflex on the neck of the toes where tension collects.

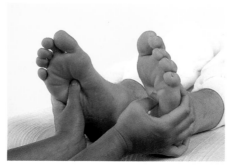

8 Ease stress from anger by working the solar plexus reflexes on both feet.

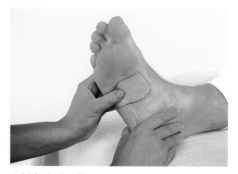

9 Work the liver area.

BACK PAIN

1 Work along the spine and find the tender parts. Work these to try to disperse some of the congestion.

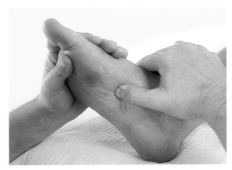

2 Work the adrenal gland reflexes on both feet. These glands deal with inflammation and aid good muscle tone when working effectively.

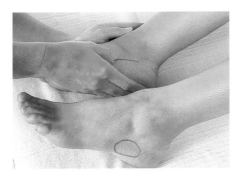

3 For lower back trouble, work the helper area by carefully rotating with your thumb.

NERVE PAIN

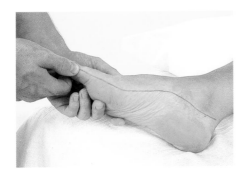

1 Thumbwalk along the spine for the central nervous system in the spinal cord.

2 Find the local area, for example, for the neck, work the cervical vertebrae and find the part of the neck of the toes that is tender.

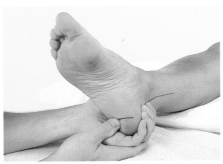

3 To treat sciatic pain, begin working the sciatic reflex as clearly shown in the foot chart.

CRAMP

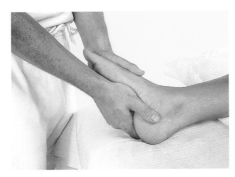

1 Hold the area and massage the appropriate cross reflex. For example, for cramp in the calf, massage the cross reflex on the lower arm.

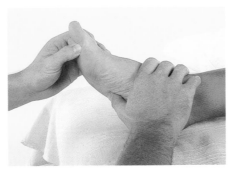

2 Work the parathyroid reflexes round the neck of the big toe.

TOOTHACHE

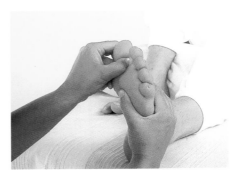

1 Find the toe or finger that has much tenderness, and work that area carefully but thoroughly.

headaches, breathing and sleeping

The three key elements to our continued health and well-being are breathing and sleeping, and a clear head. Poor breathing, possibly caused by too much tension, can easily result in headaches though. A bad night's sleep can also have unpleasant side effects, leading to a heavy head the next day. The following techniques are all excellent ways of helping overcome such problems.

1 Ease headaches by working the hypothalamus reflex, which controls the release of endorphins for pain relief.

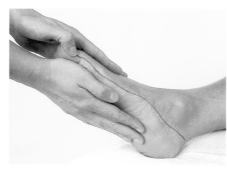

2 Work down the spine to take pressure away from the head. This will draw energy down the body.

3 Work the cervical spine on the big toe. Work the neck of all the toes to relieve any tension.

4 Aid efficient breathing by working the whole chest area on the bottom of the feet to relieve the chest and lungs.

5 Work the air passages. This prompts them to clear themselves.

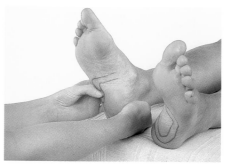

6 Work the ileo-caecal valve and the whole of the colon because this will help balance mucus levels.

7 For a good night's sleep hold the foot with your outside hand and bring it down on to the thumb of your other hand and lift off. Move your thumb one step to the side and repeat.

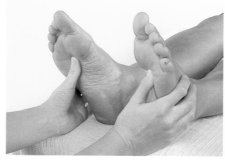

8 Do the solar plexus breathing exercise: take both feet together and position your thumbs in the centre of the diaphragm line. Press in on the in-breath, and release on the out.

Self-help

For self-help gently massage the solar plexus reflex in the palms of your hands.

reproductive problems
Reflexology is an excellent way of keeping your reproductive side in good working order. Surprisingly, it is far too often ignored, yet there are simple but highly effective techniques that will cover a wide range of problems including menstrual cramps, painful breasts, and even attacks of nausea. Note that all these reflexology movements concentrate on the feet, particularly on the area around the ankle.

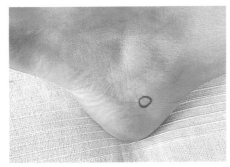

1 Work the ovaries or testes on the outside of the feet.

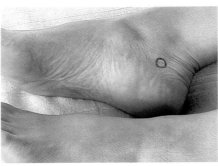

2 Work the uterus or prostate gland on the inside of the feet.

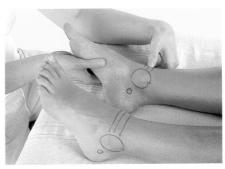

3 Work the fallopian tubes or vas deferens across the top of the ankle.

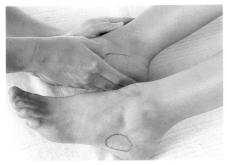

4 Ease menstrual cramps by working the lower spine for nerves to the uterus.

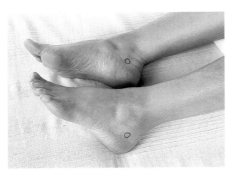

5 Work the uterus reflex area on the inside of the feet.

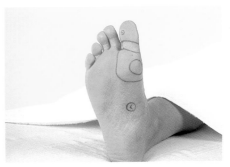

6 Work the glands on both feet, on the areas marked above.

7 Ease painful breasts by fingerwalking up the chest area on top of the foot with three fingers together.

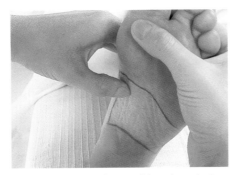

8 Relieve nausea by working the whole abdomen, especially where it seems tender. Do this gently and with care.

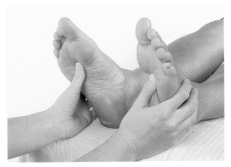

9 Do the solar plexus breathing exercise: press in with your thumbs, and release on the out.

colds, throats and sinuses

It is virtually impossible to avoid minor colds and the whole battery of side effects that go with them. Suddenly you are laid low by relentless outbreaks of sneezing and then sore throats and sinus problems. Fortunately, you do not have to grin and bear it. There are some excellent reflexology techniques that will help you overcome all these nasty extras. They will soon have you on the road to recovery.

1 Ease colds by working the chest area fully to encourage clear breathing.

2 Begin with the big toe and work the toe tops to clear the sinuses. Pinpoint the pituitary gland in the centre of the big toes for the endocrine system.

3 Work the upper lymph system to stimulate the immune system.

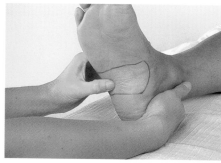

4 Work the small intestines to aid elimination of toxins and uptake of nutrients. Then work on the colon to aid elimination.

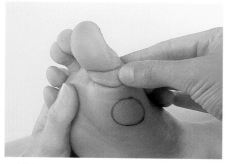

5 Help sore throats by working the upper lymph system, the throat by working the neck, and the thymus gland for the immune system.

6 Rotate the adrenal reflex in the direction of the arrow.

7 Work the trachea and the larynx to stimulate them. Work the thyroid area in the area of the chest under the big toe.

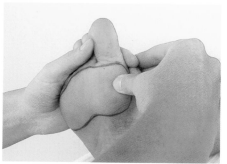

8 Ease sinus problems by working the whole chest area in order to aid good respiration.

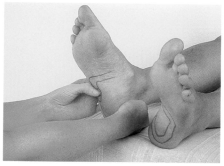

9 Pinpoint the ileo-caecal valve to balance mucus levels. Work the whole chest and rotate the adrenal reflex.

improving the digestion

The digestive system is all too frequently overlooked, yet it is vital that it is operating in a smooth and efficient way. To avoid any irritating problems, try carrying out the following quick and easy routines, and make them part of your daily or weekly reflexology session. One of the extra benefits is that they will help fine-tune the rest of you, leaving you feeling wonderfully calm, refreshed and invigorated.

1 Aid any indigestion by working the solar plexus to relax the nerves to the stomach area.

2 Work the stomach, where digestion really begins. Then work the duodenum, the first section of the small intestines.

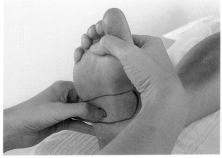

3 Work the liver and the gall bladder: the liver area is shown above, with the thumb rotating on the gall bladder reflex. These deal with digestion of fats.

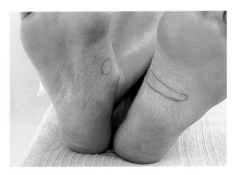

4 Work the pancreas which regulates the blood sugar levels and also helps aid digestion.

5 Ease constipation by working the diaphragm area in order to relax the abdomen.

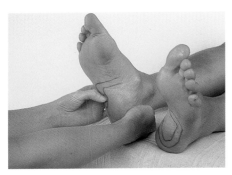

6 Pinpoint the ileo-caecal valve, which links small and large intestines. Work the colon or large intestine.

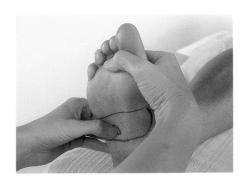

7 Work the liver and gall bladder: the liver area is shown above, with the thumb rotating on the gall bladder.

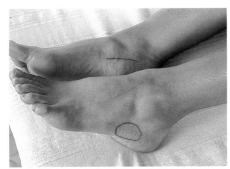

8 Work the lower spine and its helper areas for the crucial nerve supply to the colon.

9 Work the adrenals for muscle tone. Rotate the reflex with your thumb in the direction of the arrows.

charts
The foot charts are marvellous guidelines for interpretation. When you find a tender part of the foot you can look for that part on the charts and see approximately which reflex the tenderness lies on. Do bear in mind though, that every pair of feet is different and will not be the same shape as your chart. Also, the charts are two-dimensional and your body is three-dimensional. Nonetheless, the charts are every reflexologer's means to success.

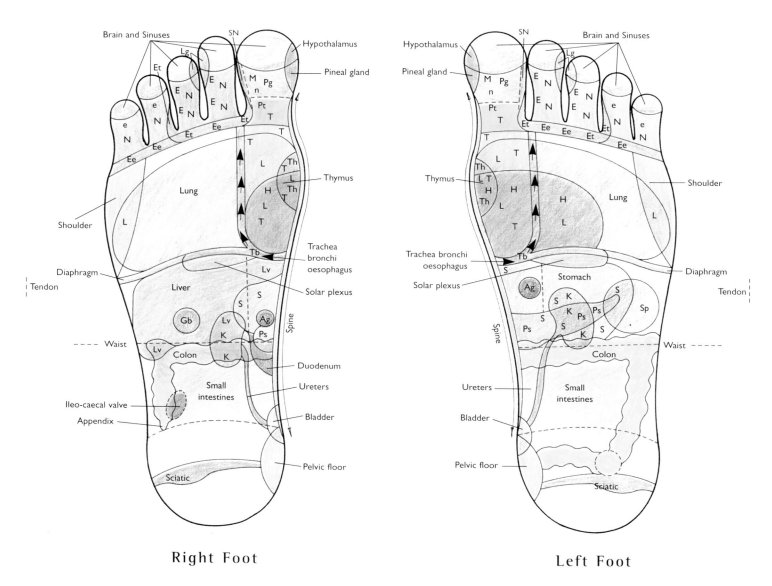

Right Foot   **Left Foot**

Key

Ag	Adrenal glands	**H**	Heart	**N**	Neck	**Sp**	Spleen
e	Ears	**K**	Kidneys	**n**	Nose	**S**	Stomach
Et	Eustachian tubes	**Lg**	Lachrymal glands	**Ps**	Pancreas	**Tb**	Trachea bronchi oesophagus
Ee	Eye/Ear helper	**Lv**	Liver	**Pt**	Para-thyroid	**Th**	Thymus
E	Eyes	**L**	Lungs	**Pg**	Pituitary glands	**T**	Thyroid
Gb	Gall bladder	**M**	Mouth	**SN**	Side of neck		

TOP AND SIDES OF FOOT

The spinal reflex (bottom) is especially important and should always be massaged, and the reflex worked thoroughly. Not only is our spinal column our main boney support but it also contains the spinal cord, and through the central nervous system the whole body may be treated on the spinal reflex.

HAND CHART

The hands reflect all the body, as do the feet. They are a very different shape to feet, but once you have adjusted to that and learnt the basic layout, the location of reflexes is quite straightforward. Use the reflexes on the hand when it is impossible to work the feet, such as when only the hands are accessible or when the feet are damaged or diseased.

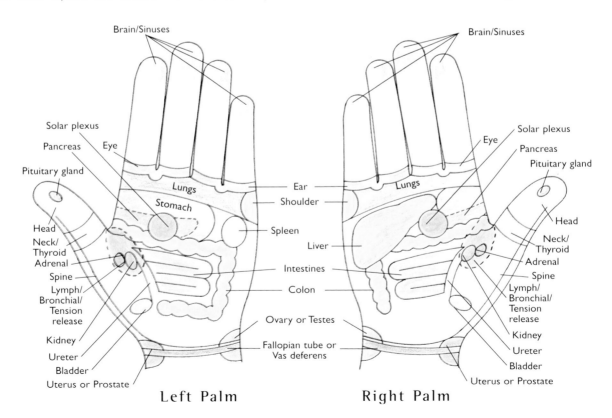

the path to inner harmony

T here are many keys to creating the right you, the you that is healthy and alert, that can relax and stay calm, that sails confidently through interviews, and that knows when to step out of everyday life and enter an inner world of harmony and meditation. The secret of success starts within, knowing how to build up a strong, confident you that is in touch not just with the world out there, but your own private world of spiritual quiet. In the following pages the Alexander technique, t'ai chi, yoga, and the art of meditation all bring special ingredients to help you understand your own being, and the ways it can be helped.

a l e x a n d e r t e c h n i q u e
alexander techn

alexander technique

People tend to associate the Alexander technique with relaxation, alternative medicine, body massage and with "posture". Yet it is actually much more than that.

One way towards a clearer understanding of the technique is to begin by stating what it is not. The Alexander technique does not train its teachers to make a medical diagnosis of their students, nor does it focus on any division between the mind and body. The technique believes in the indivisibility of the two and in their psycho-physical unity. Above all, the technique's main objective is to encourage people to use themselves, their bodies and minds more effectively in their day-to-day lives.

The technique's preventive role is an efficient tool which maintains tone and general well-being. It also helps to improve posture and relieve related pain. In fact it can assist people with stress-related illnesses such as respiratory and gastro-intestinal problems, as well as psychosomatic conditions. It can help those who suffer from psychological distress, such as depression, as well as facilitating recovery from accidents and injuries. The technique can even assist people with mechanical problems, such as frozen shoulder, tennis elbow and arthritis. Above all, it helps promote muscle tone and general well-being while encouraging poise and flexibility. The technique aids the well in addition to those with ailments.

the alexander technique principles

Once you start studying the technique, it quickly becomes clear that it helps you in all kinds of ways that other alternative remedies do not. That is not because it is superior, but because of its key agenda. As shown here, it helps us focus on our minds and bodies in new ways, and on aspects of our being that we might take for granted. The technique gets us back to basics.

Primary Control

"Misuse" occurs by contracting the muscles of the neck and pulling the head back and down into the shoulders. This has the twin effect of actually compressing the spine and narrowing and shortening the stature, creating tensions throughout the body. It is definitely something to be avoided.

Frederick Matthias Alexander discovered that the relationship between the head, the neck and the back, or "primary control", mechanically controlled movement and co-ordination in the whole body. To make ourselves aware of this consciously in our daily activities is the basis of good use.

See how this model is misusing himself. He is leaning over to the right, shortening and creating an imbalance in his body.

Inhibition

In its psychological-physiological sense, inhibition means a fast-moving yet natural control of your reactions, suppressing and smothering any possible spontaneity.

However, Alexander discovered that if he managed to stop himself from behaving in his habitual way, he could choose how he wished to respond to a stimulus. If someone rings the doorbell, your immediate response may be to go straight to the door. In doing so, you will be responding habitually. If you stop yourself from responding automatically, you then choose exactly how you will approach the door with the minimum effort.

Concepts

The concept of end-gaining is extremely important in the work of Alexander technique teachers. Alexander realized that the habits he was encountering were far more deep-rooted and powerful than he had at first thought. The most serious of these was the tendency to try to react impulsively – end-gaining. End-gaining means reacting immediately and too quickly to a stimulus, without thinking. You respond by wanting something to happen, and become interested in the end result instead of being in the present. A typical example is if you are going to be late for an appointment and start to worry about the consequences. You get worked up during this process, forgetting that you might be sitting on a train, and that things are happening around you. In effect you are letting your thoughts take the situation into the future, instead of being in the "here and now", in the present.

Cutting yourself off from your environment has inevitable consequences for body positioning. It tends to lead to a pulling back of the head, a rounding of the back, a tightening of the legs and a loss of connection between the arms and the back. The gaze becomes fixed, the breath held. Essentially, the whole person is affected, both in mind and in body.

Alexander suggests you should use your "means-whereby". To put Alexander's conclusion into context, if we accept that we cannot change circumstances, we can change our approach to our bodies and allow ourselves to experience the new. It is then possible to learn to be in the moment rather than the past or the future, and to maintain a sense of inner balance and unity.

Direction

Directions are signals given by the brain to parts of the body prior to or during physical action. It is possible to alter these signals to promote a positive change. You will find that the combination of direction and inhibition enables one to transform habitual ways of moving and eliminate old patterns of misuse.

Note how this model is walking. Her head, neck and back are all correctly aligned. Her arms are free to move in a relaxed way.

Natural Poise

Nothing is more elegant and enviable than someone with perfect poise. It is something most of us have when young, but sadly it can be quickly lost to laziness and bad postural habits. In fact, it is quite easy to be totally unaware just how bad our posture is. At various times during the day it is worth freezing your movements, and taking a good look at yourself. You will be surprised at how often you fall well short of the ideal. Sitting at work is probably the one situation when your back is almost always wrongly positioned, becoming increasingly hunched, tense and stiff. Once you have ascertained exactly when and how you are going wrong, you can start putting matters right. If in any doubt, just look at young children. They instinctively know how to move gracefully and effortlessly without strain. That is something we should all try to emulate.

This child carries his toy close to his body, allowing it to lengthen and relax. This ensures good nervous energy and blood flow and allows full expansion of the lungs for breathing.

Primary Directions

- Think of freeing the neck.
- Let the head go forward and up.
- Let the back lengthen and widen.

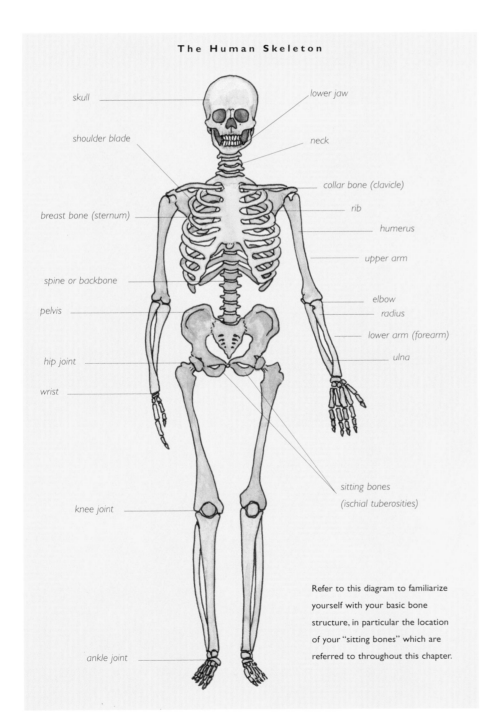

The Human Skeleton

skull
lower jaw
shoulder blade
neck
collar bone (clavicle)
rib
breast bone (sternum)
humerus
upper arm
spine or backbone
elbow
radius
pelvis
lower arm (forearm)
hip joint
ulna
wrist
knee joint
sitting bones
(ischial tuberosities)
ankle joint

Refer to this diagram to familiarize yourself with your basic bone structure, in particular the location of your "sitting bones" which are referred to throughout this chapter.

Note how this child is using his joints to squat, and how he simultaneously holds the plastic bag quite effortlessly.

"Possession of property ... a means to happiness not an end."
Thomas Jefferson

putting the alexander technique into practice
putting the alexander technique

putting the alexander technique into practice

A certain, rightful degree of commitment is paramount during a course of lessons because the older and more set in your ways you are, the longer it can take to change, to release unnecessary muscular tension, and to re-educate the system. Success, however, is not hard to achieve but note that it will not happen overnight, and that some slight pitfalls are always going to be inevitable, so do not be put off.

For example, you may well find yourself trying to do the directions as a routine mechanical exercise when in reality success lies in the power of the body and mind uniting as one, and in the power to think about what you are doing. Do not imagine there are any short cuts, there are not. There is also the distinct possibility that you might be tempted to give up out of sheer frustration because your time scale is too unrealistically short and limiting, and you have not allowed sufficient time for a significant, quantifiable improvement. Do not be hard on yourself, and do not imagine that you can become an expert in a ridiculously short space of time. The technique deserves more respect.

What therefore follows is the identification of the main procedures that we use most often in daily life, the areas that most concern us. In fact, the use of the word "procedure" is quite deliberate because it totally avoids the suggestion of a mind-body split and maintains a sense of psycho-physical unity. The emphasis throughout is on the means of achieving these procedures, but with the minimum of muscular tension and effort. Many students have said that a course of lessons in the technique could be compared to learning to drive or learning a new language. Dedication and determination are a sure basis for total success.

use of the eyes

If you want to know something about someone, just look straight into their eyes. They reveal an amazing amount about their current frame of mind. You can easily spot the depressed, dull and lifeless by their deadpan, almost one-dimensional eyes; the totally alert looking for a lively reply; the sad; the plaintive; the cheeky; and the happy. The technique reminds you how to stay lively and alert, and in touch with the rest of the world.

STAYING ALERT

If you observe people when they are either standing or walking, they often seem to be completely locked in a private world of their own, totally unaware of their own surroundings. They have stopped communicating with that is out there. When the gaze is fixed, the breathing also tends to suffer. It becomes rather restricted and there is less freedom in the body. The gaze should therefore be directed towards the outside world, taking in information so that you are not exclusively concentrating on what is happening within.

One of the strongest habits that a teacher perceives is the tendency of certain pupils to look down, not with their eyes, but by a general collapsing motion from the neck. This is the result of a fundamental misunderstanding of the alignment of the head, the neck and the back, and the position of the joints in the body.

Note how the models in this sequence of photographs (*below*) are using their eyes. Which do you think is the correct position? Can there be any doubt?.

> "It's no good shutting your eyes if you're crossing a busy road."
> F. M. Alexander

Here children are using their eyes to look at their toys. They have not disturbed the alignment between their heads, their necks and their backs, thus maintaining their good use.

In this position, the model is breaking the alignment between her head, her neck and her back as she looks down, thus using her neck inappropriately.

Note how the model is correctly aligned. She is maintaining her length and her width. Her eyes are alert and taking in her surroundings.

Here the model is breaking at the neckline and pulling her head back to look up, disturbing the alignment between her head, neck and back.

the semi-supine position

Standing for long periods easily compresses the spine. Lying down in a semi-supine position is a way of alleviating unnecessary tensions in the muscles and joints, and should be practised every day for at least 20 minutes. It encourages a better awareness of the head-neck-back relationship. This position does not necessarily need monitoring by a teacher, and it also gives you much needed time for yourself.

THE POSITION

Try to keep your eyes alert and open. It is preferable to avoid closing them because you will probably find it quite difficult not to fall asleep, which is definitely not the point of the exercise!

During your daily 20-minute session try and give yourself the time to practise some sharp, well directed thoughts to avoid your mind from wandering and spreading out, covering other possible important issues. This session can also encourage you to put into practice your excellent skills of observation. A good practice is to go over the primary directions, and to notice if you are aware of any tension in your body and to address it without trying to correct it. That is the secret of success.

Books are used to support the head. If you have too many, however, your chin will drop and you will feel pressure on your throat.

Correspondingly, if you do not have enough books your head will tilt back and will not be properly supported.

MOVING INTO THE SEMI-SUPINE

It is preferable to lie down on a hard, carpeted surface or alternatively on a rug on the floor. Avoid beds as they will not offer you adequate support. The number of books you need will depend on their thickness, and will also vary from person to person.

To lie down on the floor, place the books far enough behind you to give enough space for the whole of your torso and your bottom. When sitting, you can place your hands palms down on the floor behind you to help you lower your back. Take care not to stiffen the arms or to hold your breath in the process. To get up, it is preferable to roll over to one side, leading with your eyes rather than your head, and following with your torso and legs. Then place the free hand flat on the floor and go on to all fours. Be careful to maintain the alignment between your head, your neck and your back and not to hold your breath. Walk your hands back so that you move your bottom back towards your heels.

Make sure that your legs are about hip-width apart and that your knees are directed towards the ceiling.

If your knees are falling out, you will probably lose the contact between the inner side of your foot and the floor.

sitting and standing

Correct posture is as much about what is right as what is wrong. It is vital that you know what to do, and what not to do. It is easy to start out with correct posture, but fall into bad habits. You must know when to correct yourself. Remember to keep a straight alignment between head, neck and back, and to keep your legs hip-width apart with knees pointing forward, in the same direction as your feet.

SITTING

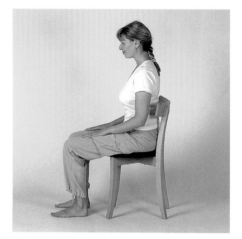

Correct: think of the shoulders going away from each other.

Incorrect: rounded shoulders and feet wrapped around chair legs.

Incorrect: arching the back, folding legs and leaning to one side.

FROM SITTING TO STANDING

It is well worth practising this basic technique several times to perfect it. You will be surprised how ingrained bad habits are. Start by placing your legs about hip-width apart. Avoid pushing firmly up with them; that is not the object. Also, make sure that your feet are flat and are not placed so far forwards that coming up to stand is in any way difficult. Finally, remember to lead with the head; that is the key to getting this technique right.

1 Here the model is relaxed, feet apart, hands resting comfortably, ready to go into the standing position.

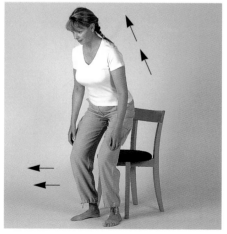

2 As she stands she has managed to keep the correct alignment between her head, neck and back.

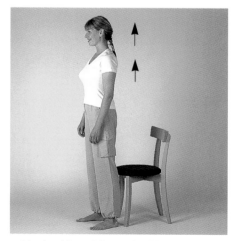

3 Having hinged from the hip, sending her knees forwards and away over her feet, she is now properly upright.

reaching and handling

It is impossible to avoid two basic movements, reaching and handling. Yet how many of us know how to do them properly, according to the Alexander technique? Reaching means keeping the alignment between the head, neck and back, whether you are low down or standing up. If you are indeed squatting, it is important that you allow your hand to lead your movement. Let everything else follow behind.

HANDLING

See how the model's weight is balanced over the feet, and how she is allowing her hand to lead her wrist and arm.

Here, the legs are straight and the head is pulled back, causing a lot of strain on the neck, and the shoulders are tense.

See how the arms remain well connected to the shoulder blades and back. Also, there is no tension in the arms and wrists.

GOING UP ON TIPTOES

When going on tiptoes correctly, the weight that is placed on the middle of the feet when standing is placed on the balls of the feet, as the head leads the body forwards and upwards. It is important to maintain the alignment between the head, the neck and the back. The breath is not held, and the eyes are alert.

Look at how this model is going on tiptoes to enable her hand to lead her arm to close the window.

Note how the model is well poised and correctly aligned. There is no undue stress on the body.

Here the head contraction is severe. The model is holding his breath, causing unnecessary tension in the body.

"monkey" or bending

The position known as the "monkey" enables us to move with more flexibility in our daily activities. It is a useful means of moving from standing to sitting or squatting, as well as helping with lifting, picking things up, working at a desk, washing, ironing, and participating in sports such as skiing and golf. The "monkey" respects the relationship between the head, neck and back.

THE POSITION

The "monkey" position might sound tricky, but it really is not. Try it slowly, see how it works, then try it again at a more natural speed. It basically involves the head moving forwards and up, and then the knees moving forwards and away over the feet to counterbalance the bottom going back over the heels, enabling the arms to move freely. It is also important to remember that when you go into "monkey" you must review your primary directions. What is more, stay alert at all times, and avoid fixing your gaze or holding your breath. Such moves will quickly undermine the marvellous effects of the "monkey".

To be more precise then, stand with your legs hip-width apart, with the feet slightly turned outwards. Your weight should be evenly distributed, neither too far forwards nor too far back on your feet. To start going into the "monkey", allow the knees to bend slightly over your feet as you tilt forwards from your hip joints, making sure your head, your neck and your back are aligned. Avoid collapsing over yourself!

One final point is to make sure you think of widening and lengthening your back as you widen across the shoulder girdle, to allow free movement and your arms to hang freely. This extra tip will ensure you enjoy the full effect of "the monkey".

This model is in the correct "monkey" position. Her head, her neck and her back are aligned. Her knees are bent forward and away from her hips.

When going into the "monkey" avoid retracting the head back and down into the spine. Note how the model has rounded her shoulders and pulled in her knees.

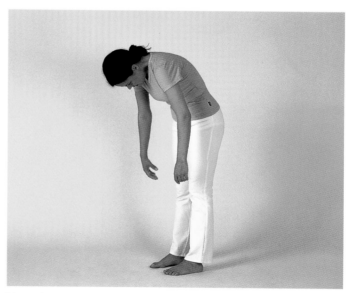

Here the model is not bending her knees as she bends forwards. Her back is collapsed over her body, and her legs are straight and braced.

everyday situations

In everyday situations it is important to pause before reacting, to make sure you are so positioned that you do not misuse yourself. The more aware you are, the more likely you will encourage muscular release through your whole system. Equally, the more at peace you are, the easier it is to apply the principles of the Alexander technique. The following excellent examples show how the "monkey" can keep you healthy.

Note how the model's back is correctly aligned, keeping to the head-neck-back principle. See how she is using her joints and allowing her widening arms to handle the dish.

How things can go wrong. Here the model has started pulling her head back. Also, her back is rounded, her legs are braced and her arms have become much too tense.

In this highly incorrect stance, the man is collapsing from his waist down as he begins works in the garden. His shoulders are far too rounded, and his head is being pulled back.

In this correct procedure, the model is neatly poised and balanced, and she is well aligned to begin her ironing. Her hand, wrist and arm are also free as she holds the iron. The other crucial point to note is how she is widening across her upper arms. It is clear that she looks balanced and feels alert.

See how the model is using the whole of his back quite correctly. He is sensibly allowing his weight to come back on to his heels, and his knees go forwards and away over his feet.

An example of how not to do it. Here he is completely out of alignment. You can sense it is not right, but why? He is actually pulling his head back, rounding the back, and holding in the arms. This position is entirely the result of bad habits. Without the Alexander technique, he would never know how to right this.

"lunge monkey"

The "lunge monkey" is similar to the "monkey" because the knees go forwards and away, and the torso tilts slightly forwards from the hip joints. Also, one foot is placed behind the other, and the legs are placed hip-width apart, enabling you to balance the upper part of your body on to the forward or the back leg whenever the need arises. In this way, your weight is placed forwards or backwards according to your activity.

BENDING

The "lunge monkey" is extremely useful when you need to lift something heavy from the floor; when you need to move an object from one side of a surface to another, for example during cooking; or when you need to push or pull something rather heavy into place.

When you adapt the "lunge monkey" it is important to remember to keep your head, your neck and your back correctly aligned. The legs must be hip-width apart, with the arms hanging freely on either side of your torso.

Also, allow your weight to move to the right on to the right foot (or to the left, as the situation demands). If moving to the left, reverse the instructions.

See how the model has collapsed badly from the waist down. Her shoulders are rounded, the legs are straight and the knees are braced, causing tension.

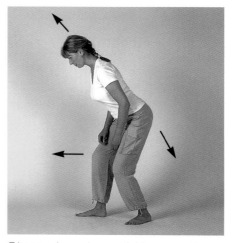

Observe how the model has gone into the "lunge monkey". Her head, neck and back are neatly aligned, and her knees are going forward away from her hips.

Note how the model has completely lost the correct alignment with her back as she squats. Her head has dropped, and her shoulders are hunched and rounded. Furthermore, she looks ill at ease and uncomfortable. There is no poise or grace. This position is definitely one to avoid.

In this correct procdure, observe how the model's head, neck and back are correctly aligned. Her shoulders are widening across her upper arms. She looks well. balanced, and fully in control of her movements. Also note how her heels are tucked in under the bottom. The position is also easy to get into.

SQUATTING

In Western societies most people find it difficult to squat in their everyday lives. Young children have very little difficulty in doing so, but as we grow older we lose the necessary flexibility to squat as our joints become less mobile.

A low "monkey" or semi-squat is the best way that an Alexander teacher can re-introduce a student to squatting over a series of lessons. To squat, follow the same guidelines as for the "monkey", but with a wider stance. Remember to maintain the alignment between the head, the neck and the back, and to allow the joints in the hips, the knees and the ankles to be free. As you go into a deeper squat you might find that your heels come off the ground. This does not present a problem as far as the technique is concerned, so long as you keep your balance. As a general rule, go only as far as you feel comfortable.

the technique in the home

The key point to note about the Alexander technique is that it is not an abstract theory that you can apply when the mood takes you. It is a specific, practical everyday guide that will help you enormously whether you are bending, squatting, lifting or carrying. It gives you terrific control whatever you are doing, injecting extra confidence that will keep you alert and relaxed.

BENDING

Note how the model is tilted forwards to get a greater range of movement. His arms are free, supported by his back.

Now he is incorrectly bending forwards from the waist. His legs are braced, and his head is pulled back.

Here the model has aligned herself nicely to make the bed. Her legs are bent, creating a greater range of movement.

SQUATTING

This model is lunge squatting to brush up dirt from the floor. She has maintained her good use, giving herself a maximum range of movement. She looks good and feels good.

Here, in an incorrect example of how you should sweep the floor, the model is badly restricting his range of movement. He is quite clearly unbalanced, and feels totally uncomfortable.

Note how this man is squatting sensibly to plant a rose bush in his garden. By placing himself at the same level as the rose, he is allowing himself a greater range of movement.

lifting and carrying
A lot of back pain is the result of lifting heavy weights. To avoid back strain, stand near to the load by placing your feet either side of it, and maintain the alignment between head, neck and back. Go into the "monkey" or "lunge monkey" and squat. Then bend your arms so that your elbows are close to your body. Make sure that you widen out across the upper arms, and avoid tension in the arms and wrists.

LIFTING

1 Once you are holding the load as closely to your body as you can, come out of a squat or lunge squat into a "monkey" before standing.

2 Lift the weight in a flowing action, that does not jar or suddenly pull against the back. If the weight proves too heavy, it is easy to bend and put it down.

3 To place the load back on the ground, reverse the process and apply the same principles, making sure that your head, neck and back are aligned.

CARRYING

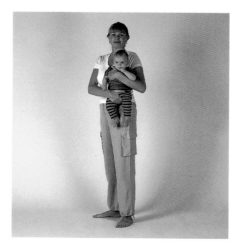

Here the model is carrying all her shopping bags in one hand, creating an imbalance as she is pulled down to the left. She is raising her right shoulder in an attempt to support her handbag.

This model is carrying her shopping bags sensibly and correctly so that they are evenly distributed on both sides. She is well balanced and able to walk freely. She looks content.

Look at the excellent way this mother is carrying her child. Her weight is evenly distributed and she is holding the child close to her body, firmly supporting his upper and lower body.

daily routines

The most surprising point about the Alexander technique is that it is not just for big, set piece movements such as lifting heavy weights, when doing it incorrectly can obviously lead to back problems. The technique even extends to the minutiae of life, routines that we completely take for granted, such as eating, drinking, and driving. If you had always wondered how they should be done, read on. These tips will make all the difference.

EATING AND DRINKING

If you are standing upright while you are drinking remember that you still need to be fully alert at all times. Therefore, make sure that you do not fix your gaze rigidly and thereby lose all communication and contact with the outside world. You also need to ensure that your head leads you away from your heels (see the section on Standing for further guidance). You will find that your shoulder girdle brings mobility to your arms, and that the pelvis provides stability which simultaneously facilitates mobility in your legs.

The very same principles also apply to eating. Whether you are going to eat something from your hand or use a fork, it is all too easy to forget your posture completely. Remember that you should not totally focus on the matter in hand, but that you must also consider your stance, alertness and poise.

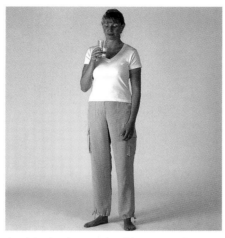

Avoid gripping or clutching your glass. Be aware of the connection with your arm, which links to your back and then into your heels. As you raise the cup to your lips, bring your weight back on to the heels, so as not to pull in your lower back. Also, bring the glass to the lips, rather than leaning down into it.

Take some time to consider how you are seated at the table and then bring the food up to your mouth, rather than the reverse. Your feet should be correctly positioned on the floor. You should also be aware of both your sitting bones, and how your back should be lengthening and widening. This position also aids digestion.

DRIVING

Most of the problems experienced by drivers are due to fixed postures, long journeys and poor seating support.

Too many people who spend huge amounts of time driving find themselves constricted by the position of the steering wheel and the pedals. Such a cramped environment is bound to lead to stress and strain on the back, and equally on the arms and legs.

When choosing a car take time to see whether the seat is firm and supportive. If you already own a car and it does not have a lumbar support adjustment, you can use a wedge-shaped cushion to give you adequate support in the lumbar area and the pelvis. It makes a vital difference.

You should be able to reach the pedals quite easily. A wedge-shaped cushion is extremely useful to avoid a poor, slumping position.

See how the model is badly collapsing forward, how the neck is being strained and the arms are rigidly tense. Such a position will cause lots of discomfort.

office work
Before reading it is important to spend some time considering exactly how you are going to sit in order to avoid badly slumping, which is very easy to do, especially in a big old comfortable armchair. Once you get drawn into what you are reading it is virtually certain that you will completely forget about your posture. It is vitally important that you do not end up creating all kinds of stresses and strains in your body.

READING AND WRITING

When you are sitting at your desk or at a table, it is important that you adjust your chair in such a way that your lower arms and hands can be placed on the surface of your table or desk at a right angle. If your chair is too close you are likely to end up lifting your shoulders to adjust your arms. If your chair is too high, you will probably find that you start slumping. You must also avoid crossing your legs, and do make sure that your feet remain comfortably flat on the floor.

A useful trick when reading is to use a sloping board to avoid slumping over your desk or table.

Note how the model is holding her body badly with her arm, and how her legs are folded, offering no support.

Keep the alignment between your head, your neck and your back.

This model is firmly gripping the pen, causing tension in her wrist and hand.

Here the model is tensing her wrist, hand and arm, restricting her movement.

DESKWORK

An increasing number of people are complaining of neck and shoulder tension, wrist problems and back pain resulting from their working environment. Some cases are directly linked to badly designed furniture, awkward or unfavourable sitting positions and immobility. In other instances, although chairs and work surfaces are good, the posture is poor. You must therefore remember your primary directions: the head, neck and back should be aligned, and the head should be lengthening away from the sitting bones.

How not to do it. See how the model is slumping badly, causing unnecessary tension in the spine, so weakening the muscles surrounding the torso.

Here the spine is correctly aligned, and the head is poised gracefully above the neck. The feet are well placed on the floor, nicely apart.

office equipment

The office is not what it used to be. It now offers amazing improvements in high-tech equipment, but also plenty of opportunities for repetitive strain injury, aching backs and tense necks. The temptation is to spend far too long in one awkward position. So always be aware of what you are doing, how long it will take, and the best position you need to adopt. Such awareness makes all the difference between a good and bad day.

MOBILE PHONE USE

Here the model is pulling her head down wrongly towards her mobile phone to talk, and slouching.

In this example the model has maintained her balance throughout her body. She looks poised and relaxed.

Observe Yourself When the Telephone Rings

Do you snatch and grab it? Or do you try to give yourself some time before you pick up the receiver? Next time the telephone rings, stop and go over your primary directions. Make sure that you bring the receiver up to your ear rather than suddenly leaning down towards it, thus compromising your position.

WORKING AT A COMPUTER

If you are working at a computer or portable computer, use your eyes to look down towards it. Avoid lurching at the neck as you will lose the correct alignment with your back.

Here the model badly collapses over her computer. She has lost the correct alignment between her hands, her wrists and her lower arms. Her shoulders are far too hunched.

Here the model is incorrectly holding in her wrist, arms and shoulders, causing unnecessary strain and discomfort. She will soon feel very uncomfortable, and have to adopt a new position.

t'ai chi

t'ai chi
t'ai chi

T'ai chi ch'uan is an ancient form of slow, graceful and rhythmic exercise which originated in China, where it is still extremely popular, often being performed in public parks in the fresh morning air. It has its roots in Taoist philosophy. The movements of the t'ai chi form gently tone and strengthen the organs and muscles, improve circulation and posture, and relax both mind and body. Its name translates as "supreme ultimate fist", but this is not its true meaning. "Strength within softness", "poetry in motion" and "moving harmony" all come closer to expressing the spirit of t'ai chi.

T'ai chi has been variously described as a system of health, medicine, physical co-ordination, relaxation, self-defence and consciousness raising, as well as a means of exercise and self-development. It is all these things. The style shown here is the Yang-style short form, as developed by Professor Cheng Man-Ch'ing, which is the one most practised in the West.

Unlike the "hard" martial arts which rely on force and speed, t'ai chi is "soft" or "internal". Its emphasis lies in the yielding aspect of nature when overcoming the hard – like the waterfall which eventually wears away the rock beneath. It teaches patience and relaxation, and fosters an understanding of the co-ordination of mind, body and spirit. It is the perfect antidote to the stresses and strains of today's modern lifestyles.

t'ai chi for health or self defence If you

simply want to go out and strike a pose, jumping about like Bruce Lee, t'ai chi is not for you. It is a very serious, highly regarded ancient technique that has two major qualities. It improves your health, and teaches you how to overcome stronger hostile forces when you are under attack. The most amazing part of t'ai chi is the way its movements are almost balletic.

The Benefits of T'ai Chi

Although t'ai chi can eventually be used in self-defence, and most classes do incorporate some of its practical applications, it is initially practised mainly for its health-giving benefits. It is particularly useful for increasing alertness and body awareness, and for developing concentration and sensitivity. It helps with balance and posture, and enhances a sense of "groundedness". However, all the postures can also be used when defending yourself against an attack by an opponent. Its gentleness and subtlety do not preclude its use as a very effective form of self-defence.

It is not easy to separate the physical and mental aspects of t'ai chi, as they are closely interrelated. In Chinese medicine, the interdependence of mind, body and spirit is seen as integral to well-being.

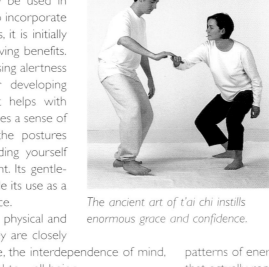

The ancient art of t'ai chi instills enormous grace and confidence.

The Theory of T'ai Chi

Like music, t'ai chi cannot be appreciated purely on an intellectual level. It also has an enormous spiritual side, and when you watch any highly experienced t'ai chi practitioners you will see how they are almost in a kind of trance, in a separate world where they cannot be touched. Correctly done, it is quite hypnotic.

For now, we must look at some of the concepts that are fundamental to the martial arts, as well as to medicine and philosophy. Although these disciplines are all treated quite separately by those in the West, they are all inseparable in the Eastern view. From thousands of years of close observation of patterns of energy, the Chinese successfully evolved a way of life that actually ropes all three ingredients together.

Chi

Chi is the prime driving force of human life, the spark behind thought, creativity and growth which maintains and nurtures us. It can be felt as movement of energy in the body, like the ceaseless flow of an electrical current. Chi flows through the body along channels called meridians.

The Tan Tien

The Chi is stored in the Tan Tien. This is an area about the size of a golf ball, located four finger-widths below the navel, and about one-third of the way from the front to the back of the body. It is the centre of gravity of the body, and in t'ai chi all movement emanates from it. Try to let the breath and the mind sink to the Tan Tien.

Yin and Yang

Yin and Yang describe the complementary yet opposing forces of nature. Their relationship has a harmony and balance: both Yin and Yang are necessary, are constantly moving and balancing each other, and this interaction creates Chi. The Chinese observed that when the balance of Yin and Yang is disrupted so too will be the body's Chi, leading to ill health.

One of the key requirements for t'ai chi is excellent balance.

warm-up exercises

Perform these exercises slowly and gently, with the mind and the breath focused in the Tan Tien. Notice any differences between the right and left sides of your body, and between the upper and lower parts. The object is gradually to enter the world of t'ai chi, and to warm up all your muscles so that you do not get any strains. The more you warm up, the better your technique will be. The movements will flow like a stream.

1 Gently shake out any tension in your wrists and hands. Gradually work up to include your shoulders. This is especially useful after long periods at work.

2 Make increasing circles with one shoulder. Change direction and decrease the size of the circles. Repeat for the other shoulder. Rotate both shoulders.

3 Place both hands lightly on your hips. Keeping your head up, begin by spiralling your hips slowly outwards, feeling for any restriction, tightness or lack of ease.

4 Place your palms lightly on your upper kneecaps. Feel the Chi from your palms radiating deep into your knee joints. Circle your knees clockwise.

5 Turn out your left foot and step forward with your right. Raise your toes. Drop forward, keeping your right leg straight. Hold then repeat on the left.

6 Stand on one leg while gently shaking tension from the other leg. Do this for 10–15 seconds and then repeat with the other leg. Repeat several times.

yang-style short form
yang-style short form

yang-style short form

After completing all the warm-up exercises, and having a moment or so quietly standing to see if you can find a point of equilibrium, a few minutes of t'ai chi walking may now follow. This is known as walking with an "empty step", rather in the manner of a cat tentatively putting out its paw before committing its full weight on to the front leg.

In fact, it is well worth studying an adult cat that is gracefully walking, or gliding forwards when it has spotted its prey. Its whole movement is one of ceaseless flow, of elegant, unforced movement when every part of its body seems to be an extension of another part, and nothing is hurried or rushed.

As you progress through the form, use the following pages as an aide-mémoire for your practice, especially for the transitions from one posture to the next. Remember to keep your movements slow and smooth, like clouds drifting gently by on a summer's day, and relax. If you worry about this new exercise, you will not succeed.

In many ways that is the key problem for the new Western practitioner. Doing these exercises initially means that you will be highly self-conscious because there is nothing like it in our culture. Yet gradually, after a few lessons, and above all after watching expert t'ai chi practitioners, it becomes clear that this is something which you can do successfully, and without having to worry about what you look like.

Once you launch into the first few movements, the rest follow, and you find that an awkward state of self-consciousness is quickly replaced by an inner calm as you become less aware of the outside world, and more aware of inner ones. The key to t'ai chi is being able to make seamless flowing moves, with the emphasis not so much on specific poses as on the linking means of getting there. Ultimately, you too may be able to go into a park in the early morning, as they do in the East, and carry out t'ai chi utterly unselfconsciously, gaining spiritual refreshment.

ATTENTION, PREPARATION AND BEGINNING

1 Stand in a relaxed and upright posture, feet pointing diagonally outwards, making a right angle. Distribute your weight evenly through your body.

2 Bend your right knee and sink all your weight down through your right leg into the foot, without leaning across. Then move the "empty" left leg a shoulder-width away, with the toes pointing straight ahead.

3 Transfer 70% of your weight to your left leg, simultaneously turning your waist and therefore your whole body diagonally to the right.

4 Keeping 70% of your weight in your left leg, turn your whole body back to face the front. Bring your right foot around to the front as your waist moves. Your feet should be shoulder-width apart and parallel. Your hands also move with your body, the palms facing the ground as if resting on a cushion of air.

5 Relax your wrists and let your arms float up and away from your body. When your hands reach shoulder height, gently extend the fingertips.

6 Draw your hands back in towards your body by dropping the elbows. This penultimate posture is one of relaxed, graceful ease.

WARD OFF LEFT

7 In the final position, relax your wrists and let your hands float down the front of your body, just in front of and below the waist. The bulk of your weight is in your left leg.

1 Sink all your weight on to your left leg, and turn your body to the right, pivoting on your right heel. Imagine you are holding a large ball, with the right hand in front of the chest.

2 Sink all your weight on to your right leg, as if carrying the ball forward. Pick up your "empty" (weightless) left leg and step forwards, toes pointing to the front.

WARD OFF RIGHT

3 Turn the waist to the left, facing the front. Your left hand comes up, palm facing the chest, and the right floats down with 70% of your weight now on your left leg, as your right moves around.

1 Sink all your weight into your left leg. Turn to the right: the left palm turns face down, the right palm turns up as if both hands are again holding the large ball. The heels should be slightly apart.

2 Turn your waist to face the right-hand side and shift 70% of your weight on to your right foot, and turn your left foot to 45°. Raise your right arm so that the palm faces your chest.

ROLL BACK, PRESS AND PUSH

This posture, together with the one that follows it, "Single Whip", is also known as "Grasping the Sparrow's Tail".

1 Turn your body to the right. Point the fingertips of your right hand to the sky in a relaxed way. Your left arm moves horizontally with the fingertips almost touching the right elbow, palm facing the body. Your weight remains 70% on the right leg, 30% on the left.

2 As you turn your waist to the left, begin to shift weight to your left leg. Follow the movement of the body with your arms until your right hand is horizontal. Your left hand begins to flow down with the movement of your waist. Your weight settles on your left leg.

3 Turn your waist back to the right and let your left arm follow this movement. All your weight remains in the left leg. Bring your palm gradually across to rest against your right wrist, opposite the centre of your chest.

4 Press forward, keeping the hands in full contact. Shift 70% of your weight into your front (right) leg. Ensure that your heels are still shoulder-width apart, and that the right foot is pointing forward, and the left foot at 45°.

5 Separate your hands and sink all your weight back into your left foot. Your fingertips are now shoulder-width apart at shoulder height.

6 Move your weight forward 70% into your right leg. Your arms and hands keep the same position.

SINGLE WHIP

1 As your weight shifts back into the left leg, leave your fingers where they are in space, effectively straightening – but not locking – your arms. The palms now face down towards the ground.

2 Turn your whole body to the left and shift all your weight into your left leg. Your right heel remains on the ground while your toes turn through 120°, following the body round.

3 Sink your weight back into your right leg. Bring your left hand under the right to hold the imaginary ball in front of your body. Then form a "hook" with the fingers and thumb of your right hand.

LIFTING HANDS

4 Ensure all your weight is in your right leg. Bend the right knee and turn your body to the left, sending out the hook in line with, and at the same height as, your shoulder. Take an "empty" (weightless) shoulder-width step with your left foot.

5 Shift 70% of your weight on to your left leg, adjusting your right foot to 45° Ensure that your heels are shoulder-width apart, your left hand in line with your left shoulder and your right hand hook at 90° to the rest of your body.

1 Place your weight on the left leg, open your hands and palms inwards, the left palm facing the right elbow. Pick up your empty right foot and place down the heel without weight, directly in front of the left heel.

WHITE CRANE SPREADS WINGS AND PUSH

2 Turn your waist to the left, your hands following the movement of your waist. Bring your right toe by your left heel, touching the ground but weightless.

3 Take an "empty" step to the right, and transfer 70% of the weight to the right foot. The left palm ends up opposite your inner right elbow. Your right arm is curved, guarding the groin, and your feet are at right angles to each other.

1 Drop all your weight into your right leg. Turn your waist to the left. As your right hand begins to rise, your left hand sweeps down in front of your left thigh.

2 Pick up your "empty" left leg and touch the toe on the ground but without shifting your weight. Bring your right hand up to guard your temple, turning to face diagonally outwards as it moves up. Your left hand floats down.

3 As you turn your waist to the left, your right hand follows and sweeps down; your left palm opens outwards.

4 As you turn your waist to the right, your right hand continues in a circle. Your left hand follows the move of your waist and faces down in front of your chest. As your waist returns to the centre, the right hand is level with the shoulder.

PLAY GUITAR. BRUSH LEFT KNEE AND PUSH

This posture is also known as "Strumming the Lute".

5 Take a shoulder-width step with your left foot, heel first. Move 70% of your weight into your left leg as your left hand brushes down across it. Meanwhile, your right hand follows a concave curve into the centre to finish by the mouth.

1 As all your weight sinks into your left leg, adjust the "empty" right foot by drawing it slightly nearer the left foot, toe first. Bring your weight into the right foot. Your left leg and arm float up simultaneously – imagine a thread connecting them.

2 Turn to the right, dropping your right hand down while your left hand follows the movement of your waist to the centre of your chest, palm facing down. As your waist returns to the front, your right hand comes to shoulder height.

STEP FORWARD, DEFLECT, INTERCEPT AND PUNCH

3 Take a shoulder-width step with your left foot, heel first. Move 70% of your weight into your left leg as your left hand brushes down across it. Your right hand follows a curve ending by your mouth.

1 Turn your waist 45° to the left and sink all your weight into your right foot. As the weight shifts back, lift the toes of your left foot and pivot 45° on the heel. Bring your hands down by your left leg.

2 Shift all your weight into your left leg. Form a loose fist with your right hand, but check that the fingers are not wrapped around the thumb. The right toes are behind the left heel.

3 Arc both of your hands and your right foot simultaneously towards the centre line, as your waist turns around to the right. The right foot now lands "empty", in line with the left instep. Check that your position is correct. Note that your left thumb should roughly be in line with your left eye.

4 Continue to turn your waist to the right, bringing the right fist palm upwards to rest on the right hip. You should now commence transferring all your weight on to your right foot. Your eyes should skim across the tops of your left fingers.

5 Place your left foot a shoulder width from the right foot. Shift 70% of your weight to your left leg and bring your right fist forward as if to punch, rotating it through a quarter turn in a corkscrew motion. Then bring your left arm across your body, with the palm facing your inner right elbow.

WITHDRAW AND PUSH. CROSSING HANDS

1 As you turn your waist to the left, your right arm follows your body to an angle of 45° and the fist opens up. Meanwhile, cup your left hand gracefully a couple of inches under your right elbow, as if supporting it.

2 Draw your right arm across your left palm as your weight sinks into your right foot, and your waist turns to the right.

3 Bring your waist back to the centre and turn both palms to face the front.

4 Move your weight forward 70% on to your left leg. Your hands remain at shoulder width and shoulder height.

5 Turn your waist to the right and simultaneously sink all your weight into your left leg. Draw your hands in towards your chest in a softly inverted "V" shape, as if holding the top of a ball.

6 As your whole weight shifts into your right leg, turn your waist to the right. Your left toes turn with your waist and your right hand travels out both diagonally and upwards.

EMBRACE TIGER, RETURN TO MOUNTAIN

7 Sink all your weight back into your left leg. Your left hand now travels out diagonally. Though the position might seem slightly awkward and lopsided, it actually flows naturally into the final step.

8 Finally, bring your right foot shoulder-width away from and parallel to the left, but maintain your weight 70% in the left leg. Both hands circle down and up, stopping opposite your chest, palms facing the body. The wrists are touching, with the right wrist outside the left one. Hold this stance for a few seconds.

1 Keeping all your weight in your left leg, turn your waist to the right. Open your hands outwards. Step diagonally back with your right foot. Move your weight 70% on to your right foot. As your waist completes its turn, move your left hand so that the fingertips are in line with your left shoulder; palm facing forward.

ROLL BACK, PRESS AND PUSH: SINGLE WHIP

PUNCH UNDER ELBOW

1 Now repeat the sequence in "Roll Back, Press and Push". This time, perform this section from one diagonal corner to the other rather than from one side to the other. This picture shows your position at the end of the sequence.

1 Sink all your weight back on to your right foot. Turn your waist 45° to the left, lifting the left toes and letting your left foot and both arms pivot 45° to the left.

2 As you turn your waist slightly to the right, allow your left hand to come across so that the fingertips point to your right elbow. Meanwhile, your right hand travels upwards so that the fingertips point heavenward.

2 Lower your left foot, gradually shifting your weight forward into it. When all your weight is on your left foot, step forward with your right foot so that the heel is in line with your left instep.

3 Rotate your upper body 90° to the left. Your arms follow this waist movement, so that the hook (your right hand) is now out in front level with your right shoulder, and your left hand is level with your face at 90° to the front. Your weight is in your left leg.

4 Transfer all your weight to your right leg, turning your waist to the right and letting your left hand move down, then up, until the fingers are in line with your left shoulder. Your left arm and leg move around simultaneously. Rest your left heel on the ground without any weight.

STEP BACK TO REPULSE THE MONKEY

1 As you turn your waist further to the right, your right hand opens and moves down by your hip, then floats up to shoulder height. The palm of your left hand turns over to face down.

2 Step back with your left foot as your waist turns to the left. Your right hand travels forward, palm facing down, while your left hand travels down towards the left hip with the palm facing up.

3 The right toes also straighten as the waist turns. As you continue to turn to the left, your left hand floats up to shoulder height, while your right hand comes forward, palm facing down.

STEP BACK TO REPULSE THE MONKEY (RIGHT). DIAGONAL FLYING

1 Turn your waist to the right, step back with your right foot and let your left hand travel forward, palm down. Your right hand moves down to rest on your hip, palm up. Your left foot turns to face the front as the waist moves. Your right hand now comes up to shoulder height.

2 With your weight on your left foot, turn your waist to the left. Turn your right hand palm upwards as it travels round in front of your waist, while your left hand, palm downwards, comes in front of your chest. Your hands are now holding an imaginary ball in front of you.

3 Turn your waist 90° to the right, maintaining the position of your arms and hands in front of your chest, as if carrying the ball.

WAVING HANDS IN CLOUDS (RIGHT, LEFT, RIGHT)

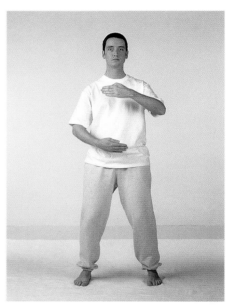

4 Stepping with your right foot, turn a further 135° to the right, and then transfer 70% of your weight into the right foot. Your waist also turns to the right and your right hand moves with it, travelling to shoulder height, arm extended and facing diagonally upwards. Your left hand moves simultaneously to just outside your left thigh, palm facing down.

1 Bring all your weight on to your right foot. Turn your waist to the right and move your left hand across near your right hip. At the same time, your right hand turns palm downwards at shoulder height. Raise your left foot and move it forward until the left heel is now level and in line with the right.

2 As your waist turns to the front, move your right hand to face it and your left hand to face your chest. The right toes swivel round to face forwards so that your feet are now shoulder-width apart.

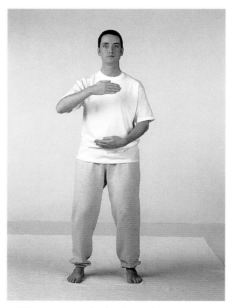

3 As your waist turns to the left, turn your palms towards each other, as if holding a large ball to the left of your body. All your weight is in your left leg and your right foot steps in to about half shoulder width.

4 Turn your waist back to the centre. Your hands again change position, the left hand descending to be opposite and facing your waist, and the right hand opposite and facing your chest.

5 Turn your waist to the right, your hands holding the imaginary ball, with the right hand uppermost, palm facing down, and the left hand below it, palm facing up. When all your weight is on your right foot, step back to shoulder-width apart.

WAVING HANDS IN CLOUDS (LEFT, RIGHT, LEFT). THE WHIP

1 Turn your waist back to the centre, bringing your right hand down to face your waist and your left hand up to face your chest. Repeat Steps 3, 4 and 5, then Steps 2 and 3 from "Waving Hands in Clouds, Right, Left, Right".

2 Turn your waist back to the centre and form a hook with your right hand, as it moves in level with your chest, directly above your left hand. It is located in front of your waist, palm upwards.

3 Step forward with your right foot. Turn your waist to the right, then to the left as you transfer your weight to your right foot, sending out the hook at 90° to the front of your body.

GOLDEN ROOSTER STANDS ON ONE LEG (LEFT). SQUATTING SINGLE WHIP

4 Continue turning your waist around towards the left, and then step with your left foot to about shoulder-width apart, with your left palm now facing your left shoulder.

5 Shift your weight 70% on to your left foot, turning away your left palm at shoulder height, and turning the right toes to 45°.

1 Sink all your weight into your left leg, turning your left hand over so that the palm faces upwards. Simultaneously turn out the right toes. This is a nicely balanced, elegant position.

2 Move your weight across into your right leg, bringing your left palm in towards your chest. The left toes turn 45° to the right.

3 Sink down into your right leg, keeping your back straight. Move your waist to the left, brush open your left knee with your left arm and turn your left toes out 90° to the left.

4 Transfer all your weight into your left leg. Open the right hand hook, lower the hand then bring it up in front of your chest. Raise your right leg as your weight shifts forward into your left leg, so that your right thigh becomes parallel with the ground. Bend your left knee.

GOLDEN ROOSTER STANDS ON ONE LEG (RIGHT). SEPARATE RIGHT FOOT

1 Place your right foot down and move all your weight on to it. As your weight sinks into your right leg, your right hand descends to rest on a cushion of air by your right thigh. Your left arm and left leg simultaneously move up to form a mirror image of the previous posture.

2 Step out with your "empty" left foot diagonally to the left, and form a ward-off position with your left arm horizontally positioned across your body, opposite your chest.

3 Shift all your weight into your left leg, bringing your right arm up to cross in front of your left arm, with the wrists touching. Bring your right toe to your left heel. Turn your wrists, maintaining skin contact as you do so, so that your left arm now crosses your right.

SEPARATE LEFT FOOT.
BRUSH LEFT KNEE
AND PUSH

4 Then turn your hands away from your body, and open them out in a fan-like action. Your eyes should be level with the tips of your fingers.

5 Keep your left hand level with your left ear, palm facing away. Open out your right hand to the corner, below shoulder height, and simultaneously kick gently with your right leg, to knee height. You should be so balanced that you do not fall over.

1 Keeping all your weight in your left leg, turn to the left-hand corner, forming a ward-off position with your right arm.

2 Turn your waist to the right and step to the right with your right leg. As you transfer weight into it, bring your left hand up outside the right so that the wrists meet. The left toes come up to meet the right heel.

3 Open out your hands, the right hand this time remaining level with the head and the left hand travelling to below shoulder height. The left foot follows, kicking gently to the corner.

4 Turn your waist and left knee to the front again. Take a shoulder-width "empty" step with your left leg, toes pointing in the forward direction.

NEEDLES AT SEA BOTTOM

5 Brush your left hand across and above the front of your left leg, to just outside your left thigh. Your right hand curves in, fingertips forward, to finish with the fingers in line with your mouth.

1 Move all your weight into your left leg. Pick up your empty right foot and make a small adjustment step forward.

2 Place your right toes down, then bring your left hand across your body so that the left palm rests above your right wrist. At the same time, pick up your left leg and place the toes down.

IRON FAN PENETRATES BACK. TURN BODY, CHOP AND PUSH

3 Move your right arm forwards and diagonally downwards with your body, then vertically downwards. The arm remains in line with your right leg, and all your weight remains in your right leg.

1 Your weight remains in your right leg and both hands assume a ward-off position. Take a shoulder-width step with the left foot. Shift your weight 70% into your left leg and turn your hands outwards, the left hand by your chest, the right guarding your temple.

2 Turn your waist to the right and sink all your weight back into your right leg, bringing your left toes round. Bring your left hand up, turning the palm diagonally outwards to guard the temple. At the same time, form a loose fist with your right hand, palm facing downwards.

3 Sink all your weight back on to your left leg. As you transfer the weight back, the fist descends in front of your groin.

4 Step to shoulder width with your right foot. Your right arm pivots at the elbow and your left arm folds across so that the left hand faces the right inner elbow. All your weight remains on your left leg. You are nicely balanced as shown above.

5 Transfer your weight forward 70% into your right leg. Your left arm pushes forward, fingertips in line with your left shoulder, and your right fist descends to your right hip, palm upwards. The left toes are at 45°.

STEP FORWARD, DEFLECT DOWNWARDS, INTERCEPT AND PUNCH, KICK WITH HEEL

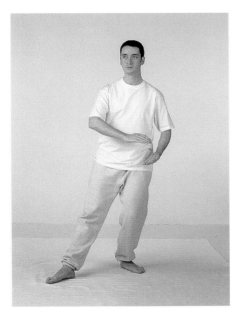

1 Sink all your weight into the left leg as your waist turns to the left. Bring the right toe to the left heel. The right hand comes across the body, and the palm faces down by the left hip. The left hand is below the right hand, palm up. Go to "Step Forward, Deflect, Intercept and Punch" and repeat Steps 3, 4 and 5.

2 Sink your weight into your left leg, turning your waist to the right. Cross your wrists, the right outside the left. Sink the weight back into your right leg. Your waist turns left and your left foot pivots on the heel 45° to the left. Shift all your weight forward into your left leg, turning your hands palms outwards.

3 Open your hands out gracefully like a fan, the right hand to below shoulder height, the left hand at head height, palms facing away. Your right foot now comes up from the ground, and the heel kicks diagonally away.

BRUSH RIGHT KNEE AND PUSH. BRUSH LEFT KNEE AND PUNCH DOWN

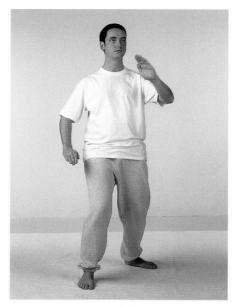

1 Place your "empty" right foot on the ground, toes forward. Your right hand curves down to rest on a cushion of air outside your right thigh. Your left hand curves forward to push to the centre, fingertips in line with your mouth.

2 Sink back into your left leg, turning your waist to the right, with the palm of your left hand facing towards your body in the Yang-style ward-off position.

3 Transfer your weight forward into your right foot, with your left palm turning so that it faces downwards.

WARD OFF RIGHT. ROLL BACK, PRESS AND PUSH. WHIP

4 Take a shoulder-width step with your left foot and bring 70% of your weight onto it. Your right hand forms a loose fist, which comes over your hip and punches down the centre. Your left hand brushes your left leg and rests by the left knee.

1 Sink back into your right leg. Your left hand now assumes a ward-off position, the fingertips of your right hand pointing towards the centre of the left palm. Your right palm faces downwards. Gaze steadily and confidently forwards.

2 Turn your body 45° to the left, pivoting neatly on the left heel. Shift all your weight forward into your left leg. Your left arm should remain in this position, while your right hand now presses smartly down.

FAIR LADY WEAVES SHUTTLES (RIGHT AND LEFT)

3 Step through at shoulder width with your "empty" right foot. As you transfer 70% of your weight into it, your right hand comes up into a ward-off position opposite your chest, with the left fingertips now pointing towards the right palm, left palm downwards. Repeat "Roll Back, Press and Push" and "Single Whip".

1 Transfer your weight to your right leg as you turn your waist to the right, and turn the "empty" left toes through 90°. Bring your left hand across your body and under your elbow. Open the hook of your right hand and lower the right arm, palm turning to face upwards.

2 Sink your weight back into your left leg, turn your waist further to the right and turn out your right foot so the heel is in line with the left instep.

3 Sink your weight into your right leg, drawing your left arm across your right palm, and step at shoulder width to the left corner with your left foot. As you shift your weight forward into your left leg, turn both palms outwards.

4 Transfer your weight into your right foot and turn your waist and left foot to the right as far as possible (135°). Turn your palms to face your body, the right palm by the left elbow.

5 Sink your weight back into your left leg and draw your left arm across your right palm.

FAIR LADY WEAVES SHUTTLES (RIGHT AND LEFT)

6 Turn a further 135° right, to the corner. Step to shoulder width with your right foot, and shift 70% of your weight into it, pushing towards the centre of your mouth with your left hand. Bring the right hand up to guard your forehead, palm facing diagonally.

1 Turn to the left, sinking all your weight into your left leg. Pick up your right foot and draw it in. Transfer all your weight to your right foot, then step to the left (45°) with your left foot. Turn your palms in and draw your right arm across the left palm, left arm in a ward-off position.

2 Your left hand then moves up and turns outwards by your head, while the fingers of your right hand come into the centre in line with your mouth. Now repeat the postures described in Steps 4, 5 and 6 of the previous exercise.

WARD OFF LEFT. WARD OFF RIGHT. ROLL BACK, PRESS AND PUSH. SINGLE WHIP

1 Sink your weight into your left leg as your waist turns to the left. Both arms come round with the movement of your waist, the left hand lower than the right. The right toes come round to the front.

2 Sink your weight into your right leg as your left hand presses down, palm facing downwards. Take a shoulder-width step with your left foot.

3 Transfer your weight 70% into your left foot. Your left hand comes up in front of your chest. Your right hand floats outside your right thigh. Repeat as in above heading, from "Ward Off Right".

SQUATTING SINGLE WHIP. STEP FORWARD FOR SEVEN STARS   RIDE TIGER

1 Repeat the postures described in Steps 1, 2 and 3 of "Golden Rooster Stands on One Leg (Left). Squatting Single Whip", ending by brushing open the left knee.

2 Transfer all your weight into your left leg. The right hand hook opens and the hand descends, then comes up in front of your neck, where it forms a loose fist. At the same time, your left hand rises up to form a loose fist, and connects at the wrist inside your right hand. Move your right toes forward to touch the ground without any weight whatsoever.

1 Keep your weight in your left leg and step back with your right foot, toes touching the ground first. Sink your weight into it and turn your waist to the right. The fists open and then move down by your right hip, with the wrists still connected.

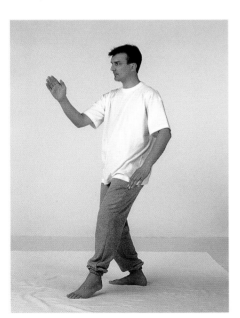

2 Pick up your left leg as your waist turns right, then place your toes down as your waist turns back to the left. Your right hand comes round to the front, fingertips level with your right ear, and your left hand rests by your left thigh.

3 Pick up your left toes, turn your waist to the left corner and place the toes down empty of any weight. Your right palm faces your inner left elbow. Your left hand is at the height of your left shoulder, elbow relaxed.

4 Lift your left toes and swing your waist clockwise, pivoting on the ball of your right foot. Your arms swing to the right with the movement of your waist.

5 Drop your left foot and transfer all your weight into it straight away. Look closely at the photograph above to check how you should be standing.

6 When your arms and waist reach the front (the arms at shoulder height and shoulder width with the palms facing downwards), your right foot lifts up and circles clockwise.

7 After circling, your right leg comes to rest with the upper leg parallel to the ground and the foot comfortably relaxed. Your left leg is bent while the arms are still pointing ahead.

BEND BOW TO SHOOT TIGER. STEP FORWARD, DEFLECT DOWN, INTERCEPT AND PUNCH

1 Turn your waist to the right. Your arms follow your waist, dropping down parallel, and your right foot is placed facing the right corner.

2 As your waist turns to the right, shift the weight into your right leg and circle your arms round to the right. As your waist turns back to the left, raise your arms and circle round with the waist. Form loose fists. Bring the right hand up to the right of your forehead, knuckles facing the right eyebrow. The left hand is at shoulder height.

3 Sink your weight into your left leg and pick up your right foot, placing the toes by your left heel. Open the left fist as your arms move across your body following the waist movement.

WITHDRAW AND PUSH. CROSSING HANDS. CONCLUSION.

4 Both hands and your right foot simultaneously arc in towards the centre line, as your waist turns to the right. The right foot lands "empty", completely in line with the left instep.

5 Continue to turn your waist, bringing the right fist palm upwards to rest on your right hip and shifting your weight to the right foot. Step through at shoulder width with your left foot. Shift 70% of your weight to the left and bring your right fist forward to punch in a corkscrew. Your left arm comes across your body.

1 Repeat the postures described in "Withdraw and Push. Crossing Hands". Ensure your weight is 70% in your left leg when crossing hands.

2 From crossing the hands, turn both palms down to face the ground as your body now rises up.

3 Bring all your weight into your left leg, turn your waist to the right and pivot on your left heel, turning the foot out to an angle of 45°.

4 Move all your weight into your right leg. Step in with your left foot so that the feet make a right angle. Bring half your weight to the left foot. Rest your arms and hands by your side with shoulders relaxed. You may now begin again.

yoga stretches

yoga stretches
yoga stretches

Have you ever watched a cat waking up? More often than not, it will give an exaggerated yawn, then arch its back until stretched to its limit, before loosely letting go and gracefully moving off on its way. Have you ever stopped to wonder why it makes these movements? The cat knows instinctively the value of stretching in maintaining flexibility and improving circulation to the muscles; you too can become stronger and more flexible with regular stretching exercises.

Most of us tend to hold in patterns of tension arising from everyday cares and worries, bad posture, lack of exercise and so on. These patterns make us feel stiff and unbending, and directly interfere with our movements. Inflexibility within our bodies can in turn affect mental flexibility, and we can become stuck in thought as well as in action. Regular stretching exercises not only free our bodies, allowing us to move easily, but can also help us to think and act without being so restricted. They are excellent improvers. In fact, by stretching muscles, ligaments and tendons, we make them much more efficient and stronger. The lengthening actions also help us to stand and walk taller, and even with added grace. The joints are better supported and are more able to go through their full range of movements, while the muscles are better nourished from the increased blood supply. The stretches give you that extra edge.

warm-up exercises
As any athlete will tell you, before starting to do any serious stretching or exercise, such as tennis, it is important that you first do some gentle warm-up exercises. They ensure that your muscles are nicely warmed and loosened, and will help to prevent any sudden strain or injury. The best thing is they only take a few minutes, and they can also be practised at any time if you are feeling stiff and need to loosen up.

SHRUGGING SHOULDERS

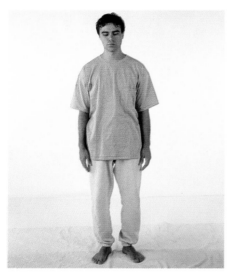

1 Stand upright with your feet slightly apart and your shoulders relaxed.

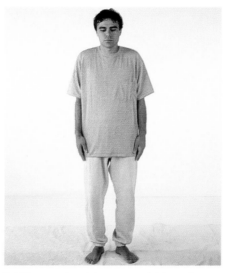

2 Lift your shoulders up as high as they will go, then let them fall down again. Stay relaxed and repeat a few times.

ARM CIRCLING

1 Wheel your arms around from the shoulders in slow, large circles.

2 Do this a few times going backwards, then repeat circling your arms forwards.

SQUATS

1 Stand with your feet slightly apart, hands on hips. Go slowly into a squat.

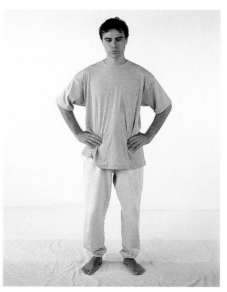

2 Slowly return to a standing position, then repeat. Your back should be upright.

LOOSE TWISTS

▌ In a standing position with feet comfortably apart and knees relaxed, swing your arms loosely backwards and forwards around your body. Keep your head and body facing forward all the time, and keep your feet and pelvis still. Repeat a few times to loosen your arms and shoulders.

ARM STRETCHING

▌ Stand with your arms straight out in front of you, at chest height. Take in a deep breath and exhale.

SIDEWAYS BEND

▌ Stand with your feet at least shoulder-width apart and your arms hanging down at your sides. Bend down to one side, trying not to twist. Slowly return to the upright and then bend to the other side. Straighten up and now repeat.

SHAKE

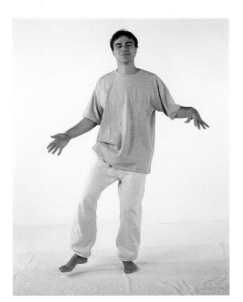

▌ Try to relax and let your whole body go completely floppy. Shake your limbs to release any tension. Continue for as long as you feel comfortable. If you prefer, shake each limb in sequence, starting with your right arm.

CAT STRETCH

1 Kneel on all fours, with your hands and knees shoulder-width apart. As you start to inhale, bring your head forward and slightly hollow your back.

2 Now breathe out and, as you do so, arch the back upwards like a cat, allowing your head to drop down. Repeat a few times.

therapeutic movements
therapeutic movements

therapeutic movements

One of the best things about stretches is that you can do some simple, straightforward exercises anywhere, at any time: at home, in the office, standing in a queue or even sitting in the car; there are no restrictions. However, in order to get the most benefit from regular stretching, and particularly from doing yoga practice, it is important to create a quiet, comfortable space and to give yourself plenty of time to do the movements without any pressure or interruptions from the telephone or colleagues. In fact, making this space is in itself a relaxing, unwinding step, and will enhance the effectiveness of the actual exercises.

Ideally, make an area that feels quiet and calming to you, perhaps with softer lighting if it is needed, maybe with a thick, soft mat for the floor-based stretches. If you have any back discomfort, or just need extra support when lying down, then a couple of cushions may be extremely useful. It is helpful to wear loose fitting, airy clothing so that you can move freely and easily. If the weather permits try to let in some fresh air, but do not risk getting cold. These exercises are not intended to work up a good sweat or strain the heart, but to make you feel altogether less stiff and tense, and generally much more flexible. They are great for loosening you up, releasing tensions, improving circulation, toning the body, and generally making you feel much freer and more confident with your own body. They can really perk you up. After each exercise 'you will also need time to relax quietly, before you plunge back into everyday life

If you find them an enormous benefit and become inspired, and want to try out more exercises, then do find a good, local class. Yoga exercises are generally best learnt in such a class, with a skilled, experienced teacher for maximum benefit. Alternatively you could create your own class at home, inviting friends and family on a regular basis.

tension and backache relievers In the great

majority of cases back trouble is the result of chronic tensions which can build up around the spine. Tired, tight muscles are also much more prone to strain or injury. The stretches that are shown here are intended to aid flexibility of the spine, and to make you feel much more supple, but if you already suffer from back pain or an injury then you must seek professional advice.

COBRA

1 Lie on your front, with your arms bent and your hands under your shoulders.

2 Slowly lift your head and push down on your arms to help raise your trunk.

3 If you can, tilt your head backwards and stretch up and back, then relax.

SIMPLE TWIST

1 Sit on the floor with your legs stetched straight out in front of you.

2 Bend one leg and place the foot on the floor across the other knee.

3 With your opposite arm, reach around the bent leg to catch hold of your foot.

FULL TWIST

1 Bend one leg so that the foot rests on the inner thigh of the other leg.

2 Bring this leg over the first one, then grasp your foot with the other arm.

3 Twist as far around as you can, hold, then relax. Swap over your legs. Repeat.

TRIANGLE

1 Stand with your feet shoulder-width apart and your arms straight out to the sides. This should be a well-balanced, easily held position. Your head should feel like a ball balancing on your neck. Stare straight ahead.

2 Bend down to one side without twisting your body, letting the opposite arm rise in the air. If you find this awkward or uncomfortable, do not strain yourself. The object is to loosen the body, not injure it.

3 Stretch the raised arm, look up and hold. Slowly straighten and repeat on the other side. If you can, repeat several times, but be careful to move slowly into position to avoid a strain.

BENDING TWIST

SLOUCH STRESS

1 Stand with your feet shoulder-width apart and your arms straight out to the sides. Bending forward, try to touch your foot, or the floor in front of it if you can, with your opposite hand. Slowly uncurl and return to the starting position. Repeat on the other side.

1 Sit on a tall stool so that your feet are just off the floor. With your hands behind your back, slouch so that your back is rounded, with your head now lowered down towards your chest.

2 Flex one foot, and lift the leg to straighten it if possible. Release the leg, relax, then repeat a few times. Repeat with the other leg. Note that the object is to build up a slow pace, not to go fast.

soothing and removing tension

Many of us suffer at some time from tension headaches and know that they begin with a gradual feeling of pressure in the head or neck, or a taut sensation in the facial muscles. Once you are aware of such tension, tackle it immediately. A few simple stretches can help to relieve these muscular spasms and prevent them leading to a severe headache. They can be done almost anywhere.

SIDEWAYS NECK STRETCH

1 Slowly stretch your head down to one side, feeling the pull in the neck muscles. Return the head to the upright position and repeat on the other side.

2 To make this stretch of the neck muscles more effective, use your hands to give extra leverage. Place one hand under your chin and the other on top of your head; repeat the other side.

HEAD TO CHEST

1 Lower your head towards your chest, feeling the pull on the back of the neck. Hold at your furthest stretch before slowly raising the head again. Repeat two or three times.

LION POSTURE

1 To stretch the facial muscles and release tension, open your mouth as wide as possible and push out your tongue. At the same time, open your eyes into as wide a stare as you can manage. Repeat a couple of times.

SEMICIRCLE ROTATION

1 Turn the head to one side, then steadily rotate it in a semicircular movement, letting the chin drop down across the chest.

2 Dropping the head backwards compresses the neck, so it is best not to make this a full circle rotation. Repeat, going back in the opposite direction.

posture enhancers
One of the great benefits of an exercise system such as yoga is the fact that it gradually and increasingly gives you considerable grace and poise. In addition it will make a huge difference to your overall posture. If it was previously a bit lax, and you ended up slouching, you will really notice the difference. In fact, learning to hold yourself properly can help you to look and feel much younger, and reduce muscle strain.

1 Stand with feet slightly apart and arms raised in front. Slowly twist to one side. Repeat on the other side.

2 Stand with your feet apart, and hold your arms out. Bend over, sliding one hand down the inside of the same leg.

3 Reach as far as is comfortable, then slowly return to the upright and repeat on the other side.

4 For the tree routine, stand on one leg and bend the other knee, as shown.

5 Either place your palms together above your head, or raise the hands.

6 For the arm and leg stance, stand on one leg and hold the other foot behind.

tired and aching leg revivers

Most of us spend too long each day with our legs stuck in fixed positions, and stiffness of the lower limbs from inactivity or tension can make you feel quite tired. Legs benefit from being stretched, keeping them toned and supple. These exercises prevent the legs, thighs and lower back from getting too tense. Since some of these positions are quite difficult, do beware of straining yourself.

ALTERNATE LEG PULLS

1 Sit on the floor, with one leg out straight and the other bent so that the foot rests on the inner thigh of your extended leg. Do it with care.

2 Lean forward and clasp the straight leg as far down as is comfortable; pull your chest down a little further and hold for a moment. Change legs and repeat.

FULL LEG PULLS

1 The previous stretch can be extended by starting with both legs straight out in front of you. Repeat as described.

SIDE LEG RAISE

2 Lean forward and hold the legs with both hands; pull yourself down a little further and hold for a moment. If this is difficult, bend the legs slightly.

1 Lie on your side with your legs and body in a straight line. Support your head with one hand and place your free hand on the floor for balance.

2 Without twisting your hips, steadily raise the upper leg as far as is comfortable. Hold, then lower slowly. Repeat with the other leg.

CAT STRETCH

1 Kneel on all fours with your hands and knees shoulder-width apart. Raise your head and look straight ahead.

2 Breathe in, and as you exhale lift and arch your back. Hold for a moment before relaxing back into the original position. Inhale, then repeat.

BACK PUSH-UP

1 Lie on your back with your knees bent and your feet on the floor, hip-width apart. Now place your hands on the floor by your shoulders.

SIT UP/LIE DOWN

2 Push up with your hands and feet, arching your back at the same time. Hold for a moment, then lower your body back to the floor. Do not strain yourself with this movement – it works on lots of muscles at the same time.

1 Sit on the floor with both legs straight out in front of you. Your torso should be at right angles to your legs, with your eyes looking forward.

2 Slowly lower your back to the floor, then start to bend the legs and raise them off the floor.

3 As you raise the legs, slowly start to straighten them until they are as close to the vertical as you can manage. Again, take care not to strain yourself.

4 Keeping the legs straight, slowly lower them to the floor.

5 Continue the movement by sitting up and clasping your legs with your hands to bend forwards. Slowly return to the original sitting position.

abdominal tension relievers

We tend to hold and lock up too much tension in our abdomen, especially if we are the kind of people who always bottle up our feelings. Even simple muscular tension can leave us feeling stiff and rather uncomfortable, and much less flexible around the waist. Consequently exercises aimed at reducing stiffness and increasing flexibility in the abdominal region are extremely useful.

LOTUS

1 Sit with one leg bent so that the foot rests on the inner thigh of the other leg. Bend the second leg and place the foot on top of the opposite thigh. Keep the spine upright to avoid straining.

2 For the full lotus, the first leg should be bent with the foot on top of the other thigh, and the second leg bent so that the foot goes over the other leg on to the opposite thigh. Hold if possible.

ABDOMINAL MOVEMENTS

1 Either sit cross-legged or kneel, and place your hands on your waist or thighs. Breathe out completely.

2 Without inhaling, pull in your abdomen as far as you can, then "snap" it in and out up to five times before taking a breath. Relax for a few moments, breathing freely, before repeating.

LEG OVER

1 Lie on your back, with your legs out straight. Raise one leg as close to the vertical as is comfortable, then move it across the body, keeping your hips in contact with the floor.

2 Push the leg as far over as possible, then slowly return to the original position. Repeat with the other leg.

LYING TWISTS

1 Lie on your back, hands behind your head and legs together, knees bent.

2 Twist the legs from side to side, keeping the back and hips on the floor.

SIDE BENDS

1 Stand with feet apart and hands on hips. Bend down to one side.

ROLL TWIST

2 Slowly return to the upright position and bend to the other side. Repeat.

1 Keeping the legs and hips still, roll your upper body around in a clockwise circle.

2 Move slowly and carefully, and bend only as far as is comfortable.

SIT UP/LIE DOWN

1 Sit on the floor with both legs straight out in front of you.

2 Slowly lie back, then start to bend the legs and raise them off the floor.

3 Sit up, bend forwards, clasp your legs and slowly return to the sitting position.

office tensions and stiff muscles

For people who spend their working day sitting at a desk it is very easy to get stiff, aching muscles. Badly designed chairs do not help, and as you get tired, so posture suffers and you can end up getting round-shouldered. It is therefore absolutely essential that every now and again you get up and walk around, relax your body, and try some of these excellent loosening-up exercises.

SEATED CAT STRETCH

1 Pull the chair back from the desk slightly to give yourself more room, then bend forward and clasp your ankles.

2 Carefully arch your back to stretch, then relax back and repeat.

CALF STRETCH

1 Sit fairly upright, then lift and straighten each leg alternately. Repeat a few times.

NECK TWISTS

2 Flex the foot to stretch the calf muscle. Repeat a few times.

1 Turn your head to one side, feeling the extension in the neck muscles.

2 Repeat, turning the head from side to side. Do both steps quite slowly.

ARM AND CHEST STRETCH

❚ Sitting upright, link your hands together, palms away from your body, and push your arms straight out in front of you. Hold for a couple of seconds, relax and then repeat.

ARM AND BACK STRETCH

❚ Link your hands together behind your back, over the top of the chair, and lift your arms slightly. Do not strain yourself. Push away from your body, hold, then repeat the exercise.

FOREARM STRETCH

❚ Hold your arms straight out to the sides and stretch them. Alternately flex and extend your hands. Feel the pull on the upper and lower sides of your forearms as you do so.

BACK/SHOULDER STRETCH

❚ Stretch your arms up in the air over your head. As you breathe in, arch your back ever so slightly. Relax with the exhalation and repeat the exercise a couple of times.

POSTURE CLASP

❚ Put one arm behind your back and bend it up, with the hand reaching the other shoulder. With your other arm raised and bent down over your shoulder, try to clasp your fingers.

SHOULDER RELEASE

❚ Finally, link your fingers together and stretch your arms high above your head. Repeat several times.

meditation

meditation meditation

Meditation has been in use from the beginning of time: people have always sought inner quiet and physical relaxation, whether for reasons connected with the spirit, self-realization or health. You do not have to be a physical contortionist to achieve and enjoy the benefits of meditation at both physical and mental levels.

What, then, is meditation? As one speaker put it recently, it is just sitting and relaxing. Many people find that their lives are so full of the demands of work, family, friends and organized leisure pursuits that they have no time to "stand and stare". Many are so caught up in planning and working towards the future that they take little pleasure from the here and now. In their bustle to "get on" they miss out on the simple pleasures of life. But beauty and joy are there to be seen and experienced, even in industrial cities.

The benefits of meditation come from regular use. If you are under stress, you may find that meditating twice daily will be effective in restoring composure. Make a time and space you can call your own, and use breathing and relaxation exercises to ease yourself into the meditative state. The more you practise meditation the less time you will need to spend on these, but they remain useful in calming and preparing you. Allow at least 10 minutes, ideally 20, for meditation in each session.

the benefits of meditation

Human beings were never designed to cope with the high-pressure demands of life in the 21st century; life when you are constantly in demand, having to make vital decisions at breakneck speed right through the day, and even during the night. You might say it cannot be done, but it can, with help. Knowing how as well as when to switch off makes all the difference, and even scientists now agree.

PSYCHO-PHYSICAL LINKS

A period of meditation can often lead to a feeling of being refreshed, with a more positive attitude and a general feeling of well-being. Things that had been bothering you may now be seen in a new and more helpful way. You gain a different, wider perspective on things and feel very much more in control.

These beneficial reactions have been well known for years, but only in recent times has anyone found a physiological explanation. Detailed, extensive knowledge of brain scans and even brain wave patterns has given extraordinary new information about what is commonly called the "alpha state".

Mind and body work together in meditation to promote health and well-being in the whole person.

Endorphin Release

When we are truly relaxed, both mentally and physically, there are changes in the brain wave pattern until it is predominantly located and fixed within the alpha state. Within this particular state the brain triggers chemicals known as endorphins. It is in fact this chemical trigger that has the benefits that are experienced as a feeling of well-being. Indeed, endorphins have frequently been called "nature's very own special opiates". Meditation is one of the easiest ways to achieve this, and these good feelings can easily linger for some time after the meditation has ended, the length of time varying considerably. There is also a real physical benefit, as these endorphins boost and recharge the immune system, helping you to fight off all kinds of infections.

Meditation and Work

The tensions of modern working practices often mean that people are so bound up in meeting all the vigorous demands placed upon them that they maintain a high level of mental and physical activity right through the day. This frequently means that they are not only cutting off their extremely important emotional responses and their enjoyment of the simple things in life, but they are also pushing their physical and mental health right to the very limit. Much has now been written about the management of stress, and the significant need for periods of mental and physical relaxation during the working day.

The 20-minute Rule

One writer, Ernest Rossi, has formulated the 20-minute rule which is based on the theory of ultradian rhythms. Ultradian rhythms are biorhythms that the body works through during each day – a little like hyperbolic curves of energy which repeat every 90 to 120 minutes. Naturally, it would be best to work only at peak performance times, but this is just not possible. However, timing work breaks to coincide with the mind/body slow-down pattern every 90 minutes does ensure maximum productivity and restricts the potential build-up of stress.

Rossi suggested the pattern of working for 90 minutes and then taking a brief 20-minute break. He himself usually lies down and meditates during this period because it is the best form of total mental and physical relaxation, and is good preparation for returning to optimum mental processing.

It is important that these breaks take place every 90 minutes or so, and in such a way as to completely change the mind/body state. Ideally, you should stop all work activity and experience a change of physical status (standing rather than sitting, looking into the distance rather than close up, for example) and mental focus. A 20-minute meditation is ideal and the benefits will be felt immediately. On returning to work after the 20 minutes, you will see things afresh and deal with them more efficiently, as you are ready to climb to peak performance on the biorhythmic curve. The feeling of well-being lasts into the next 90-minute period.

To be at your best for meetings ensure you take regular breaks.

gaining the meditative state
Many religious groups, as well as adherents of Transcendental Meditation, talk of using a sound, or "mantra", to help with meditation. The constant repetition of a phrase, word or sound ("aum" is commonly used in Hinduism) creates the alpha state by an almost hypnotic focus of attention upon that particular sound. In fact chants repeated again and again can lead to its members reaching a "high".

Sound

An effortless sound, repeated with the natural regular rhythm of breathing, can have the same soothing, liberating effect as the constant natural sound of running water, rustling leaves or a beating heart. The single sound, or mantra as it is known, is used to blot out the "chatter" of intrusive thoughts, allowing the mind to find deep repose. Speaking or chanting a mantra as a flowing stream of endless sound is a very old method of heightening a person's awareness by concentrating the senses. The simple gentle sound "om", or "aum", is sometimes known as the first mantra, which is literally an instrument of thought. The curving Sanskrit (the ancient language of Hindus in India) symbol for this primordial word represents the various states of consciousness: waking, dreaming, deep sleep and the transcendental state.

However, the actual sound need not be a special word or incantation; something simple and meaningful will be as effective. The sound of the word "calm" spoken or thought with each exhalation can be very effective, especially while imagining tension leaving your body. Any word that appeals to you will do.

Make sure that you are sitting quite comfortably and then start breathing in the colour of your choice.

Touch

You can use your sense of touch in a lulling, soothing way to induce a state of meditation at times of stress. Young children do this when they adopt a satisfyingly smooth ribbon or piece of fabric to hold and manipulate when they are feeling tense. The same technique is seen all over the Middle East, where strings of worry beads are rhythmically passed through the fingers at difficult moments to focus the mind and calm anxiety. Their uniform size, gentle round shapes, smooth surfaces and rhythmic, orderly clicking as they are passed along their string all assist the meditative state. Use one or two smooth, rounded stones in the same way, passing them slowly from hand to hand.

Colours

Some colours are associated with relaxation and can be a helpful way to clear the mind of tension and allow meditation to start. Sit with your eyes closed, and be aware of the colour that comes into your mind: it may be any colour of the rainbow – red or purple are common. Then slowly and gradually allow that colour to change to a blue or green colour, allowing it to fill the whole of your mind's eye and replacing all other colours. The colour pink is also recommended by colour therapists and this may prove helpful. You will find a feeling of relaxation growing as the new colour builds in your mind, and when the relaxed colour is complete, you will experience feelings of inner peace.

Establish a comfortable rhythm of breathing and then focus on it until your mind is completely still, relaxed and clear. Colours are associated with all kinds of qualities, so choose the best for your own particular moods and needs. Red: vitality, energy, strength and willpower (complementary colour turquoise). Orange: happiness and laughter (complementary colour blue). Yellow: intellect and objectivity (complementary colour violet). Green: cleansing and harmony (complementary colour magenta). Turquoise: boosts and strengthens the immune system, counteracts disease (complementary colour red). Blue: peace and relaxation, restful sleep (complementary colour orange). Violet: beauty, dignity, assured self-respect (complementary colour yellow). Magenta: the liberating release of all obsessional thoughts and memories (complementary colour green).

Repeating a mantra takes you into a world of peace and harmony.

how to use meditation

how to use meditation

how to use meditation

The key to using meditation lies in recognizing that you actually need it. Once you get into the whirlpool of work and stress, they can both all too easily become an integral part of your lifestyle. In fact, they can be such a formidable cornerstone that you cannot imagine what life could possibly be like without them. But once you stand back and see clearly and exactly what is happening to you, what your life has become, then suddenly you see you actually need a way out. One of the best ways involves deep meditation.

Meditation needs to be done like regular exercise. In fact you might say you are exercising the ways in which you relax. The very first step involves switching off, like switching off a light in a room, and concentrating on what could be called the "Inner Other", that is to say the marvellous, relaxed, empty inner spaces inside your head and body. This stage, put crudely, means sweeping out all the noise and mayhem and chaos of everyday life and getting ready to enter another world.

The second stage involves being carried along what one expert teacher calls "a moving but going nowhere sound that coils round and even through itself in a perpetual state of being". Perhaps the best way of evaluating it is by hearing what people have to say after meditation. "As good as a holiday" or "like a wonderful deep refreshing sleep" is what most people say. If you are to get its full, continuous benefits then you really must make sure that meditation is something that you do regularly every day, at certain times, because like almost all forms of exercise the more often you do it, the better you are at it; the quicker you can switch off and tune in, and enter that fantastic deep state of total energizing, refreshing relaxation.

You must use meditation with care though. It is not like switching on and off a tap. It needs to be respected. Few people who meditate try, even if they could, to describe its ultimate power. That would be like divulging a wonderful private secret; to have it is quite enough.

simple meditation techiques

While meditating might sound like something that everyone can do in just a few minutes, when you start learning to meditate you need an experienced teacher to help you understand what you have got to do. There is no point in sitting there and closing your eyes and hoping. Nothing will happen. The following techniques give a great understanding of exactly what happens. Try them and see.

Introduce a child to meditation by using the Numbers Game.

THE NUMBERS GAME

This is a very simple form of meditation using a blackboard, real or imaginary. It is a good "game" to use with children (or adults), giving them a taste of meditation, and they really enjoy it. It is described here as if you are leading a group, but it can be easily used on one person, and provides an excellent way to clear the mind through concentration, imagination and patterns: all wonderful ways of gaining a real experience of deep meditation.

What you must do is this …

1 Get the children to sit or lie comfortably. Once they have found a really comfortable position ask them to remember it.

2 With chalk on the blackboard, draw a diagram of numbers, making sure that there are no mathematical links, like this:

$$\begin{array}{ccc} 3 & 1 & 5 \\ 8 & 6 & 9 \\ 4 & 7 & 2 \end{array}$$

3 Give the children one minute to memorize this sequence.

4 Ask them to return to their relaxed position, eyes closed, and concentrate on the numbers alone.

5 Rub out the numbers, telling them to do the same in their minds. Do this slowly saying "That leaves just four numbers", etc.

6 Then rub out the last number, saying "Now concentrate on what is left" … Let them remain in silence until you notice a restlessness – this is often three or more minutes.

7 Wake them gently with an instruction to "Sit up". Ask them what the last number was and for their reactions.

THE HAVEN

Once you have managed to achieve complete physical relaxation and calm, gradually allow your mind to enter a place, whether real or imaginary, that is quite special to you. Now you can allow your mind to drift … drift to a pleasant, peaceful place. A place that you know and where you always feel able to relax … completely. A safe … secure … place … where no one … and nothing can ever bother you.

It may be a place you have visited on holiday, a beach or a place in the countryside. Or it may be a room … a room you have had … a room you do have … or a room you would like to have … an imaginary place. But it is a place where you can always feel able to let go … completely … a haven, a haven of tranquillity, unique and special to you.

In order to help you imagine this place … notice first the light: is it bright, natural or dim … is there any particular source of light … natural or man-made? Notice also the temperature level … hot, warm or cool … and any particular source of heat. Be aware of the colours that surround you … shapes … and textures … the familiar objects that make that place special. Begin to see it in all its detail. You can just be there … whether sitting, lying or reclining, enjoying the sounds … the smells … the atmosphere … with nobody wanting anything, nobody needing anything and no one demanding anything from you. Relax.

Everyone has their own haven, a quiet magical place like this.

Try to imagine your perfect country house.

A GUIDED VISIT TO A COUNTRY HOUSE

Imagine that you are visiting a beautiful country house … a really beautiful old country house or a stately home with magnificent sweeping lawns on a warm, sunny, summer's afternoon. You are standing on the staircase that leads into the entrance hall, one of those wide ceremonial types of staircase. And as you look down across the entrance hall you can just glimpse, through the open doors opposite, a gravel drive, and the sunlight on the gravel. It is a beautiful, sunny, summer's afternoon and there is no one around to trouble or bother you as you stand alone on that staircase …

Now you are moving down the last ten steps to the hallway, relaxing more and more with each step down.

10 Taking one step down, relaxing and letting go …
9 Taking another step down, feeling at ease …
8 Becoming more relaxed, letting go even more …
7 Just drifting deeper … and deeper … everything is getting darker and darker, and even deeper down still …

6 Becoming calmer … and calmer … even calmer still …
5 Continuing to relax, continuing to let go and feeling good …
4 Relaxing even more … letting go even more …
3 Sinking deeper … drifting even further into this welcoming, relaxed state …
2 Enjoying those good feelings, all those feelings of inner peace and relaxation …
1 Nearly all the way down now, feeling very good … beautifully relaxed … and **0**.

You are wandering across that hallway now, towards the open doors and the gardens beyond, soaking up the atmosphere of peace and permanence in that lovely old building. You wander out through the doors and down the stone steps outside … and find yourself standing on the gravel drive outside, a wide gravel drive that leads down to the entrance gates.

As you stand there you notice the lush green lawns, so flat and well-clipped … and there are shrubs and trees, different shades of green and brown against a clear, blue sky … and you can feel the warmth of the sun on your head and shoulders as you enjoy this beautiful summer's afternoon in this lovely old garden … There are flowerbeds with their splashes of colour so carefully arranged and neatly tended. And there's no one else about … nobody needing anything, nobody wanting anything and nobody expecting anything from you, so you can enjoy the peace and serenity and solitude of this afternoon in this beautiful garden that's been so well looked after for so many, many years.

A little way down on the right-hand side of the driveway, you notice an ornamental fish pond. So you decide to wander down and have a look at those fish. Sometimes they seem almost to disappear behind the weed and shadows, but always they reappear, with their scales catching the sunlight, red, gold, silver or black. And as you watch those fish your mind becomes even more deeply relaxed …

THE WELL

This continues from the previous visualization of the beautiful country house and is intended to take you to even deeper levels of meditation.

… As you watch those fish you notice that the centre of the pond is very deep. It could be the top of a disused well. You take from your pocket a silver-coloured coin, and toss that coin so that it lands over the centre of the pond, and then you watch as it swings down through the water. The ripples drift to the edges of the pond, but you just watch that coin as it sinks deeper and deeper through that clear water, sometimes it seems to disappear as it turns on edge, at other times a face of the coin catches the sunlight and it flashes through the water … sinking, drifting deeper and deeper, twisting and turning as it makes its way down … Finally it rests at the bottom lying on a cushion of soft brown mud, a silver coin in that still, clean water on its own cushion of mud … And you feel as still as that coin, as still and cool and motionless as that water, enjoying that feeling of inner peace and stillness.

Watch the ripples as the coin lands in the very centre of the pond. Look even more closely as it tumbles down through the water …

personal development
Affirmations are a deceptively simple device that can be used by anyone and they are remarkably effective. Try to use this method while in the meditative state, having planned and memorized the affirmations involved. These powerful, positive phrases will improve communication with all parts of your mind. All you need is a simple phrase summing up how you want to be.

THE POWER OF WORDS

To make affirmations effective, they should

- be made in the present tense
- be positively phrased
- have an emotional reward.

Now contrast the power of such phrases with what happens if you are asked not to do or think of something. The words "no", "not", "never" and so on generally have the opposite effect to that intended, and why? Yours is the most influential voice in your life because you believe it. It comes live, straight out of the personality and intellect, and is fuelled by your dreams and language. The power you have over yourself is extraordinary. That is precisely why you must be careful to avoid any negative or demeaning statements you regularly make about yourself, either to others or to yourself – "I am shy", "I lack confidence", "I cannot", "I get nervous when" and so on – they are self-limiting beliefs that you are reinforcing each time they slip into your conversation or mind. You become what you say.

The point about affirmations is that instead of running yourself down, albeit in a subtle, insidious way, you actually start building yourself up. You start creating the inner psychological scaffolding to support the new you. Such affirmations are best used while in a wonderful state of meditation.

Thinking through what you want to be is the big key to success.

IMPROVED SELF-WORTH

We all have attributes and qualities in which we can take pride and pleasure. This exercise is about emphasizing these positive aspects to allay the doubts that only serve to limit our potential.

- I like my [physical attribute].
- I am proud of my [attitude or achievement].
- I love meeting people – they are fascinating.
- My contribution is valuable to [name person].
- I am lovable and can give love.
- Others appreciate my [opinions, assistance, a personal quality].
- I enjoy being a unique combination of mind and body.

Now imagine yourself speaking to colleagues, boss, employees or friends … See yourself behaving and looking confident, standing and looking a confident person … Notice how you stand … your facial expression … hear the way that you speak … slowly, calmly, quietly, clearly and with confidence. You are communicating your needs … ideas … opinions in a positive way. Notice how your words flow easily, and how others are listening attentively to you … valuing what you have to say. Now "climb aboard" … be there – know how it feels to stand like that … to speak like that … and to have that positive reception from others. Get in touch with the stance … expression … and feelings … and know that you can use these any time in the future to gain those same feelings or that inner strength in everything you do. See yourself in different situations: at home, in a social setting, in all the parts of your life, confident and assured, going from strength to strength.

The difference affirmations can make is extraordinary. From shy and introverted to open, confident and winning.

If you want to be No. 1, then take time to concentrate on seeing yourself as the best. Give yourself the power to come out top.

VISUALIZATION

In the same way that you can utilize your voice, so, perhaps more powerfully, you can use your imagination. The imagination can stimulate emotions, and they can register new attitudes in the mind. It can be a direct communication with the deeper levels of the mind, providing a powerful influence for improvements in your attitudes, behaviour patterns and overall confidence.

Visualization requires that you imagine yourself in a situation, behaving, reacting and looking as you would wish to do at an interview, an important meeting, a social gathering, a one-to-one situation, or perhaps a sporting event. Imagine what that will mean for you, your reactions, the reactions of those around you and, importantly, feel all the good feelings that will be there when this happens in reality.

It is like playing a video of the event, on that screen on the inside of the forehead, the mind's eye, from the beginning of the situation through to the perfect outcome. Should any doubts or negative images creep into your "video", push them away and replace them with positive ones. Keep this realistic, and base it upon real information from your past.

CONFIDENCE IN FUTURE SITUATIONS

The meditative state, affirmations and visualization can be a valuable rehearsal and preparation for a future event. Athletes and other sportsmen have proved that it actually does work. We can all use these extraordinary techniques to achieve our own optimum performance during any situation. Now consider the following phrases, and how they relate to you …

- I am quietly confident in meetings.
- I speak slowly, quietly and confidently so that others listen.
- My contribution is wanted and valued by others.
- I enjoy meetings, as they bring forth new ideas and help to renew my enthusiasm.

Imagine an important meeting that is about to happen, and see yourself there, filling in all the details that you know, and the people too; imagine yourself there looking confident and relaxed, concentrating on what is happening. Be aware of the acute interest you are giving to what is happening with complete, concentrated attention, and then imagine yourself speaking, to give information or to ask a question: hear yourself speaking quietly, slowly and calmly …

Notice people listening to what you are saying; they wish you well and support you, as you are expressing your viewpoint or raising a question they may well have wanted to ask, too. Notice how you are sitting or standing, how you lean slightly forward when speaking, that expression of calm confidence on your face. When this is clear in your mind, just like a film playing in your mind's eye, play it back and forth. When you are feeling comfortable with it, get into that imaginary you, "climb aboard" and be there in your mind, seeing things from that perspective, hearing things from that point in the meeting. As you speak, get in touch with those calm feelings, and the attitudes that allow you to feel calm, in control, and quietly confident … It is like a rehearsal; the more you manage to rehearse the better the final performance will be. You will acquire the right attitudes, stance and tone of voice, so that when you are in that situation all of these will be available to you, and it will be just as you imagined, as if you had done it all, successfully, before.

In short, what this technique does is take you step by step through a rehearsal. Imagine every possible scenario, and how you will deal with it. That is the key to a successful outcome.

The preparation was worth it; you went into a meeting knowing you could do it, and that is exactly what happened.

enjoyment and achievement
The mind and the body are so completely interlinked that if we keep physically fit we are also mentally alert. The one boosts the other, but it also works the other way around. If we really utilize our mental capacities we can affect and improve our physical health and performance. So it is up to you to make sure that these twin forces keep functioning at full power. Do not let either slip.

A well-tuned lively body keeps you feeling well and alert.

THE BODY/MIND LINK
Regularly say to yourself …
- I feel safe, happy and content in the knowledge that my body is constantly renewing itself. It is alive and well.
- It feels marvellous to know that every damaged cell is replaced by a healthy one.
- My immune system is strong and fights off any infections easily.
- My mind and my body are working in harmony to keep me healthy, well and alert.

Now, imagine yourself lying or sitting comfortably. As you see yourself there you notice a healing glow of coloured light surrounding your body, but not touching it. Let that colour become stronger, until it has a very clear pure colour, which is the colour of healing for you.

Now, as you watch, that healing, coloured light begins to flow into the top of your head. You can see it slowly draining into all parts of the head, face, ears, and starts its journey down through the neck and shoulders, into the tops of the arms … It continues to flow down through the arms and the chest area, that healing, coloured light, penetrating all the muscles and organs … even as you watch you can also feel a healing warmth coming into your body … NOW … as it flows down into the stomach area, the back, right the way down to the base of the spine. Then you can allow the light to disperse again and gradually return to your normal wakeful state, knowing that in those areas that need it, the healing process will continue.

STRESS REDUCTION
Stress is a factor in everyone's life and can even be a major motivator in some circumstances. Meditation can be a great help in coping with it, and combined with visualization, it can change your whole response to stressful demands. Keep saying …
- I enjoy solving problems.
- I work well under pressure.
- I am a calm, methodical and efficient worker.
- I love that feeling of having achieved so much in a day.
- I enjoy being calm when others around me are not.

Imagine yourself in a situation that has in the past caused stress. Picture the situation, and the other people involved … See yourself there … and notice a slight shimmer of light between yourself and those other people … a sort of bubble around you … a protective bubble that reflects any negative feelings back to them … leaving you able to get on with your tasks … your life, with an inner strength and calmness that surprises even you. A protective, invisible bubble surrounds you at all times. It will only allow those feelings that are positive and helpful to you to pass through for you to enjoy and build upon. Others may catch stress from each other … negativity, too, can be infectious … but you are protected … you continue to keep things in perspective … and to deal with things calmly and methodically. You are able to see the way forward clearly … solve problems … find ways around difficulties … by using your own inner resources and strengths, born of experience. In you alone lies the secret of success. You can and you will succeed.

Imagine yourself leading a healthy lifestyle and it will happen.

LIVING NOW

Although we cannot change the past, we can learn from it and build up a range of skills and useful insights from it. The future is that unknown world of possibilities and opportunities before us – but all that we can truly have any effect upon is the present. Keep saying to yourself …

• I have learned a great deal from the past.
• The future is an exciting range of opportunities.
• I enjoy laying good foundations NOW on which to build a better future.

Imagine yourself standing on a pathway. As you look around the left, right and above is brilliantly illuminated, and sounds are amazingly clear. As you check over your shoulder you notice the path behind is unclear. You hear a clock chime in the distance and take a step forward. You notice the slightest of noises, movements or shifts of light, and take pleasure even in the pure sound of silence, too. You can hear that same clock ticking now, and with each tick you can take a small step forward, effortlessly, along the path, and that illumination and awareness moves with you. At any fork in the path you can make decisions easily as you are truly involved in the moment, rather than looking over your shoulder at what might have been, or staring blindly into the future at what might happen. You enjoy being in the brilliantly illuminated, acute awareness of sound, hearing, feeling, taste and smell that is NOW.

For a complete experience, be more acutely aware of shapes and textures as well as sounds, colours and scents.

GOAL ACHIEVEMENT

A goal, in all areas of life, is vitally important in order to focus your attention and inner resources. A goal provides a sense of direction and ultimately the joy of achievement. Without it you might flounder, so keep saying to yourself …

• I direct my energies to achieve my goals.
• I enjoy directing my energies positively.
• I know where I am going and how I am getting there.
• Step by step I am moving in the right direction.
• I have the ability, I have the determination, I shall succeed.

Keep your eyes firmly fixed on your goal and you will achieve it.

Be aware of the different areas of your life: work, social, leisure activities, emotional and spiritual. Select one of these for this exercise … and be aware of what you want to happen in that area of your life, what you want to achieve … Make it realistic and clear in your mind. It may be useful to write it down and describe it fully before beginning this visualization.

While in the meditative state, imagine yourself having achieved that goal, imagine yourself there, in that situation. Surround yourself with all the things or people that indicate that you have achieved that goal. Be as specific as you can … be aware of all the senses … what are you seeing … hearing … touching or sensing … smelling … tasting. Be there … make it real … be specific … about colours … temperatures … lighting, to make it more and more real in your mind.

Now, from where you are at that moment of achieving that goal … look back … as if along a path, a pathway of time … to where you were … and notice the different stages of change … of movement towards achieving that goal … along the way … along that path … the different actions you have taken … the contacts you have made … and the people involved. Be aware of all the stages along the way … and as you return to the here and now … you remain in touch with the feelings that will make it all worthwhile … and you feel more and more determined to take one step at a time … make one change at a time … along that path to the successful achievement of your goal. And as you return from the meditative state so you are more determined to be success-ful in the achievement of your goal.

Herbalism

UK
National Institute of Medical
Herbalists
56 Longbrook Street
Exeter
Devon
EX4 6AH

The Herb Society
134 Buckingham Palace Road
London
SW1W 9SA

The School of
Phytotherapy/Herbal Medicine
Buckstreep Manor
Bodle Street Green
Hailsham
East Sussex
BN27 4RJ

US
The Herb Research Foundation
1007 Pearl Street, Suite 200
Boulder
CO 80302

American Botanical Council
PO Box 144345
Austin
TX 78714

Blazing Star Herb School
PO Box 6
Shelburne Falls
MA 01370

Outlets for Herbs
Cameron Park Botanicals
Highway 64 East
Raleigh
NC 27610

Caprilands Herb Farm
Silver Street
North Coventry
CT 06238

Seeds Blum
Idaho City State
Boise
ID 83706

AUSTRALIA
National Herbalist Association
PO Box 61
Broadway
NSW 2066

Homeopathy

UK
The Homeopathic Society
2 Powis Place
Great Ormond Street
London
WC1N 3HT

The Society of Homeopaths
2 Artizan Road
Northampton
NN1 4HU

**Outlets for Homeopathic
Remedies**
*Most chemists and health food shops
will stock a limited supply of
homeopathic remedies. The list below
will stock a complete range.*

Buxton and Grant
176 Whiteladies Road
Bristol
BS8 2XU

Freeman's Pharmacy
7 Eaglesham Road
Clarkston
Glasgow
G76 7BU

Goulds the Chemist
14 Crowndale Road
London
NW1 1TT

Helios Pharmacy
97 Camden Road
Tunbridge Wells
Kent
TN1 2QR

US
Homeopathic Educational Services
2124 Kittredge Street
Berkeley
CA 94704

National Center for Homeopathy
801 N Fairfax No 306
Alexandria
VA 22314

AUSTRALIA
Australian Institute of
Homeopathy
PO Box 122
Roseville
NSW 2069

Massage

UK
The Massage Training Institute/
The Academy of On-site Massage
24 Brunswick Square
Hove
BN13 1EH

London College of Massage
5 Newman Passage
London
W1P 3PF

Clare Maxwell-Hudson Massage
Training Centre
PO Box 457
London
NW2 4BR

The School of Holistic Massage
c/o Nitya Lacroix
75 Dresden Road
London
N19 3BG

US
American Massage Therapy
Association
820 Davies Street, Suite 100
Evanston
IL 60201

Pacific School of Massage and
Healing Arts
44800 Fish Rock Road
Gualala
CA 95445

Body Therapy Center
368 California Avenue
Palo Alto.
CA 94306

AUSTRALIA
Association of Massage Therapists
3/33 Denham Street
Bondi
New South Wales

Aromatherapy

UK
International Society of
Professional Aromatherapists
The Hinckley and District
Hospital
Mount Road
Hinckley
Leicestershire
LE10 1AG

International Federation of
Aromatherapists
4 Eastmearn Road
Dulwich
London
SE21 8HA

US
Institute of Aromatherapy
3108 Route 10
West Denville
NJ 07834

Aromatherapy School and Herbal
Studies
219 Carl Street
San Fransisco
CA 94117

AUSTRALIA
Australian School of Awareness
251 Dorset Road
Croydon
Victoria 3136

International Federation of
Aromatherapists
83 Riversdale Road
Hawthorn
Victoria 3122

Shiatsu

UK
The British School of
Shiatsu-Do
3rd Floor
130-132 Tooley Street
London
SE1 2TU

The Shiatsu Society
Interchange Studios
Dalby Street
London
NW5 3NQ

The European Shiatsu School
Central Administration
Highbanks
Lockeridge
Marlborough
Wiltshire
SN8 4EQ

US
International School of Shiatsu
10 South Clinton Street, Suite 300
Doylestown
PA 18901

School of Shiatsu and Massage at
Harbin Hot Springs
PO Box 889
Middletown
CA 95461

AUSTRALIA
The Shiatsu Therapy Association
of Australia
2 Caminoley Wynd
Templestowe
Victoria 3106

Australian Natural Therapies
Association Ltd.
Suite 1, 2nd Floor
468-472 George Street
(PO Box A964)
Sydney
New South Wales 2000

Reflexology

UK
Association of Reflexologists
27 Old Gloucester Street
London
W1N 3XX

Holistic Association of
Reflexologists
92 Sheering Road
Old Harrow
Essex
CM17 0JW

The British Reflexology
Association
12 Pond Road
London
SE3 6JL

US
International Institute of
Reflexology
PO Box 12462
St Petersburg,
FL 33733

Reflexology Center
Scarborough Professional Center
136 Route One
Scarborough
ME 04074

AUSTRALIA
Reflexology Association of
Australia
15 Kedumba Crescent
Turramurra
New South Wales 2074

RASA (Australia)
73 Illawong Way
Karand Downs
Brisbane
Queensland 4306

Australian School of Reflexology
and Relaxation
165 Progress Road
Eltham North
Victoria 3095

Tai Chi

UK
Tai Chi Union of Great Britain
69 Kilpatrick Gardens
Clarkston
Glasgow
Scotland
G76 7RF

Golden Rooster Tai Chi School
19 Albany Road
London
N4 4RR

Rainbow Tai Chi Kung Centre
Creek Farm
Pitley Hill
Woodland Ashburton
Devon
PQ13 7JY

British Tai Chi Chuan & Kung Fu
Association
28 Linden Farm Drive
Countesthorpe
Leicestershire
LE8 5SX

USA
Mind, Body, Spirit Academy
PO Box 415
Chadsford
PA 19317

Tai Chi Cultural Centre
PO Box 8885
Stanford
CA 94309

Sarasota Shaolia Academy
4655 Flatbush Avenue
Sarasota
Florida
FL 34233-1920

AUSTRALASIA
Australian Academy of Tai Chi
686 Parrametta Road
Croydon
NSW 2132

Shaolin Wahnan Tai Chi
RSD Strathfelsaye Road
Victoria 3551

Yoga

UK
Iyengar Yoga Institute
223a Randolph Avenue
London
W9 1NL

Manchester & District Institute of
Iyengar Yoga
134 King Street
Dukinfield
Tameside
Greater Manchester
M60 8HG

Edinburgh Iyengar Yoga Centre
195 Bruntsfield Place
Edinburgh
EH10 4DQ

The British Wheel of Yoga
1 Hamilton Place
Boston Road
Sleaford
Lincolnshire
NG24 7EI

USA
Satchidananda Ashram - Yogaville
Buckingham
VA 23921

International Yoga Association
92 Main Street
Warrenton
VA 20186

BKS Iyengar Yoga National
Association of the United States
Inc.
8223 West Third Street
Los Angeles
CA 90038

Sivanda Yoga Vedanta Center
1246 Bryn Mawr
Chicago
IL 60660

AUSTRALASIA
BKS Iyengar Association of
Australasia
1 Rickman Avenue
Mosman
NSW 2088

Sivananda Yoga Vedanta Centre
409th Avenue
Katoomba
NSW 2780

Meditation

UK
Gateway Books
The Hollies
Wellow
Bath
Somerset
BA2 8QJ

Western Zen Retreats
Winterhead Hill Farm
Shipham
Winscombe
Somerset
BS25 1RS

Transcendental Meditation
Freepost
London
SW1P 4YY

The Community Health
Foundation 188 Old Street
London
EC1V 9FR

USA
Greater Washington DC
Association of Professionals
Practising the Transcendental
Meditation Program
4818 Montgomery Lane
Bethesda
MD 20814

Institute of Noetic Sciences
PO Box 909
Sausalito
CA 94966

First Zen Institute of America
113E 30th Street
New York
NY 10016

American Buddhist Association
1151 West Leland Avenue
Chicago
IL 60640

AUSTRALASIA
Transcendental Meditation Centre
68 Wood Street
Manly
Sydney
NSW 2095

The Barry Long Centre
Box 5277
Gold Coast MC
Queensland 4217

Transcendental Meditation Centre
New Zealand
5 Adam Street
Green Lane
Auckland 5

*The publishers would particularly like to
thank the following photographers for
the use of their pictures:*
Michelle Garrett, Alistair Hughes, Lucy
Mason and Debbie Patterson.

*Thanks also to the following libraries for
supplying pictures:*
A-Z Botanical Collection Ltd: 27BL;
39TR; 44 BL; 52BL; 53 BL, BR; 54BR;
55TL; 57TM; 244ML. Bruce Coleman
Collection: 54BM; 55TM; 56BM. Frank
Lane Photographic Agency: 31BM.
Garden & Wildlife Matters: 30TL;
51BM; 128TL,TM, BM, BR; 251TR. The
Garden Picture Library: 28BL,TR;
30TM; 31BR; 55BL; 127BM, BR,TR;
128TR; 129TR,TM. Images Colour
Library: 66B. Harry Smith Collection:
45BL; 53TM; 56TL,TR; 57BM. Tony
Stone Images: 27BR; 60T, B ,63B; 64B;
70B; 74B; 242BL; 243BL; 245TR;
246TL, BR; 247TL, BR; 248BL; 249T;
251BL.